Modelling and Assessir

THE CAMBRIDGE APPLIED LINGUISTICS SERIES

Series editors: Michael H. Long and Jack C. Richards

This series presents the findings of work in applied linguistics that are of direct relevance to language teaching and learning and of particular interest to applied linguists, researchers, language teachers, and teacher trainers.

Recent publications in this series:

Modelling and Assessing Vocabulary Knowledge

Edited by

Helmut Daller, James Milton and Jeanine Treffers-Daller

CAMBRIDGE
UNIVERSITY PRESS

CAMBRIDGE UNIVERSITY PRESS
Cambridge, New York, Melbourne, Madrid, Cape Town,
Singapore, São Paulo, Delhi, Tokyo, Mexico City

Cambridge University Press
The Edinburgh Building, Cambridge CB2 8RU, UK

Published in the United States of America by
Cambridge University Press, New York

www.cambridge.org
Information on this title: www.cambridge.org/9780521703277

First published 2007

A catalogue record for this publication is available from the British Library

Library of Congress Cataloguing in Publication data
Modelling and assessing vocabulary knowledge / edited by Helmut Daller,
James Milton, and Jeanine Treffers–Daller.
    p. cm. – (Cambridge applied linguistics series)
Includes bibliographical references and index.
ISBN 978-0-521-70327-7 (pbk.) – ISBN 978-0-521-87851-7 (hardback)
1. Language and languages–Ability testing. 2. Vocabulary–Ability testing.
I. Daller, Helmut, 1957– II. Milton, James, 1955–
III. Treffers–Daller, Jeanine, 1959– IV. Title. V. Series.
P53.9.M63 2007
418.0076–dc22   2007020745

ISBN 978-0-521-87851-7 Hardback
ISBN 978-0-521-70327-7 Paperback

Contents

Contributors

Frank Boers, *Erasmuscollege, Brussels, Belgium*

Helmut Daller, *University of the West of England, Bristol, UK*

June Eyckmans, *Erasmuscollege, Brussels, Belgium*

Tess Fitzpatrick, *University of Wales, Swansea, UK*

Hilde Hacquebord, *University of Groningen, The Netherlands*

Nuria Lorenzo-Dus, *University of Wales, Swansea, UK*

David Malvern, *University of Reading, UK*

Paul Meara, *University of Wales, Swansea, UK*

James Milton, *University of Wales, Swansea, UK*

Paul Nation, *Victoria University of Wellington, New Zealand*

David Phelan, *University of the West of England, Bristol, UK*

Brian Richards, *University of Reading, UK*

Ellen Schur, *The Open University, Israel*

Berend Stellingwerf, *University of Groningen, The Netherlands*

Françoise Tidball, *University of the West of England, Bristol, UK*

Jeanine Treffers-Daller, *University of the West of England, Bristol, UK*

Hans Van de Velde, *Utrecht Institute of Linguistics OTS, The Netherlands*

Roeland van Hout, *University of Nijmegen, The Netherlands*

Anne Vermeer, *University of Tilburg, The Netherlands*

Clarissa Wilks, *Kingston University, UK*

Huijuan Xue, *University of the West of England, Bristol, UK*

Abbreviations

AWL	Academic Word List
BNC	British National Corpus
CHAT	Codes for the Human Analysis of Transcripts
CHILDES	Child Language Data Exchange System
CLAN	Computerised Language Analysis Program
EVST	Eurocentre's Vocabulary Size Tests
LFP	Lexical Frequency Profile
SALT	Systematic Analysis of Language Transcripts
TTR	Type–Token Ratio
X-Lex	X-Lex the Swansea Placement Test

Acknowledgements

We would like to acknowledge financial support given by the British Association for Applied Linguistics (BAAL) and the Linguistics Association of Great Britain (LAGB) for the organisation of a BAAL/CUP workshop (with the Universities of the West of England, Reading and Swansea) on 8–9 January 2004.

The authors and publishers acknowledge the following sources of copyright material and are grateful for the permissions granted. While every effort has been made, it has not always been possible to identify the sources of all the material used, or to trace all copyright holders. If any omissions are brought to out notice, we will be happy to include the appropriate acknowledgements on reprinting.

Cambridge University Press for Table 1 on p. 5: 'What is involved in knowing a word?' taken from *Learning Vocabulary in Another Language*, written by I.S.P Nation (2001); for Figure 2 on p. 11: extract from an X-Lex test of French, written by J. Milton (2006), which appeared in *Journal of French Language Studies* 16 (2); for the text on p. 90: extract taken from *Statistics in Language Studies*, written by Woods, Fletcher and Hughes © (1986). Used by permission of Cambridge University Press.

Oxford University Press for Table 2 on p. 14: example of a vocabulary profile produced by Laufer and Nation's Lexical Frequency Profile (1995), which appeared in 'Vocabulary Size and Use: Lexical Richness in L2 Written Production' in *Applied Linguistics* 16, 307–322. Used by permission of Oxford University Press.

Blackwell Publishing for the text on p. 37: 'Dialogue Vocabulary development: a morphological analysis', which appeared in *Monographs of the Society for Research and Child Development*, Serial no: 238, Vol. 58, written by J.M. Anglin. Used by permission of Blackwell Publishing Ltd.

Thomson Learning for the text on p. 43: 'Vocabulary' from *Testing ESL Composition*, 1st edition, by Jacobs 0883772256 (1981); for Table 3 on p. 129: 'Aspects of Word Knowledge' taken from *Teaching and Learning Vocabulary*, 1st edition by Nation (1990). Reprinted with permission of Heinle, a division of Thomson Learning: http://www.thomsonrights.com

University College, Swansea: Centre for Applied Language Studies for Figure 1 on p. 48: 'Vocabulary knowledge of a typical learner', taken from *EFL Vocabulary Tests* by P. Meara © (1992). Used by permission of University College, Swansea.

Table 7 on p. 99: Means scores for 20 adult L2-informants (nine-month intervals)' taken from 'Measuring Lexical Richness and Variety in Second Language Use', *Polyglot* 8, 116, written by Broeder, Extra and Van Hout.

Elsevier for the extract on p. 223: 'The language tester's statistical toolbox', reprinted from *System* 28 (4), 605–617, written by F. Davidson © (2000). Used with permission from Elsevier.

Foreword

Modelling and assessing vocabulary knowledge are two sides of the same coin. Progress in modelling will help to develop more refined ways of assessing vocabulary knowledge, and empirical data from assessments will feed into the development of models for this aspect of language proficiency. The focus of this book is on both, modelling and assessing. The initiative for this book came after a BAAL/CUP workshop in January 2004 at the University of the West of England, Bristol. Researchers from various backgrounds were discussing their way of approaching vocabulary knowledge in the development and evaluation of measures, or in the discussion of models. After an intensive discussion over two days we decided to bring our views on this topic together by replying to the keynote chapter of Paul Nation, who outlined the threats to the validity of various measures of lexical knowledge. Chapter 1 of this book gives an overview of these threats; the remainder of the book is dedicated to the approaches to overcome these methodological problems. Overall, most researchers in the field stress that a single 'one-size-fits-all' measure or a 'Holy Grail' does not exist for the measurement of vocabulary knowledge. Instead many researchers stress the importance of multiple measures to give a valid picture of the lexical richness of a person. A broad variety of these measures are discussed in this book.

Series Editors' Preface

This book explores approaches to the measurement of vocabulary knowledge and vocabulary development in second and foreign language learners. Vocabulary plays an important role in the lives of all language users, since it is one of the major predictors of school performance, and successful learning and use of new vocabulary is also key to membership of many social and professional roles. The measurement of vocabulary knowledge in second language learners is of interest not only to language teachers, who are often required to make assessments of development of their learners' language proficiency, but also to researchers and test developers who seek to develop valid and reliable measures of second language knowledge and use. While there is a considerable literature of many aspects of language testing, the assessment of lexical knowledge has received relatively little attention until recently, despite the fact that vocabulary can be viewed as the core component of all the language skills. The papers in this book show how scholars in a number of different countries are addressing fundamental questions related to vocabulary modelling and measurement.

Modelling and Assessing Vocabulary provides an overview of issues involved in vocabulary measurement in second and foreign language learning. The central question which the contributors to the book explore is, how can one assess the extent and richness of a person's vocabulary knowledge and use? Lexical competence is difficult to assess with a single measure since vocabulary knowledge is multi-faceted. Multiple measures are needed across a variety of tasks and settings in order to provide an adequate picture of the extent of a learner's vocabulary. In this book a number of approaches to the measurement of the L2 lexicon are illustrated. Many standard vocabulary tests are shown to reflect a partial view of the nature of lexical competence, and the papers demonstrate how researchers are attempting to develop more sophisticated and representative measures of lexical competence. The contributors show that among the factors affecting the validity of vocabulary measures are the definition of a word itself, individual variables learners bring to the testing process, test-taking strategies employed by learners, learners' motivation to complete a test, the characteristics of the test itself, the source of the items included in tests, and the choice of first language versus second language test formats.

As a whole the papers in this book throw valuable light on the issues involved in measuring vocabulary learning in a second or foreign language and illustrate ways in which vocabulary tests can seek to capture the complex and multi-dimensional nature of lexical knowledge.

Michel H. Long
Jack C. Richards

Editors' introduction

Conventions, terminology and an overview of the book

Over the last 20 years vocabulary research has grown from a 'Cinderella subject' in foreign language teaching and research, to achieve a position of some salience. Vocabulary is now considered integral to just about every aspect of language knowledge. With this development have come standard and widely used tests, such as vocabulary size and lexical richness measures, and very commonly accepted metaphors, such as 'a web of words' to describe the mental lexicon. Less widely known outside academic circles, however, is the extensive work on learners' lexis and the utility, reliability and validity of the tests we use to measure and investigate vocabulary knowledge and growth. Vocabulary is a lively and vital area of innovation in academic approach and research. The penalty we pay for working in so vital a subject area is that even recent, and excellent, surveys of the field are rapidly overtaken by new ideas, fresh insights in modelling and testing, a healthy re-evaluation of the principles we work under, and an ever-growing body of empirical research. The intention of this volume, therefore, is to place in the hands of the reader some of these new ideas and insights. It brings together contributions from internationally renowned researchers in this field to explain much of the background to study in this area, and reconsider some of the ideas which underpin the tests we use. It introduces to a wider audience the concerns, new approaches and developments in the field of vocabulary research and testing.

To place these ideas in context, and to provide a point of entry for non-specialists in this field, this introduction will survey the conventions and terminology of vocabulary study which, if you are not familiar with them, can make even simple ideas impenetrably difficult. The background this introduction provides should allow the chapters which follow to be placed in context and help to explain why the concerns they address are of importance to researchers. The second half of this introduction provides summaries of the chapters.

1

Conventions and terminology

What is a word?

One of our colleagues used to begin lectures on vocabulary learning by asking his audience how many words they thought they knew in English. Most people had no idea of course, and had to guess, and the answers they suggested varied enormously – from 200 words to many millions. These extremes are unusual but in truth it was a question without a clear answer, because the answer depends on what you mean by a word and therefore what your unit of counting is. According to context and need, researchers can consider *types*, *tokens*, *running words*, *lemmas*, and *word families* as words.

In one sense it is obvious what a word is. Words are the black marks you are reading on this page and you know when one word ends and another one begins because there are spaces between words. There are occasions when it is appropriate to use a definition of this kind in making word counts, for example, in counting the number of words in a student's essay or the number of words in the huge corpus that a researcher will collect so that they can use real examples of word use. When counting words in this way we often refer to them as *tokens* so it is clear what we are talking about. Sometimes we also refer to *running words* with much the same meaning, for example, if you consult a dictionary corpus you may be presented with the information that the word *maunder* occurs on average only once every several million running words.

In addition to knowing the number of words in a text or a corpus, researchers sometimes want to know the number of *different* words that occur in a given text. The terms *tokens* and *types* are used to distinguish between these two ways of counting. *Tokens* refers to the total number of words in a text or corpus while *types* refers to the number of different words. In the sentence:

> *The cat sat on the mat*

there are six *tokens* (a total of six words), but the word *the* occurs twice so there are only five *types*.

But there are problems even with a catch-all definition of this kind. How do you count contractions such as *don't*, *it's* or *won't*? Should they be counted as single words or two? Is the number at the top of this page a word or not? Are the names we have put on the title page of this book words? And if you are counting words in speech rather than writing, how do you count the *ums* and *ers* which always occur? Practice can vary according to the needs of the researcher but often, numbers, proper nouns and names, and false starts and mistakes are excluded from word counts.

Once you start counting the number of words a person knows more difficulties raise their heads. If a student learns the verb *to work*, for example, this will involve learning the form *works* for use with the third person singular in the present simple tense, the form *worked* for use in the simple past, and *working* for use with continuous tenses. The question arises whether the learner has learned one word or four here. These inflections or changes to the root form of the verb are highly regular and can be applied to most verbs in English. Provided a few simple rules of grammar are known, learners only need to learn a new root form to have these other forms at their disposal and available for use. It is often convenient, therefore, to think of all these word forms as a single unit since they do not have to be learned separately by the learner; learning the root form means all the others can be deduced from it and will therefore also be known. This has the profound advantage of reducing the numbers of words we have to work with in describing vocabulary knowledge to manageable levels: to a few thousand or tens of thousand instead of hundreds of thousands. A collection of words such as *to work, works, working, worked*, comprising a root form and the most frequent regular inflections, is known as a *lemma*. Where a noun has a regular plural formed by adding -*s*, as in *orange* and *oranges*, for example, these two words would also form a single lemma. In most word-frequency counts and estimates of learners' vocabulary sizes, the lemma is used as the basis of counting, and *work, works, working* and *worked* would be counted as just one lemma. Rather confusingly, lemmas are often called words, and researchers are not always consistent in their use of terminology. In both Nation's vocabulary level's test (1983) and Meara and Milton's *X-Lex* (2003a) word knowledge is tested in what are called 1,000-word frequency bands. In fact, the researchers used lemmatised word lists and these should have been referred to as 1,000-lemma frequency bands.

Some estimates of a speaker's vocabulary size, however (for example, Goulden, Nation and Read's (1990) estimate of 17,000 words for educated native speakers of English) use a larger unit still and are actually estimates of the number of *word families* a person knows. The forms of a word which can be included in a lemma are fairly limited. But words often have lots of other forms which are clearly related to the root form. The lemma *work*, for example, includes *working, works* and *worked* but does not include *worker* although this is obviously a derived form which is very closely related. The lemma *govern* would include *governs, governing* and *governed* but not *governor* or *government*. Closely related words like this would be called a *word family*. Clearly, estimates of size based on the *lemma* and on the *word family* will be quite different.

At first sight this may appear confusing and quite unnecessarily complex. Certainly, researchers often contribute to the confusion both by being unclear as to the units they use, and by adopting idiosyncratic definitions. The divisions between a word, a lemma and a word family are not entirely arbitrary, however, and are based on Bauer and Nation's (1993) frequency-based groupings of affixes in English. *Lemmas* will generally be words made by using affixes from the top three groups, and *word families* from the top six. Thus, *lemmas* would include only the most common affixes and would not generally involve changing the part of speech from that of the head word, while a *word family* would be much more inclusive. The *lemma* of a word such as *establish*, for example, would include *establishes, establishing*, and *established* but not *establishment* which would change the part of speech and includes a suffix at Level 4 in Bauer and Nation's hierarchy, while the *word family* would include *establishment* and many other words using less frequent affixes such as *interestablishment* or *antiestablishment*. Further, this hierarchy of word units is not the product of whim on the part of researchers but rather a result of the need to reduce the figures we work with to manageable proportions. In measuring distance we use millimetres, centimetres, metres and kilometres, to name just a few, according to the size of what is being measured, and in measuring vocabulary we are behaving no differently.

What is 'knowing a word'?

If defining a word has presented problems, then deciding when a word is actually known is no easier. There are a number of qualities which might be included in the definition of *knowing* and this has been added to over the years. Nation's list, in Table 1, is the latest and most comprehensive incarnation.

Depending on how you define *knowing*, you will have very different ideas about what constitutes a learner's knowledge of words, and statistical counts of a learner's vocabulary size will then also vary according to the definition of *knowing* used. Perhaps the most basic, catch-all definition would be simple, passive, word recognition; the learner recognises the form of a word and that it is a word rather than a meaningless jumble of symbols. This aspect of knowing is clearly identified in Nation's table. There are several tests (e.g. Meara

Table 1   What is involved in knowing a word? (from Nation, 2001: 27)

Form	spoken	R	What does the word sound like?
		P	How is the word pronounced?
	written	R	What does the word look like?
		P	How is the word written and spelled?
	word parts	R	What parts are recognisable in this word?
		P	What word parts are needed to express meaning?
Meaning	form and meaning	R	What meaning does this word form signal?
		P	What word form can be used to express this meaning?
	concepts and referents	R	What is included in the concept?
		P	What items can the concept refer to?
	associations	R	What other words does this word make us think of?
		P	What other words could we use instead of this one?
Use	grammatical functions	R	In what patterns does the word occur?
		P	In what patterns must we use this word?
	collocations	R	What words or types of word occur with this one?
		P	What words or types of words must we use with this one?
	constraints on use	R	Where, when and how often would we meet this word?
		P	Where, when and how often can we use this word?

R = receptive, P = productive.

and Jones's EVST, 1990; Meara and Milton's *X-Lex*, 2003a) which use this definition of *knowing*. In principle, a calculation made using this definition will surely include every other kind of knowledge since, presumably, a learner could not reasonably use, attach a meaning to or find a correct collocation for something they do not even recognise as a word. Most of the tests we use to calculate vocabulary size are based on written forms of knowledge and these predict a range of reading- and writing-based language abilities as well, but the ability to recognise or use the spoken form of a word is much less well investigated. Interestingly, initial results from studies using phonologically based vocabulary size tests (Milton, 2005) suggest that aural word recognition predicts oral proficiency particularly well. This ties in with Daller and Huijuan Xue's chapter in this volume (Chapter 8) which addresses the problems of finding a good measure of lexical knowledge to tie in with oral proficiency.

A second very common definition of knowing a word can be found within the 'Meaning' section of Nation's table. This rests on the idea that a word is known if the learner can attach a meaning, such as an explanation or a translation, to a foreign language word. Calculations of vocabulary knowledge and size made on this basis ought to be smaller than those made on the basis of passive word recognition. Every learner must be familiar with the sensation of encountering a word they know they have seen before but cannot, for the moment, attach to a meaning. It seems this aspect of knowledge can be surprisingly fragile in the foreign language learner's vocabulary. The link between form and meaning can disappear quite suddenly and without explanation and, just as suddenly, reappear. The chapters by Meara and Wilks (Chapter 9) and by Schur (Chapter 10) investigate the applicability of various kinds of network theory to vocabulary, and begin to make this kind of phenomenon explicable but, as their chapters show, this work is still in its infancy. It is a phenomenon which also underlies the questions encountered in Chapter 3 by Eyckmans, Van de Velde, van Hout and Boers and by Fitzpatrick in Chapter 6 where differences in translation and receptive test scores challenge easy interpretation.

Nation's table of what is involved in knowing a word draws attention to a further distinction, that of *receptive* and *productive* or *passive* and *active* word knowledge: indicated by R and P in column three (see Table 1). The distinction here lies in the difference between the words you can handle in the context of reading or listening to speech, and those you can call readily to mind when you need to speak or write in the foreign language. Usually the additional context information which comes with written or spoken language means that a learner's passive or receptive vocabulary appears to exceed the productive or active vocabulary. The relationship between the two types of knowledge is not clear, and may vary according to a variety of individual learner characteristics or the type of test used. But it is quite extensively researched, going back to Stoddard in 1929. Estimates vary but the range of studies reviewed in Waring (1997) suggest that productive vocabulary size is about 50% of receptive vocabulary size; and presumably one is a subset of the other. There are, of course, methodological problems inherent in measuring these two different kinds of vocabulary in a way which is strictly equivalent and these problems haunt several of the contributors to this volume such as Richards and Malvern (Chapter 4), and van Hout and Vermeer (Chapter 5). These methods are considered in more detail later on in this introduction.

Other aspects of word knowledge seem much less well researched and standard tests are lacking, in some cases we even lack an agreed approach to testing. For example, in his section on 'Form' (Table 1) Nation suggests that word knowledge can include knowledge at the level of the morpheme. Our concentration on calculating word knowledge using the *lemma* or the *word family* as the basic unit means that our tests cannot tell us about knowledge at this level of detail. But the testing problems experienced by Eyckmans et al. described in Chapter 3, may result to some extent, from learners' abilities to make educated guesses about the meaning of words from their different parts or components. Our concern is that this kind of guesswork may destabilise some tests of vocabulary knowledge and make the scores they produce less useful than we may think they are. Again, knowledge of a word's collocations, connotations and preferred associations is an area where we struggle to find a single, simple way of characterising this knowledge in a way in which it can be usefully quantified and tested. Further, our concentration on tests which use the lemma, and the fact that we often investigate infrequent vocabulary, means that all of the most frequent linking words tend not to be investigated. Such information falls below the radar of the tests we use. Chapters 9 and 10 by Wilks and Meara, and by Schur respectively, are a direct attempt to suggest models of analysis and testing methods which might help fill in these gaps in our knowledge.

What is the lexical space?

It is clear from this discussion that vocabulary knowledge is complex and multi-faceted. The qualities we investigate are not easily described or tested and we tend to resort to analogy and metaphor to try to illuminate the way words are learned and stored. One such idea is that of *lexical space* where a learner's vocabulary knowledge is described as a three-dimensional space, where each dimension represents an aspect of knowing a word (see Figure 1).

In Figure 1 the horizontal axis represents the concept of *lexical breadth* which is intended, in essence, to define the number of words a learner knows regardless of how well he or she knows them. This would include the 'Form' and the *form and meaning* elements of Nation's table. Vocabulary size tests, passive/receptive style tests and translation tests are all tests of lexical breadth, although they may produce varying estimates of size and knowledge. Chapters 2 and 3 by Milton and Eyckmans et al. respectively, are directly concerned with how to make estimates of vocabulary breadth.

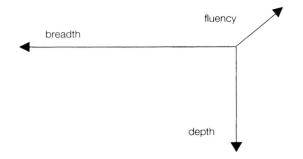

Figure 1   The lexical space: dimensions of word knowledge and ability

The vertical axis in Figure 1 represents the concept of *lexical depth* which is intended to define how much the learner knows about the words he or she knows. This would include the elements of *concepts and referents, associations, grammatical functions, collocations* and *constraints on use* from Nation's table (Table 1). These elements tend to be tested separately, probably because this is a disparate list of word qualities, for which we have not as yet succeeded in pinning down a unifying idea or model which can provide the basis of a comprehensive test of depth. This is not for want of trying, however, and the precise relationship between the lexicon and grammar has been the subject of considerable research (e.g. Hunston and Francis, 2000). This area might properly be the subject of an entire but separate volume. Space in this volume permits only limited reference to this area based on a further metaphor, that of a web of words, which is often used to describe this axis and the way the words interact with each other. Chapters 9 and 10 by Wilks and Meara and by Schur, deal with precisely this issue and investigate the possibility of turning this metaphor into a model of lexical depth which can be empirically tested with real language users. Meara and Wolter (2004) have developed a test which allows learners to activate these webs of grammatical and lexical knowledge so that a score can be assigned to it. At first sight this looks like a promising innovation but it is early days.

The final axis is that of *fluency* and this is intended to define how readily and automatically a learner is able to use the words they know and the information they have on the use of these words. This might involve the speed and accuracy with which a word can be recognised or called to mind in speech or writing. It would probably be true to say that we have no widely used or generally accepted test of vocabulary fluency. Some very promising ideas are emerging (for example, Shiotsu, 2001) but it is interesting to note that this field is still somewhat inchoate, so much so that no papers were presented at the Vocabulary Workshop giving rise to this volume.

These three axes define the lexical space and, in principle, it becomes possible to locate a learner's vocabulary knowledge within this space. Some learners may have large vocabularies but are very limited in the speed and ease with which they can recall these words and put them to use communicatively. These learners ought to be placed well along the breadth axis but less far along the fluency or depth axes. Other learners may appear to have different characteristics and possess comparatively few vocabulary resources but considerable fluency in calling these to mind and using them in communication. These learners would occupy a different location in the lexical space, less far along the breadth axis but further along the fluency axis. This way of describing lexical knowledge is both attractive and convenient as it makes it easier to define, briefly, the nature of a test or what defines a learner's knowledge of words. But the notion of lexical space is still fundamentally a metaphor with all the drawbacks that go with that. The nature of the lexicon is not really a three-dimensional space and attempts to turn the metaphor into a detailed model which can be tested empirically run into trouble. The precise nature of the depth axis is a case in point and Read, who uses the term in his (Read, 2000) review of the field, questions the nature of this axis in later work (Read, 2004).

What are the conventional ways of measuring knowledge in this lexical space?

While we lack a comprehensive range of tests across the whole field of vocabulary knowledge, we do have a small number of well-established tests in the area of vocabulary breadth and, more particularly, passive receptive vocabulary knowledge. At first sight, testing how much a person knows from the enormous number of words in the English language (for example) appears a daunting task. There are tens or even hundreds of thousands of words, depending on how you define *word*, potentially available for learners to acquire, and taking a reasonable sample of these words to test a learner's knowledge should be difficult. A learner may only know a few of these words so the task is like searching for a needle in a haystack. Nonetheless, it does appear possible to compile a representative sample of words and this is because of the way words are used in language. Words do not occur randomly in speech or writing and some occur very much more frequently than others. Thus, verbs such as *make* or *do*, prepositions such as *in* and *on* and pronouns such as *I* or *you* are used a lot by every speaker, while other words such as *anamnestic* and *mitogenic* are very uncommon and might not be used at all even by native speakers except in the most specialised of situations. Where learners are exposed to a new language, therefore, they encounter some words much more often than others, and some words they never encounter at all. Unsurprisingly, learners are more likely to learn the frequent words than the infrequent words, or words so rare they never even see or hear them. Tests such as Nation's Levels Test and Meara and Milton's *X-Lex* take advantage of this reality to produce samples of the most frequent words in a given language to make credible estimates of overall vocabulary knowledge in learners. A good test is possible because it can be focused on areas where learning is likely to occur, rather than on areas where there is no knowledge to be detected. Although these tests work well, the frequency effect is an assumption which does not appear to have been empirically tested and the second chapter in this volume addresses this issue directly, asking not only whether or not the effect really exists, but also how strong it is and whether all learners are affected equally.

The idea of counting the frequency of words in a language tends to be thought of as a recent innovation and something we can now do because we have computers which can process millions of words. But the idea is, in reality, very old and goes back at least to the study of the writings of the Prophet Mohammed in the eighth century. The earliest counts made for pedagogical reasons were made in the 1930s and 1940s and these still provide useful lists, but modern resources such as the Bank of English and the British National Corpus now make very large corpora available to researchers and other organisations and these can be broken down so it is possible to investigate, say the frequencies of only written English or of only spoken English. Modern tests tend to be based on corpora and frequency counts of this kind and, for convenience draw on the most frequent vocabulary only, often in 1,000-word bands.

While the Levels Test and *X-Lex* estimate knowledge within the same area of the lexical space and are based on frequency counts of English, they are nonetheless two very different tests. *X-Lex*, for example, samples the 5,000 most frequent words of English drawing 20 words from each of the five 1,000-word frequency bands within this list and uses this to make an estimate of the number of words known out of these 5,000 words. This is probably the most general and all-encompassing kind of estimate of vocabulary size possible since it is a Yes/No or checklist test which requires learners merely to say if they recognise a test word as a word. An example from a paper version is shown in Figure 2 and gives an idea of the format.

Please look at these words. Some of these words are real French words and some are invented but are made to look like real words. Please tick the words that you know or can use. Here is an example.

☑ chien

Thank you for your help.

☐ de   ☐ distance   ☐ abattre   ☐ absurde   ☐ achevé   ☐ manchir

---

Figure 2   Extract from an *X-Lex* test of French (Milton, 2006: 190)

Any objective, or forced-answer test of this kind is open to guess-work on the part of the test-taker. The Yes/No tests attempt to estimate the amount of guesswork on the part of the test-taker and to adjust the scores the tests give, through the inclusion of pseudowords in the test. Pseudowords are words which look and sound like real words but do not really exist. In the French example in Figure 2, *manchir* is such a word. Usually this system works well and gives reliable results but in some learners the pseudowords attract very high numbers of Yes answers and it is less clear in these circumstances that the test is working as it should and is giving results which are useful. This question is addressed in Chapter 3.

Nation's *Levels Test* has many similarities with *X-Lex* in that it tests vocabulary breadth and takes advantage of frequency information in its construction. But it appears different since it adopts a complex multiple-choice format. An example of the question type it uses is shown in Figure 3.

This is a vocabulary test. You must choose the right word to go with each meaning. Write the number of that word next to its meaning.

1 business
2 clock   _____ part of a house
3 horse   _____ animal with four legs
4 pencil   _____ something used for writing
5 shoe
6 wall

Figure 3   Levels Test example taken from Nation (2001: 416)

There is no adjustment for guesswork but the presence of a range of answers means that learners who take the test must use the kind of test strategy which Eyckmans describes in Chapter 3 in order to try to maximise their marks. Even if they do not know the meaning of test words they will be in a position to pick a likely answer, because that is the nature of a test and choosing an uncertain answer is more likely to gain marks than not answering at all. Kamimoto (2005) recently reported speak aloud protocols conducted with learners taking this test. The feedback he received suggests that the learners' choice of guessing strategy can produce considerable differences in score and the Levels Test might have much more variation according to guesswork than any of us imagined. However, there is no explicit way in the test for taking account of this phenomenon.

Like *X-Lex* the Levels Test samples a range of frequency bands in order to gauge learners' overall vocabulary knowledge. Eighteen words are tested at each of the second, third, fifth and tenth 1,000-word frequency bands. In addition it samples knowledge of the University Word List (Nation, 1990) or the Academic Word List (Coxhead, 2000): lists of words which are particularly frequent in academic learning such as school or university.

Both these tests have been able to take advantage of frequency to sample the words in a language and form a picture of the learners' vocabulary resources. Because they are receptive tests the test-maker has the opportunity to manipulate the language being tested and can control the words being investigated. We are not only interested in estimating receptive or passive knowledge, however. We also need to be able to estimate the vocabulary resources which learners are able to use productively in speaking or reading. Testing this is much more difficult because we are reliant on the language which the learners themselves produce. As language users we are very adaptable with regard to the words we choose to speak or write. We may adjust our use of words according to who we are speaking to. For example, a doctor talking to an adult patient may mention *acute abdominal pain* but to a child the same condition might be *tummy ache*. Our use of language also varies according to the task we are called upon to perform. A letter or an essay will contain lots of highly frequent function words such as *make, can* and *do*, but a shopping list will omit these verbs and consist entirely of a list of nouns. The significance of this is that a single short piece of writing or speech, and most learners can only produce small amounts of language, may be untypical of what a learner knows and can do in other circumstances. So a single, short piece of writing or speech may tell us very little about the extent of productive word knowledge a learner possesses. It is a difficulty which is addressed in two questions which are pertinent to the whole of Part III in this volume. How do you collect a sample of productive language that is in some way typical or representative of the learner's vocabulary productive ability? And, how do you analyse the language which is produced to create a measure which you can use to compare one learner's knowledge with another in some meaningful way?

Attempts to arrive at such a measure, and answer the second question, usually revolve around the concept of *lexical richness*. The term covers several aspects of vocabulary use (see Read, 2000: 200 ff.) such as *lexical diversity*, which is 'the variety of active vocabulary deployed by a speaker or writer' (Malvern and Richards, 2002: 87), and *lexical sophistication* (the number of low frequency words) or *lexical density* (the ratio of content and function words). These notions are best understood through the example:

The cat sat on the mat.

We have already established that the above sentence has six tokens but only five types giving a Type–Token Ratio (TTR) of 5:6 or 0.833. Calculating TTR this way would be a simple measure of *lexical diversity*.

By looking at the numbers of function and content words we can make a calculation of lexical density for the same sentence. Function words are words like *and*, *of* and *is*, which do not carry much meaning in themselves but are essential to creating a grammatical sentence or phrases. Prepositions, conjunctions, pronouns and auxiliary words would almost always be function words. Content words tend to be nouns, main verbs and adjectives and are words which contribute most of the meaning to anything that is said or written. In the example sentence there are three function words, *the* occurs twice and *on* once, and three content words, *cat*, *sat* and *mat*. The ratio of content and function words would thus be 3:3 giving a *lexical density* of 1.

By looking at the number of low frequency words it is possible to make a calculation of lexical sophistication. There are computer programs such as *P-Lex* which can do this automatically (Meara and Bell, 2001); this uses a definition of any word which is not in the 2,000 most frequent words in English in order to systematically identify low frequency words. In the example, there is only one such word out of the six in the sentence and that is *mat*. A ratio of 1:6 would give a score for *lexical sophistication* of 0.167. *P-Lex* attempts to overcome difficulties created by length by making this calculation for every successive 10-word block in a piece of writing. It appears

(Milton, 2004b) that normal, unacademic text produces scores on this scale of about 2.5. About 80–90% of normal text, it would seem, is made up of very frequent vocabulary.

Since we know, or at least we think we do, that frequency and vocabulary learning are closely associated, the significance of the numbers of low frequency words a learner can use is potentially of great interest. Laufer and Nation's (1995) program the Lexical Frequency Profile (LFP) is able to take a text and produce a profile giving the numbers and proportions of vocabulary in the first 1,000-word frequency band, the second 1,000-word frequency band and the University Word List. An example of the information this program produces is shown in Table 2.

Table 2   Example of a vocabulary profile produced by Laufer and Nation's Lexical Frequency Profile (1995)

Word List	Tokens / %	Types / %	Families
one	3499/81.8	558/59.6	380
two	165/ 3.9	88/ 9.4	72
three	298/ 7.0	161/17.2	122
not in the lists	314/ 7.3	130/13.9	–
Total	4276	937	574

The results show that for the text under analysis there were 4,276 running words or tokens and 937 types. Of these, 3,499 or 81.8% of the tokens came from the first 1,000-word frequency band, 165 or 3.9% of tokens from the second 1,000-word frequency band and 298 words or 7% from the University Word List. Finally, 314 words, 7.3% of the tokens, were low frequency and did not occur in any of the other three categories. In any text, a surprisingly large number of words only ever occur once, in the text used for the example above 452 words occur only once and that is nearly half of all types, and linguistics has a name for these words – *hapax legomena* or sometimes just *hapax*.

There are, however, many methodological problems in the actual measurement of *lexical richness* in written texts or speech. The Type–Token Ratio has been under discussion for nearly a century (e.g. Thomson and Thompson, 1915; Johnson, 1944) but this is still being used today (for example, Jarvis, Grant, Bikowski and Ferris, 2003, who use this measure with controlled text length). However, the TTR has been strongly criticised as unreliable in contexts where texts with different lengths are compared (for a discussion see van Hout and

Vermeer, 1988; Broeder, Extra and van Hout, 1993; and Vermeer, 2000). The problem is that TTR is sensitive to text length. Longer texts have a tendency to produce lower values for the TTR because the chance of a new word (type) occurring gets lower as text length increases since the speaker/writer has a limited number of words at their disposal. This means that speakers who produce longer texts get systematically 'marked down' by this measure and those who produce shorter texts (often a good indicator of lower proficiency level) get higher scores. This makes the TTR less suitable for the measurement of spontaneous speech or writing where texts with different lengths have to be compared.

The studies in Part III of this volume use a variety of the measures described here, often adapted so that they are less sensitive to variations in length. They also use a variety of ways of collecting samples of productive language from which to assess lexical richness. Most common is the use of written essays and the studies used to validate both *P-Lex* and LFP rely on these. The subject matter of essays can affect scores, however, as can the register chosen by the learner, and this variation poses problems. Other researchers use transcripts of speech which has the same potential problem. In Chapter 7 Tidball and Treffers-Daller use picture cues to prompt story telling and this seems a promising way of standardising the nature of student output so scores can be meaningfully compared.

Test reliability and validity

Whatever the tests we use in measuring vocabulary, there is always a concern that the tests should work and properly. All of the studies presented in this volume are concerned with establishing what the tests tell us so that we can interpret the scores appropriately. There are two major issues which the users of any test will need to be sure of and these are *test reliability* and *test validity*.

Test reliability is the accuracy with which a test measures what it is supposed to measure. More usefully, it might be seen as a test of consistency. If you run a vocabulary test several times on a person whose vocabulary has not changed (several tests in one afternoon, for example) then the tests should give the same results. If it does this then it is said to be reliable. If a test cannot do this then you cannot place much faith in the scores it gives you. Reliability tells you nothing else about the qualities of the test, whether it is testing what you think it is testing or whether it is the right test for the use it is put to; it only says whether it is working consistently and does not give different scores for people with the same ability. Multiple-choice and forced-answer tests generally seem to have very good reliability and part of the credibility attached to tests of receptive vocabulary know-ledge is that they give very reliable results. Both Milton and Eyck-mans touch on this in Chapters 2 and 3. Part of the difficulties which we experience in tests of productive knowledge, and which are dealt with in greater depth in Part III of this volume, is that our data collection techniques, using unstandardised pieces of speech and writing, are simply not consistent enough to allow reliable results to emerge.

Test validity is the extent to which a test measures what it is supposed to measure. So, in the case of vocabulary size, can we be sure that a test measures this quantity and not something else? There may be several separate issues involved in this notion, which is quite a complex one. One such issue would be *content validity*, that is, the degree to which a test has the necessary content. Tests like the Levels Test and *X-Lex* can be said to have good content validity because they do not waste time and effort testing words which learners will never know and because they use frequency information to target testing in areas where there is likely to be knowledge. Of course, if the assumption that frequency and learning are not as closely related as we think, and Chapter 2 examines this, then the content validity of these tests will be severely compromised. Connected with content validity is *construct validity*, that is, whether the test measures the skill or construct it is meant to. This is where the whole subject becomes really challenging. Language knowledge is not easily quanti-fiable like shoe size or hat size and often has to be inferred from activities or actions which may well involve other knowledge and abilities. This is exactly the issue raised by Eyckmans et al. in Chapter 3: can a test constructed using pseudowords work well enough to be valid? It is also a leitmotiv of all this volume. While van Hout and Vermeer, and Richards and Malvern consider the construct of productive vocabulary tests from the point of view of theory, later chapters tackle the problem empirically by investigating what skills and abilities these tests predict best, for example, Chapter 8 by Daller and Huijuan Xue.

A common way of determining whether or not a test is well constructed is to test learners using two tests; a new test, for example, and a well-established test of the same language ability or skill, and to then compare the results. It is generally expected that if the new test is well constructed then the scores will correlate with the older test. This is called *concurrent validity* and it is frequently used in the consideration of new test forms. One of the attractions of this process is that it usually allows correlations between the two tests to be calculated and statistical tests of reliability to be applied. The whole basis of validity appears to be placed on a sounder empirical footing than would otherwise be the case. Within reason, this is a sensible and useful thing to do but Chapter 6, by Fitzpatrick, provides a cautionary tale in the overuse, or misuse, of concurrent validity testing. Test validity in languages is, in reality, rarely a simple or a black and white issue where a test is clearly valid or invalid. Rather, it raises questions of degrees of confidence and subtleties of interpretation and this volume endeavours to do the same.

The studies in this volume

Paul Nation's introductory chapter raises six questions about the validity of tests of vocabulary knowledge. They are all centred around the danger that one or more intervening variables can affect scores on even the most rigorously constructed vocabulary test. The tests themselves may be fine but the way learners handle the test or the ways in which users handle them or the results may result in misleading conclusions being drawn.

The first threat to the validity of a test arises from the testees' attitudes towards the test, their willingness to participate, or not, due to negative experiences with previous tests and their familiarity with the test format. Learners will therefore vary in the way they approach and handle vocabulary tests and test scores may reflect this kind of variation (in addition to variation in vocabulary knowledge), and we have very little knowledge of how this variation may work.

The second threat relates to the appropriateness of frequency data. Many tests are based on frequency lists. Frequency data gathered in formal L1 contexts are unlikely to provide a useful basis for tests in a more informal L2 setting.

The third threat has to do with the unit of counting used (e.g. word families as opposed to lemmas); an inappropriate unit of counting might lead to over- or underestimations of vocabulary knowledge.

Fourth, Nation strongly argues for multiple measures in vocabulary assessment since vocabulary knowledge is multi-dimensional. Nation discusses several studies where multiple measures show clear advantages over single measures. The aim is to use a set of complementary measures that tap into different aspects of vocabulary knowledge and give a more complete picture than a single measure can.

A fifth threat to validity is the language of instruction used in the test. It is a common finding in research on bilingualism that testees are disadvantaged if the test is carried out in their weaker language (for immigrants this is in many cases the language of the host country). The same holds true for second language testing. Scores are generally higher in bilingual test formats than in monolingual formats.

Sixth, Nation argues for measures that focus on actual language use. He discusses measures of vocabulary richness in writing but points out that similar measures can be developed for speaking and other skills. It should be pointed out that the ultimate aim of all measures is to give insight in an aspect of linguistic knowledge that is part of language proficiency and therefore of the ability to use the language effectively.

The authors of this book address the questions raised by Nation from different angles and discuss ways of overcoming potential problems with the validity of the measures currently used.

Chapter 2 by Milton addresses the first of the validity questions raised in Nation's opening chapter: the question about variability between learners. Measures of vocabulary knowledge that are based on the frequency of the words make the implicit or explicit assumption that there is a predictable relationship between the frequency of a word in the input of a given language and the probability that it is learned at a certain stage of L2 acquisition. These measures divide the vocabulary into frequency bands, the most frequent thousand words, the next most frequent thousand words and so on. It can be assumed that more words are known from band 1 than from band 2 and that more words from band 2 are known than from higher bands.

However, it is far from clear what constitutes 'input' for many learners. The frequency of words used in course books does not necessarily reflect the frequency used by native speakers in a natural setting. Milton reports on a study that found a high number of infrequent words in textbooks. The chapter lists a number of other factors that influence vocabulary learning, including different learner styles. All these factors can explain that vocabulary knowledge in L2 cannot necessarily be predicted by the frequency of the words in frequency lists that are at least partially based on L1 usage. This is especially the case with low-level learners that have little access to their L2 outside the classroom. Milton reports the findings of a study of 227 Greek EFL learners. Only 60% of the learners follow the 'normal' expected pattern whereby the knowledge of a word can be predicted from an established frequency list. Other learners show an unusual dip in the percentage of known words that belong to frequency band 2 (this is called a *level two deficit*) or show other less clear patterns, and these patterns are by no means stable. More than a quarter of a subgroup tested twice show a change in their patterns. Some learners who showed a level two deficit in the first test did not show that deficit in the second test and vice versa. There are indications that the use of guessing strategies is one of the reasons for the changing patterns.

Milton's chapter illustrates that many factors influence lexical learning in L2. All these factors lead to considerable variability among learners, and this in turn is a threat to the validity of measures that are based on frequency lists. Milton points out that high variability can be found mainly in the knowledge of the most frequent 2,000 words. The knowledge of words with a higher frequency seems to follow the expected pattern more regularly. He argues that frequency-based measures are not under threat *per se* but that we have to take variability into account, especially among low level learners.

In Chapter 3 Eyckmans et al. address the issue of test validity with regard to the Yes/No Vocabulary Test in particular. Their research findings with this test format (studies with a total of 2,000 French-speaking learners of Dutch) are characterised by a response bias that contaminates the measure of vocabulary knowledge. This means that testees generally tend to favour either the *Yes* or the *No* response and do not demonstrate the neutral attitude to test items which the test presupposes. This introduces a variability that does not reflect differences in vocabulary knowledge but instead highlights the cultural, psychological or sociological characteristics, for example, that distinguishes each individual learner. These characteristics are obviously a threat to the validity of this test as they would be to any forced-answer test. The correction formulae that have been proposed in the literature to take into account this construct-irrelevant variance do not succeed in compensating for these effects whilst maintaining a sufficient reliability.

Eyckmans et al. investigate whether the use of certain features that are only available in a computer-based Yes/No test can overcome these validity problems. These features include forced response, presenting the items in a random order, imposing a time limit per item and repeating the instruction with every item presented. In order to decide whether these features give some added value to the test format two different computer-based test formats are used, one that includes all these special features (format B), and one that does not, and is therefore not dissimilar to a pencil and paper test (format A). They then compare the *hit rate* (real words that are claimed to be known) and the *rejection rate* (pseudowords that are claimed to be unknown). For format A the *hit rate* and the *rejection rate* show a statistically significant negative correlation which can only be explained as the result of a systematic response bias. Those testees who claim that they know the correct words also claim to know the pseudowords, and those who have a tendency to claim that they do not know the correct words have a tendency to make the same claim for pseudowords. With other words candidates have a systematic bias towards a *Yes* or a *No* response. For format B there was no significant correlation between the two response rates. This does not, however, prove a higher validity for format B as both versions had a high *false alarm rate* (more than 20% of the pseudowords were claimed to be known). In order to investigate this further a translation task was used. Testees were asked to translate the items into their L1 (French). The marking of this translation was relatively lenient, wrong spellings etc. were accepted. Nevertheless almost half of the words that were claimed to be known were translated incorrectly. The question is whether correction formulae can compensate for this degree of overestimation of vocabulary knowledge by the testees. To investigate the validity issue further, correlations were computed between the Yes/No test scores obtained by different correction formulae and the scores on the translation task. The correction formulae reduce the number of *hit scores* (existing words that are claimed to be known) by 'marking down' testees who apply guessing strategies. However, this does not lead to a dramatic increase in the correlations with the translation task. In other words, concurrent validity of the correction formulae cannot be established with this group of learners. Overall, Eyckmans et al. conclude that the validity of the Yes/No format has to be questioned in that it may not be equally suitable for all types of learners.

In Chapter 4 Richards and Malvern discuss a number of studies with regard to the validity questions raised by Nation. In line with Milton (Chapter 2) the validity of measures based on L1 frequency data for lower and intermediate learners is questioned because their access to the foreign language outside the classroom may be limited. However, a study with secondary school learners showed that a frequency-based test (*X-Lex*, Meara and Milton, 2003a) aimed at lower intermediate learners yielded convincing results showing that these learners are sensitive to the frequency of words. The test is based on five frequency bands (1–5k) and there is a steady decline in the percentage of known words from the highest to the lowest frequency band. The authors discuss several other threats to the validity of vocabulary tests and identify learners' attitudes which are related to the face validity of a test as the most serious threat as this aspect is to a large extent beyond the control of the researcher.

A specific concern of the authors is that of multiple measures. Richards and Malvern argue strongly in favour of multiple measures and against the misinterpretation that the measure developed by the authors (*D*) was suggested as a single measure. *D* was originally developed to overcome the problems with the falling Type–Token Ratio (TTR) curve. The longer a text is, the fewer new words will be introduced, simply because the speaker/writer runs out of new words. This leads to a systematic decrease in the ratio between new words (types) and all words (tokens) and makes it difficult to compare texts of different lengths. *D* is the single parameter of a mathematical model for this falling TTR curve and allows comparing speakers/writers irrespective of the length of the text produced. *D* had been called a 'unified measure' but the authors stress that this does not mean 'single measure'. The mathematical modelling is unified in the sense that it can be applied to various other ratios, not only the TTR. Richards and Malvern discuss a number of studies that use the same underlying mathematical model and apply it to other ratios (e.g. research in early L1 acquisition with a focus on the relation between nouns and verbs).

In the remainder of the chapter the authors investigate the third threat to validity mentioned in Nation's opening chapter, that is, the question of the unit of counting. There can be no single answer to the best unit of counting since this might depend on the age of the learners and the aim of the study. Richards and Malvern discuss a study where the same database, transcriptions from the Bristol Corpus in L1 acquisition, was analysed according to different definitions of the unit of counting; ranging from a very broad definition of what would count as a word on the basis of the unedited transcript, to a very narrow definition at the other end of the spectrum, to a fully lemmatised transcription. The authors applied *D*, as a measure of diversity, to the transcripts with five different definitions of the unit of counting. The results show high inter-correlations between the *D*-values obtained. The authors argue, however, that these correlations do not mean that the five versions of the test measure the same thing. They bring forward three objections to such an interpretation. They argue that better edited data are always more reliable, that a high inter-correlation does not mean that the individuals score similarly (with negative consequences, if judgements were to be made on individual children) and finally, that the correlations can be misleading from a statistical point of view. Overall, Richards and Malvern make a strong case for a carefully defined unit of counting.

Chapter 5 is entirely focused on the measurement of lexical

richness. Van Hout and Vermeer discuss the validity problems with Type–Token Ratio and attempt to overcome these problems with mathematical transformation. The authors list a number of mathematical transformations that have been proposed in the past but focus in their investigation on the measure of Guiraud's Index (a simple mathematical transformation of the TTR) and D – the mathematical model that is discussed in the previous chapter, Chapter 4. The argument is complex but rich in detail.

First, they illustrate the problems that arise due to the influence of text lengths with an empirical study based on the first three chapters of Genesis (King James Bible). With increasing text length (number of tokens) there is also an increase in the number of new words (types). This increase, however, follows a curvilinear pattern rather than a straightforward linear one. This is in line with the expectations as mentioned in Chapter 4. Writers/speakers simply run out of new words and repeat words already used the longer the text gets. Therefore, the number of new words (types) does not increase in the same way as the total number of words (tokens). In van Hout and Vermeer's study this leads to an upwards curvilinear relationship because they look at the increase of types with increasing text length. This corresponds to a systematic decrease of the Type–Token Ratio. This decrease of the TTR is stronger at the beginning of growing text length before it flattens out, hence the curvilinear pattern. Van Hout and Vermeer show that this pattern cannot be modelled by a simple regression. They carry out four regression analyses on the basis of the raw data and three mathematical transformations that attempt to straighten out the curvilinear pattern. The regression analysis on the raw data leads to a constant which 'makes no sense', as the authors point out, since the model would predict that a text with a length of one token would contain 59 types (see Tables 2 and 3 in Chapter 5). Further, the regressions carried out on the mathematical transformations also lead to constants, in two cases with a negative sign. This is not interpretable because a text cannot contain a negative number of types. It remains to be discussed whether these findings rule out the use of regression analysis *per se* for modelling the relationship between types and tokens.

Van Hout and Vermeer go on to consider the TTR and two other measures for lexical diversity that have been proposed in the literature. These are Guiraud's Index and Herdan's Index, which are two mathematical transformations of the TTR. In a study on Moroccan and Turkish L2 learners of Dutch in primary education all values for the indices decrease with increasing L2 exposure. The authors make a tentative interpretation of these data by stating that an increase of high-frequency function words at a certain point in L2 acquisition might be the reason for the surprising findings. This raises questions about validity similar to those addressed by Nation about the influence of the unit of counting. Complex L2 acquisition processes might not be accessible by counting mere types and tokens without looking into the function that different types have at different stages of the acquisition process. Van Hout and Vermeer report on a further study with adult L2 learners where there was no increase in the measures of lexical richness used over time. They argue that during L2 acquisition, a complex relationship between the types and tokens used might take place.

With this in mind, they consider a theoretical approach to why and how texts differ in the number of types used using an 'urn' model of different vocabularies. Two-word categories (function words and content words) are given different probabilities of being picked from an 'urn' and end up as 'words in a text'. The number of different words in these texts depends on several parameters: the probability of the two-word categories being picked; the ratio between these word categories; and the number of items in the urn, the vocabulary size. The main finding is that even with a relatively simple model like this the TTR discriminates only poorly between the different vocabulary sizes. However, this simple model can be made a bit more 'human' by a more complex set of probabilities for the items. The function words are divided into two groups, one with a high and one with a low probability of being picked from the urn. For the content words the probability of being picked can be increased if the same item has already been chosen earlier. Three different lexicons can be modelled in this way. All have the same size but different probabilities. The number of types that are picked differs widely and the 95% confidence interval for the mean score of types picked increases the more 'human' the lexicons are made. The authors argue that these findings raise serious doubts about the reliability of measures that are based on the occurrence of types.

As a consequence, they suggest a new way of measuring richness by taking the frequencies of the types into account (the MLR or Measure of Lexical Richness). Van Hout and Vermeer are mainly concerned with the vocabulary size of schoolchildren. Therefore, they define the frequency on the basis of a corpus that was gathered in a school setting. This corpus comprises almost two million words with 26,000 lemmas that can be divided into nine frequency bands. The size of a child's productive vocabulary can be estimated on the basis of the number of words that are used from each frequency band. Van Hout and Vermeer report the findings of a study that uses

this new measure. Two groups of children were compared, 16 L1
learners and 16 L2 learners of Dutch. These children carried out a
word-recognition task and a word-definition task. In addition,
spontaneous speech was recorded. On the basis of these data several
measures were carried out, including Guiraud's Index, two versions
of MLR and *D* (computed with the CLAN command *vocd*).
Guiraud's Index and MLR show significant differences between the
groups whereas no significant differences can be found with *D*.
Extrapolation of the vocabulary size based on MLR shows a clearly
larger vocabulary for L1 learners than for L2 learners. Van Hout and
Vermeer draw the overall conclusion that frequency data need to be
taken into account in research on lexical richness. They argue that
only large corpora can provide these data. In line with Nation's
second validity question, they gather these data from the environment
of the children, the school setting.

In Chapter 6 Fitzpatrick addresses another issue of test validity:
the premature use of test formats that have not been sufficiently
scrutinised in pilot studies. Whereas in many cases researchers look
mainly at the concurrent or criterion-related validity of a test,
Fitzpatrick argues that the construct and content validity of a test
equally deserve attention. The test format under investigation in this
chapter is *Lex-30*, a vocabulary association task. Thirty frequent
words are used in this test and the subjects are asked to give three or
four word associations for each stimulus. The test score of *Lex-30* is
the percentage of infrequent word associations given by the subjects.
In order to investigate what these test scores mean two other tests
were administered with the same subjects, the Controlled Productive
version of the Levels Test (Laufer and Nation, 1999) and a translation task based on 20 randomly selected words from each of the
first three frequency bands of Nation's word list. It was assumed that
these three tests would yield high correlations as they seem to test the
same ability: to produce L2 words which represent various frequency
bands. All correlations between the three tests are statistically
significant. However, the magnitude of the correlation between
Lex-30 and the two other tests is relatively low. This means that
either the tests vary in their degree of accuracy or measure different
aspects of lexical knowledge.

Fitzpatrick pursues this idea and tries to establish the construct
validity of the tests involved by having a closer look at what is
measured and how these tests measure vocabulary knowledge. It
emerges that the Productive Levels Test as used in this study focuses
mainly on the most frequent 3,000 words and so does the translation
task. However, *Lex-30* awards marks for any word beyond the first

frequency band and therefore includes words that are beyond the first 3,000 words. Furthermore, the three tests use different stimuli to elicit the lexical response. *Lex-30* has only a semantic stimulus, whereas there is also an orthographic stimulus in the other tasks and even an additional orthographic stimulus in the Productive Levels Test and the three tests therefore activate knowledge in different ways. An argument that the three tests measure different types of vocabulary knowledge can be made on the basis of Nation's list of 'aspects of word knowledge'. This clearly indicates that some aspects (e.g. meaning associations) are only relevant for *Lex-30* and others (e.g. collocations or appropriateness of the word) only for the Productive Levels Test. Overall, Fitzpatrick concludes that more work is needed to establish the construct validity of the tests involved before they can be used by teachers and other decision-makers. This might be regrettable from a practical point of view but seems to be a necessary precaution especially for high-stakes test settings.

The multi-faceted concept of lexical knowledge is an argument for multiple measures as outlined by Nation in his chapter. In Chapter 7, therefore, Tidball and Treffers-Daller apply this concept to two groups of French learners, first-year undergraduates, final year under-graduates and a group of French native speakers. All three groups carried out a semi-spontaneous productive task based on retelling stories from two short comic strips. The transcriptions of these stories were then entered into the Codes for the Human Analysis of Transcripts (CHAT) format and analysed. In addition a C-test was administered. Two different types of measure were used to analyse the data. The first type of measure applied in this study is not based on any frequency data but on the occurrence of types and tokens (*D*, Guiraud's Index and TTR). The second type of measure is based on the distinction between basic and advanced words (Advanced Guiraud and Limiting Relative Diversity (LRD)). This distinction is made in the present study on the basis of a word list for spoken French. As Nation points out, the validity of measures based on word lists is threatened if an inappropriate list is used. The list used in this case is based on oral data but is relatively old (collected in 1959) and in principle, if oral language use changes rapidly, this might invalidate any conclusions based on such a list. In practice, however, it appears that the most frequent words in such lists do not change substantially (Nation, 2004). A further problem with frequency lists is the unit of counting. Tidball and Treffers-Daller argue strongly for a lemmatisation of the data, especially for French with its rich morphology. The question how measures can be adapted to specific languages has rarely been addressed (see also Daller, 1999 and Daller, van Hout and Treffers-Daller, 2003) but it seems logical that the structural characteristics of a language influence the way in which the unit of counting is usefully defined.

All measures in this study show the differences between the groups and yield statistically significant results when carrying out an ANOVA. The differences for the TTR are significant but the effect size (Eta^2) is much lower for the TTR than for the other measures. This is in line with the expectations. The highest value for Eta^2 is achieved with D for the vocabulary measures. It is worth mentioning that the C-test whose validity has been questioned (see Alderson, 2002) yields the highest value for Eta^2 overall. Quite astonishing are the very high correlation between D and Guiraud's Index ($r = .973$) which needs to be investigated further. Overall, the authors conclude that the word-list-based measures in this study do not show an advantage over the other measures, probably because the definition of basic items was not entirely appropriate to the task.

In Chapter 8 Daller and Huijuan Xue also use multiple measures to investigate the oral proficiency of Chinese EFL learners with different measures of lexical richness. The focus of this chapter is a methodological analysis of different measures of lexical richness: which measures can be used to describe the differences between the groups and to what extent do these findings reflect the results of Tidball and Treffers-Daller reported in the previous chapter? Two groups of Chinese EFL learners, one in the UK and another at a different level of proficiency in China, were asked to describe orally two picture stories (the same as in the study of Tidball and Treffers-Daller). These descriptions were then transcribed into the CHAT format and analysed. Two types of measures were used for this analysis: measures based on word lists (LFP/*Beyond 2,000*, *P-Lex* and Advanced Guiraud) and measures that are not based on any frequency data but only on the occurrence of types and tokens (D, Guiraud's Index and TTR). They used Nation's word list in the present study for the definition of basic and advanced words.

All measures except the TTR and *P-Lex* yielded highly significant differences between the two groups. For the TTR this was predictable as the text length of the spoken descriptions varied greatly (from 61 to 602 tokens). An interpretation for *P-Lex* is difficult. This measure is not designed to be a function of text length. It is a measure that models the occurrence of rare words according to a Poisson distribution. An interpretation of this result is not easy and more research into the use of this measure would be necessary. The other measures discriminate between the two groups with the highest Eta^2 achieved with the Guiraud's Index, followed by D and then the word-list-based measures. We do not know what the actual difference in lexical proficiency between the two groups is and therefore we do not know what an 'appropriate' value for Eta^2 would be. Guiraud's Index might exaggerate the actual differences. Nevertheless, it turns out to be the best measure because it discriminates between the groups most clearly. It might be a magnifying glass but still a useful one. This is in line with the positive results for this index obtained by van Hout and Vermeer (see Chapter 5). The fact that the word-list-based measures yield a significant p-value but a nonetheless lower value for Eta^2 than Guiraud's Index and D is probably due to the fact that the word list here is not appropriate for the task. It is not a word list that is based on spoken language and it is relatively old (roughly similar to the word list used in the previous chapter). There are two ways out of this problem: we could try to find more appropriate word lists or we could base our decisions about basic and advanced words on a different criterion, e.g. teacher judgements (see Daller et al., 2003). Overall, Chapters 7 and 8 come to the same conclusions. Firstly, the word lists used have to be selected very carefully as Nation already points out in his chapter. Secondly, more than 50 years after it was proposed, Guiraud's Index still appears to be a good measure of lexical richness.

In Chapter 9 Wilks and Meara challenge the metaphor of a 'network' as a suitable concept for vocabulary research. They argue that the metaphor itself might shape our concept of lexical organisation rather than explain it. They ask whether the attitude and actual behaviour of test-takers in the test situation shape the construct of a network that does not exist in this form outside the test situation. In this way a network is a construct which develops 'a life of its own'. This would certainly undermine the validity of these tests and is quite similar to the validity question about learners' attitudes raised by Nation. To investigate the concept of lexical networks further Wilks and Meara carry out a study on word associations. Two groups of French learners and a group of French native speakers were asked to identify word associations in 20 sets each containing 10 words that were randomly selected from a French basic word list. The learner group with the higher proficiency identified more associations than the lower proficiency group. The highest number of associations was found by the native speakers. The number of associations for each group can quite convincingly be modelled with a Poisson distribution where the higher proficiency of the group is reflected in a higher parameter lambda (Poisson distributions are defined by a single parameter: lambda). However, when the association profiles of individual subjects are examined there are considerable deviations from the model curves and there is a 'surprising degree of individual variation'. This means that the number of associations made by the individuals does not follow predictable patterns in many cases. A further analysis including interviews with the subjects shows that a range of different strategies were applied to carry out the task and that idiosyncratic association behaviour constitutes a serious threat to the validity of the test. The main problem is that it is impossible to identify what is a legitimate association as it varies from individual to individual even in a native speaker group. Our access to lexical networks is only possible via the test-taking task and is therefore indirect. It is even possible associations are only created through the task and do not exist in this form permanently outside the task. On the basis of these findings the authors argue for a long-term approach to research on the relationship between theory and methodology.

In Chapter 10 Schur also investigates the organisation of the lexicon as a network. Her hypothesis is that the organisation of the lexicon follows the pattern of small-world networks, a concept adopted from graph theory. Small-world networks have several characteristics, such as sparseness of the connections and their clustering around a few nodes, which appear to mimic the way we think words may interconnect in a lexicon. Another useful characteristic is that the organisation of small-world networks is neither completely regular nor completely random. The nodes in lexical networks are obviously words which form the network through their connection with other words through association or collocation. Nodes in these networks are either highly connected or have only a limited number of associates with other words.

Schur's research design is based on associations of different groups of testees between a set of 50 verbs selected by the researcher. The groups included bilinguals, monolinguals and foreign language learners, and they produced clearly different association networks. This allows making a distinction between different learner types on the basis of their word association. Interestingly, there are also different network associations between EFL learners with different L1 backgrounds. The group of Chinese EFL students in Schur's study showed clearly distinct behaviour in their network associations when compared with Hebrew EFL learners. The Chinese students produced much more bi-directional associations than the Hebrew students did. An explanation of this difference is far from easy; however, this shows that a research design based on the elicitation of associations and the consequent construction of networks allows distinguishing between different learner types. This is an argument for the validity of this specific research method. All association networks produced by these groups were analysed according to graph theoretical criteria. Schur shows that the groups create different association networks but what all networks have in common is that they belong to the category of small-world networks. This is at least a tentative finding which is a strong argument for further research in this area which might lead to a new way in understanding lexical knowledge and its organisation.

In Chapter 11 Haquebord and Stellingwerf investigate the relationship between vocabulary knowledge and reading competence in a Dutch school setting. They discuss the development of an adaptive vocabulary test that can be used as part of a diagnostic test battery for reading proficiency at secondary school level. This is a very important area of research because an increasing number of pupils in the Netherlands in particular and in Europe in general are L2 learners. One important research question is whether the difficulties such learners often experience in reading are due to a small vocabulary or a lack of appropriate reading strategies. An answer to this question obviously has important pedagogical implications for remedial programmes. The authors argue that reading proficiency is based on vocabulary knowledge (e.g. word recognition) *and* a combination of top-down and bottom-up reading strategies. Good readers combine these two strategies to extract meaning from the text. The authors identify three types of weaker readers with different needs for remedial programmes. The first group of weak readers relies mainly on top-down strategies (e.g. guessing) which can compensate for a lack of lexical knowledge. However, if texts become more difficult these readers fail and need additional vocabulary training. The second group of weak readers have sufficient vocabulary knowledge but lack successful reading strategies. This group needs additional reading instructions. A third group has problems in both areas and needs special attention. Haquebord and Stellingwerf developed an adaptive vocabulary test that can, in addition to a well-established reading comprehension test in Dutch, draw a detailed picture of the reading profile of secondary pupils. This allows an informed judgement on remedial teaching for pupils with different reading profiles. The vocabulary test developed by the authors is adaptive in the sense that it can be adjusted to different reading levels. An empirical investigation with more than 2,700 pupils in secondary education in the Netherlands shows that the vocabulary test differentiates sufficiently between students at different levels. This is an argument for the reliability and the validity of the test. The fact that the vocabulary test in combination with the established reading comprehension test allows identifying different reader types as mentioned above is an additional argument for the construct validity of the test. More than 50% of the pupils in this study are classified as fluent readers. It is, however, a worrying fact that about 15% of pupils have severe reading difficulties. It is perhaps no coincidence that this percentage matches the percentage of L2 first year students in secondary education in the Netherlands. This large number of pupils with severe reading difficulties makes it clear that valid vocabulary tests and research on vocabulary knowledge are of vital importance in our present school environment.

In Chapter 12 Lorenzo-Dus argues strongly in favour of integrated methodologies in vocabulary research. She points out that it is essential to combine qualitative and quantitative approaches to draw a comprehensive picture of foreign language proficiency. To make the point for qualitative approaches Lorenzo-Dus reports a study carried out by Koike (1998) where two interview techniques are compared, the oral proficiency interview (OPI) and the simulated oral proficiency interview (SOPI). In the first technique an examiner is present during the interview, in the latter technique the candidate has to carry out a series of oral tasks without an examiner being present. It would be expected that the performance of candidates would differ with the two interview techniques. However, quantitative analyses fail to show these differences whereas a qualitative approach reveals variation in candidate performance when these two different interview techniques are used. Lorenzo-Dus takes this as a further indication that qualitative approaches have to be part of research designs in vocabulary research. For this reason she combines both approaches in a study of oral interviews in Spanish. A first result which is also discussed in Chapter 13 is the fact that examiners obviously focus more on lexical sophistication than on lexical diversity. This can be shown with purely quantitative methods. However, other aspects of the interviews are only accessible with qualitative approaches. Lorenzo-Dus shows that the ratings of the examiners are not only influenced by the number of rare words used but also by their position in discourse. Examinees who receive high ratings use these words more often in natural stretches of talk rather than in 'prefabricated units' (word clusters learned and used as chunks).

Another aspect that appears to be important in the prediction of teacher ratings is the accommodation strategies used by examiners or interlocutors. The more the examiner has to accommodate to the examinee, the lower the rating of the candidate's performance will be. However, only a qualitative analysis will reveal the use of some of these strategies. The findings of Lorenzo-Dus show that the number of questions from the examiner seeking clarification does not differ significantly between interviews with students at different proficiency levels. Therefore a quantitative approach does not give further insights in the importance of this question type for rating by examiners. A qualitative analysis of the function of these questions reveals, however, that they are mainly used to check comprehension with poorer candidates and to manage turn-taking with better students. Overall, the findings of Lorenzo-Dus are a clear indication that a combination of different approaches is useful, and this is a further argument for the use of multiple measurements in research on vocabulary proficiency.

In the final chapter, Chapter 13, Daller and Phelan investigate which aspects of lexical richness are more important for teacher judgements on foreign language proficiency. The answer to this question is important, since, at least in a classroom setting, the construct of language proficiency is partially determined by the judgements of the teachers. We assume that teachers focus more on lexical sophistication than on lexical diversity because judgements based on the use of rare words allow economical marking strategies. Four experienced teachers were asked to give an overall rating of 31 essays written by EFL learners. They were also asked to judge various other linguistic aspects of these essays, including the vocabulary range. There are high inter-correlations between the ratings of the teachers as a group, which is an indication for reliable judgements overall. However, there are also high correlations between the ratings that teachers give on the different linguistic qualities of individual essays. It can be assumed that there are large halo effects and that in general teachers are mainly focused on an overall, holistic rating. This is in line with earlier findings on the assessment of oral interviews (Malvern and Richards, 2002). An obvious explanation is that teachers have economical marking strategies where holistic ratings are more efficient than more detailed judgements. The ratings of the teachers were then correlated with scores of the essays obtained by different measures of lexical richness. These are measures of lexical diversity (TTR, D and Guiraud's Index) and measures of lexical sophistication (Guiraud Advanced, *P-Lex* and the total number of Advanced Types). The teacher ratings correlate highly with all measures of lexical sophistication but only modestly and not significantly with D. This is an indication that lexical sophistication is indeed more important than lexical diversity for teacher ratings. A further finding of this study is that the TTR is not a useful measure where essays of different length are analysed. This is in line with the researchers' expectations. Quite surprisingly, Guiraud's Index, which is only a simple mathematical transformation of the TTR, seems to be a useful measure. As Chapters 7 and 8 report similar findings for Guiraud's Index in other contexts, we argue that this relatively old index should not be discarded from our repertoire of lexical measures for the time being and be included in future research designs.

Helmut Daller, James Milton and Jeanine Treffers-Daller

PART I:
FUNDAMENTAL ISSUES

1 Fundamental issues in modelling and assessing vocabulary knowledge

Paul Nation

At a recent conference on vocabulary measurement and testing (held at the University of the West of England, Bristol, in January 2004) those who took part were struck by the way independent researchers were constantly returning to the same theme in their work; that of the validity of the measures we were using. This trend was not restricted to new efforts to model and measure vocabulary knowledge, as in attempts to characterise vocabulary depth. But they extended too to areas such as vocabulary breadth where, at first sight, the measures we have appear extremely well founded and reliable, and where the qualities of the tests appear to be well known. This chapter, then, looks at a range of factors that have been shown to affect the validity of vocabulary measures and it provides an oversight of the issues which will be addressed again and again in subsequent chapters. These issues include the selection of vocabulary items, the attitude of the subjects involved, what is counted as a word, and various aspects of what it means to know a word (multiple measures, the use of the first language, and vocabulary in use). There are satisfactory ways of dealing with these factors and they mostly relate to having a clear idea of the purpose of the measure.

Learner attitude and individual variability

The importance of this is probably best made clear by an anecdote. One of the teachers studying in our MA programme had given the Vocabulary Levels Test to a group of his secondary school students. He said he thought most of them were native speakers of English. Their scores on the Academic Word List level were low, less than 15 out of 30. I was surprised at this because my belief had been that young native speakers of English increased their vocabulary size by around 1,000 word families a year, and this can be considered a conservative estimate. Their lexical knowledge by secondary school age should have included all the Academic Word List (AWL) items. I went to the school and went through the AWL section of the test that they had previously sat, individually with each learner. Initially I used the procedure of getting them to read each of the six words in a block aloud, and then to read the definitions aloud. I did this to check if their low scores were affected by their reading skills. One learner had trouble with irregularly spelled words like *foreign*, but, when asked, she could explain its meaning. I then covered up the two bottom definitions and, focusing only on the top definition, got the learner to read through the six words trying to find a match with the definition. Initially there was a hasty incorrect response, to which I said, 'Try again'. When they chose the correct answer I praised them and we carried on. If they got all three in a block correct I said, 'Great. You know all of those.' Sometimes an answer was incorrect because they had a homograph in mind, for example *seal* where they were thinking of the marine mammal and the test was looking for the verb 'close completely'.

Each learner got most of the AWL section correct. Using the previous results of the test, the school had just set up a programme to teach the AWL words to the students. It was clear from the later responses of the individuals that they already knew most of the words and that their poor scores on the test were the result of several factors. The most important was probably their attitude to taking the test. They did not take it seriously and probably did it quickly without giving it much attention. Secondly, many of them had had bad experiences with tests before and lacked confidence in their own ability. Thirdly, there was a lack of test-taking strategies. The Vocabulary Levels Test uses a matching format and the items within each block are unavoidably interdependent. If you get the first one wrong and that wrong answer is the correct answer for another item in the block, then it has a double effect. So with the six choices there is a need to consider each choice. It helps if each block is approached in a systematic strategic way, but in this case we had no idea how the test-takers' strategies were affecting the scores until they were interviewed and retested. Fourthly, there is a problem with the test itself. The test items do not have a context, so the test-taker is not guided to a particular polyseme or homograph. Fifthly, a few of the AWL words, particularly with the senses given in the test, may be unknown to 15–16-year old native speakers of English, or may not be their first choice of a meaning.

What was clear to me from this brief piece of work with some learners was that we need to check whether our tests and measures are giving us valid information. Ideally this checking would not only be in the form of pilot studies, but by checking with the individuals who sat the test as soon as possible after the sitting. Anglin (1993: 112–113) also noticed a similar phenomenon when learners sat a multiple-choice test after they had been interviewed about words. Anglin's exemplification of interviews about word meanings shows the different roles that interview tests and multiple-choice tests can play, particularly with items where there are literal meanings that are not the required answer.

I: OK. What does the word *twenty questions* mean?
C: It could mean like questions like things that are asked by people.
I: Mm-mmm.
C: *Twenty* might mean that you're asking them twenty questions.
I: OK. Can you tell me anything more about the word *twenty questions*?
C: *Twenty*'s a number, and it's the amount of questions you can ask.
I: Can you use it in a sentence to show me you know what it means?
C: The teacher asked us twenty questions in the afternoon. [*Multiple-choice question answered correctly.*]
I: Have you ever played that game?
C: Ya, I just forgot about that.

In an interview, although a learner might pursue a meaning that is on the wrong track, in a multiple-choice item they can choose the wanted answer even when one of the wrong choices is the wrong track they originally pursued.

I: What does the word *dust bowl* mean?
C: *Dust bowl?*
I: Mmm.
C: Well dust is, like, is like little dirt in the air that it'll, it'll collect on things.
I: Mmm.
C: Dust. And a bowl is like you eat your cereal out of it.
I: Mmm.
C: A *dust bowl*. Wouldn't be dust in a bowl I don't think.
I: Mmm.
C: So I don't know.
I: OK. Do you think you might be able to use it in a sentence to show me you know what it means?
C: No. These ones are getting tougher. [*Multiple-choice question answered correctly.*]

Interviews have the value of being a stringent unguided test of knowledge. A disadvantage is that the learners' initial mind-set might stop them from reaching the correct answer. Multiple-choice items also seemed to be more sensitive than the interview in that learners gained higher scores. They also allow a focus on particular meanings. Multiple-choice items provide answers and so there may be a doubt about whether the learners really knew the answer in that detail.

However, by providing choices they allow the learners to consider responses that they knew but may not have considered in the interview.

Of course, not all vocabulary tests are multiple choice. Nonetheless, the same problems of learner attitude and response to the test can affect the data. A task as seemingly simple as the Yes/No response favoured in tests such as *X-Lex* (Meara and Milton, 2003a) requires the testee to be interested enough to make a considered judgement to the test word in the first place but also, in the event of doubt, decide how big a risk to take in responding. The work of Eyckmans et al. (in this volume) on the way their Dutch learners of French respond to false words suggests that all learners may not be alike in making the same kind of choices when faced with partially known, or unknown, words. This is bound to affect the scores such learners get on these Yes/No tests but in a way we do not fully understand.

Frequency lists

Vocabulary tests generally make use of word frequency data to subdivide and sequence items in a test. Developments in corpus linguistics have added greatly to our knowledge of important factors affecting the making of frequency lists, but somewhat surprisingly has not always resulted in the creation of relevant, well-constructed lists. The most recent, accessible and substantial frequency lists are those derived from the British National Corpus (Leech, Rayson and Wilson, 2001). The lists have been very carefully made using the three essential measures of frequency, range and dispersion. The full set of these measures is noticeably missing in many other recent counts such as those done for the Longman and COBUILD learner dictionaries. The BNC list also provides lemma groupings.

A careful examination of the BNC lists reveals what is now a truism in corpus linguistics – the composition of the corpus determines the nature of what is drawn from it. Leech and Fallon's (1992) brilliantly revealing and amusing study of the Lancaster–Oslo/Bergen Corpus (LOB) and Brown corpora is an excellent example of this. The BNC lists clearly reflect the nature of the BNC, which is that it is a corpus of adult, formal, British English. Some examples will make this clear. *Literacy* is more frequent than *naughty*, *archbishop* is more frequent than *strap*. There are words which have surprisingly high frequencies in the BNC, higher than might be expected from our experience of everyday language use, for example, *infrastructure*, *allege*, and *directorate*. *Budget, campaign, client, executive, county,* and *Parliament* all come in the top 3,000 of the BNC. This suggests that if the BNC lists are used to sequence items in a test designed for people who are not British or adult, or who use language for less formal purposes, the lists will not be entirely satisfactory.

The unit of counting

Another truism from corpus linguistics is that the unit of counting should match the use to which the data is put. For example, Vermeer (2004a) has shown that in studies of learners' productive use of language, the lemma is the most valid unit of counting because different lemmas involve different collocations and grammatical constructions, and the use of word families would mask this important productive knowledge. When receptive uses are considered however, the word family is a more valid unit (Bertram, Baayen and Schreuder, 2000; Bertram, Laine and Virkkalla, 2000; Nagy, Anderson, Schommer, Scott and Stallman, 1989). The BNC lists do not have word family groupings although this is now being worked on.

If an inappropriate unit of counting is used there may be overestimation or underestimation of vocabulary knowledge. For example, if lemmas are used as the unit in frequency sequenced receptive vocabulary measures, learners may get higher scores than they should at the lower frequency levels because they can show knowledge of transparent low-frequency family members of a high-frequency family. Similarly, if families instead of lemmas are used for productive vocabulary measures learners may gain credit for family members they cannot produce or be penalised for not knowing a word-family when in fact they can use some of its members.

Multiple measures

If vocabulary growth is being measured as a result of some experimental intervention, it is important that several measures of vocabulary are used; that is, that each target word should be tested in two or three different ways. A recently published experiment by Waring and Takaki (2003) provides a very good example of the values in doing this. Waring and Takaki wanted to measure the vocabulary learning from reading a single graded reader. They used three vocabulary measures at three different levels of sensitivity – a word recognition test (*Which of these words occurred in the story?*), a multiple-choice test, and a word translation test. Not surprisingly, the immediate post-test scores were highest on the word recognition test (15.3 out of 25), and lowest on the translation test (4.6 out of

25). Waring and Takaki considered the translation test to be the most valid because in terms of external validity it most resembles what learners have to do while they read; that is, retrieve a meaning for a given word form. From this perspective, the vocabulary learning from reading was very low. However, the responses to the multiple-choice items showed that some knowledge of many words (10.6 out of 25) had been picked up and at worst this represented a good first step towards knowing the words, and it may also indicate that, with the support of context when reading, the meaning may have been retrieved. In initial vocabulary learning, it could be argued that recognising the form of a word is one of the two major first pieces of knowledge. The other is connecting this form to a first language meaning. Thus the vocabulary benefits of reading a graded reader should not be seen as being best measured by a translation test, but as being best measured by all the learning shown in the three tests.

There are other arguments for using multiple measures. Webb (2002) tested each word in his experiments with ten tests ranging across the different aspects of what is involved in knowing a word. The aim of his research was to see if different learning conditions, such as learning with or without context sentences, resulted in different kinds of vocabulary knowledge. The use of a variety of measures enabled him to show that different tasks did result in some different kinds of knowledge and that these differences would not have been apparent if only one measure had been used.

Joe (1998) used three measures for each word when assessing the vocabulary learning effects of a retelling task. This enabled her to provide a strength measure for each word on a scale of 0 to 5. This was then shown to have a close relationship with the degree of generativity with which the word was used in the retelling. Showing this relationship would not have been possible if only a single measure had been used. Another advantage of using several test formats of varying difficulty is that if one of them proves to be too easy or too difficult, then at least the remaining tests will provide usable data.

First language and second language test formats

In recent years some bilingual versions of the Vocabulary Levels Test have been developed. In these versions, the six words listed in each block remain in English but the three definitions to match with three of the words are in the form of first language synonyms. The main motive initially for this development was to allow testing of the most frequent 1,000 words where the definitions could not be expressed in words that were more frequent than the words being tested.

In using these measures it quickly became clear that learners gained higher scores on the bilingual versions (those using L1 meanings) than on the monolingual versions (those solely in English). This was particularly true for lower proficiency learners. There seem to be several related reasons for this. Firstly, it will usually be easier for learners to comprehend their first language than their second language. Secondly, giving the meaning in the second language usually requires the use of definitions rather than one- or two-word synonyms. Understanding these definitions then involves understanding the grammar involved in the definition as well as the words used. Thirdly, studies of young learners giving the meaning of words show that definitions are not favoured by such learners. Studies of learners comprehending definitions (McKeown, 1993; Nesi and Meara, 1994) show that short, simple definitions work best. First language definitions meet these criteria better than second language definitions.

At a very rough estimate, the use of first language definitions seems to increase scores on the Vocabulary Levels Test by at least 10%. First language definitions remove some of the obstacles that interfere with the measurement of second language vocabulary knowledge and thus in some studies could be more valid measures than the convenient monolingual measures. The use of bilingual measures brings other complicating factors, particularly in multilingual settings, as it would be very difficult to show that the various bilingual versions of a test were indeed equivalent. However, in a setting where learners all share the same first language, there are strong arguments for bilingual measures. There is clearly a need to make sure that the tests used are suitable for the intended learners.

Testing vocabulary in use

Read (2000) argues the importance of testing vocabulary in use in order to gain a balanced picture of a learner's vocabulary knowledge. Measures of vocabulary in use have the characteristics of having the assessment of vocabulary as part of a larger construct such as the ability to read informative texts, taking account of the total vocabulary content of the language use material, and involving the user in having to take account of a range of contextual information (Read, 2000: 7–13).

Measures of lexical richness in writing provide good examples of these characteristics. The learners do a piece of writing without being aware that their vocabulary use in that writing is going to be investigated. The lexical richness measure is likely to be only part of the assessment of the quality of the piece of writing. The lexical richness measure considers all the vocabulary in the piece of writing. In the Lexical Frequency Profile (Laufer and Nation, 1995) for example, the total vocabulary of the text is divided into frequency levels according to predetermined lists and the more vocabulary a text has from outside the high frequency levels, the greater the lexical richness rating. When learners write the texts which are analysed for lexical richness they have to take account of a range of contextual factors such as the audience for the text, the nature of the subject matter being dealt with, the degree of formality required and so on.

There are now numerous measures of lexical richness in writing (Malvern, Richards, Chipere and Durán, 2004) and the current view of these is that most are best viewed not as competing measures but as complementary views of the nature of written lexical use. This standpoint fits nicely with discrete measures of vocabulary knowledge such as multiple-choice tests, word translation tests, and word recognition tests, which are not seen as competing measures but as measures tapping different strengths and aspects of vocabulary knowledge. Having several measures provides a more comprehensive and thus useful picture of vocabulary knowledge. With each of the lexical richness measures there are usually cautions that apply to their use. For example, what was the most popular measure, the Type–Token Ratio, has been shown to be strongly dependent on text length (Richards and Malvern, 1997). Thus, if this measure is used, the texts being compared must all be exactly the same length.

Measures of language use currently cannot tell the size of a learner's vocabulary, productive or otherwise, but they indicate how skilful the learner is in drawing on vocabulary knowledge to perform communicative tasks. Even where the assessment of writing requires a consideration of the writer's knowledge and choice of words, it is unclear how this knowledge influences the final grading of ability that emerges.

By far the most commonly used measures of vocabulary in use are rating scales, where the vocabulary component is one of several subscales. The vocabulary subscale typically has four or five levels ranging from very poor knowledge of vocabulary to an excellent, sophisticated, appropriate use of vocabulary. For example, Jacobs, Zingraf, Wormuth, Hartfiel and Hughey (1981) have five subscales in their ESL composition profile – content, organisation, vocabulary, language use, and mechanics. Each subscale has four levels and the vocabulary subscale's levels are as follows:

Vocabulary

20–18 Excellent to very good: sophisticated range • effective word/idiom choice and usage • word form mastery • appropriate register

17–14 Good to average: adequate range • occasional errors of word/idiom form, choice, *usage but meaning not obscured*

13–10 Fair to poor: limited range • frequent errors of word/ idiom form, choice, usage • *meaning confused or obscured*

9–7 Very poor: essentially translation • little knowledge of English vocabulary, idioms, word form • OR not enough to evaluate   (Jacobs et al. 1981: 30)

Not surprisingly there are aspects of vocabulary knowledge in some of the other subscales – mechanics includes spelling, and language use includes word order.

Here we have looked only at writing, but such analytic scales exist for speaking, and they can be devised for rating the input material used for the receptive skills of listening and reading. Similarly, other lexical richness measures can be applied in some way or other across the four skills.

Conclusion

Of all the factors looked at in this paper, the one that troubles me the most is the one of learner attitude because this is the one where the researcher has least control. All the other factors require careful thought about the goals of the study and how best to meet these when designing the measures. They are factors relating to the preparation of measures. Learner attitude, however, is more related to the administration of the measures, and as Anglin's study shows, even with one-by-one testing, problems can occur. The lesson from this is that the measurement needs to be checked by some other form of delivery, at least in pilot testing and at worst during or after the administration of the measure. It remains to be seen if computerised testing solves this attitude problem. Early indications are that it won't and that computerisation may remove yet another source of monitoring while giving us unjustified feelings of success.

PART II:
VOCABULARY AND
LEARNER DIFFERENCES

2 Lexical profiles, learning styles and the construct validity of lexical size tests

James Milton

Introduction

This chapter will consider in more detail the first of the validity questions which Nation raises in the opening chapter: that of the individual variables each learner will bring to the testing process. Lexical knowledge, like all language knowledge, is not a directly accessible quality like a person's height or weight. In tests, therefore, we rely on the learners themselves to demonstrate their knowledge so we can assess it or measure it. In the opening chapter Nation points out that this is inherently problematic for the validity of a test and its results. If a learner is uninterested and does not try, or guesses a lot, or gives up half way through the test, then the score cannot accurately reflect the learner's true knowledge or ability. The validity of any test of this kind relies on the assumption that learners will behave reasonably, and reasonably consistently, in trying to show what knowledge they have.

In reality we know that learners faced with a test do not always behave either reasonably or consistently. Vocabulary size testing, which makes extensive use of objective style questions, is particularly open to learners using, or attempting to use, test-taking strategies in the hope of maximising their score rather than accurately reflecting their knowledge. A test such as the Eurocentre's Vocabulary Size Test (Meara and Jones, 1990) makes a calculation of a testee's guesswork based on responses to false words contained in the test and, if guessing is sufficiently high, indicates an accurate assessment cannot be made. It is clear from this test that individuals and even groups can behave differently from each other. High guessing levels have been reported among learners who are native Arabic (Al-Hazemi, 1993) and Dutch (Eyckmans et al., in this volume) speakers. By contrast, the Japanese speaking learners reported by Shillaw (1999) display remarkably little guesswork. While tests in this genre attempt to compensate for guesswork, there is no question that attitudinal factors can be a problem, even to the point of invalidating the results of the test. Eyckmans et al. consider attitudinal factors and guesswork in lexical tests in more detail in the next chapter.

But guesswork and learner attitude are not the only ways in which the qualities a learner brings to this test may affect the measure obtained from it. Learners can vary in other ways and these can also, at least potentially, affect the reliability and validity of the tests we currently use. This chapter considers individual differences in language learning aptitude or learning style and the impact these may have on the validity of the tests of lexical knowledge. The reason why these factors are relevant may not be immediately obvious, but the tests which measure vocabulary knowledge assume that vocabulary is learned in a particular way and it is possible that this is not the case for all learners. This chapter, therefore, will consider whether the frequency model which underlies this sort of test is an appropriate model for assessing vocabulary size in every case, which would in turn challenge the construct validity of the test.

The frequency model of lexical learning

So what is the model so many vocabulary tests are based on? It is a commonly accepted truth in foreign language learning that the more frequent a word is in a language then the more easily, and the earlier, it is likely to be learned. This idea can be traced back at least as far as Palmer who wrote in 1917 that 'the more frequently used words will be the more easily learnt' (1917: 123). Later writers accept this without demur, for example, both Mackey (1965) and McCarthy (1990) repeat Palmer's assertion without reservation. One of the advantages of this idea is that it can be turned into a model which can then be tested empirically. Meara (1992a) does this by graphing up the relationship which, he suggests, should look like Figure 1.

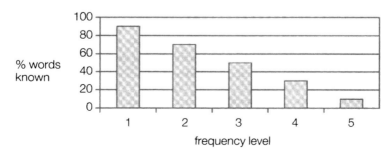

Figure 1   Vocabulary knowledge of a typical learner (Meara, 1992a: 4)

Column 1 represents knowledge of the first thousand most frequent words in a language, column 2 the next most frequent 1,000 words, and so on. A typical learner's knowledge is high in the frequent columns and lower in the less frequent columns giving a distinctive downwards slope from left to right. As learner knowledge increases, this profile moves upwards until it hits a ceiling at 100% when the profile ought to flatten at the most frequent levels and the downwards slope, left to right, shifts to the right into less frequent vocabulary bands.

It is on the basis of this sort of analysis that vocabulary knowledge tests are made. The percentage of words known at each frequency level allows an extrapolation to be made and a calculation of overall lexical knowledge in the foreign language being tested. This is exactly how tests such as the Eurocentre's Vocabulary Size Test (Meara and Jones, 1990) and *X-Lex* (Meara and Milton, 2003b) are constructed. Predictions can even be made of knowledge in frequency levels not tested. Nation's Vocabulary Levels Test (Nation, 1983) tests the 2,000, 3,000, 5,000 and 10,000 word frequency ranges in order to estimate overall lexical competence, confident in the assumption that the frequency levels in between those tested will perform predictably. The tests produced in this way are surprisingly robust. However, there are a number of caveats which need to be acknowledged with this kind of analysis.

One is that frequency information drawn from a wide variety of native speaker sources may not be relevant to foreign language learners who are not exposed to this sort of language but have only textbooks to draw on. Course books will necessarily have to be selective as to the lexis and structures used and lexis in particular is likely to be selected thematically rather than on the basis of frequency. Lexical exposure, particularly at the outset of learning, ought to be different from that which a native speaker might get from newspapers, books and so on. A study of the lexical content of course books reported in Milton and Vassiliu (2000) notes the very high volumes of infrequent vocabulary they include. In principle this might affect the usefulness of frequency-based tests. The evidence on these matters is slim. Meara and Jones (1990), for example, observe that their vocabulary size test is probably not reliable with low-level learners, and while this could be a sampling problem, it might equally well be that the standard frequency models do not reflect the vocabulary which beginners have been exposed to and have learned. But they are unspecific about the point at which it does become reliable. The most recent lexical size tests address this problem in their construction. Meara and Milton's (2003a,b) *X-Lex* Swansea

Levels Test draws on both Nation's (1984) general frequency materials, but also Hindmarsh's (1980) lists, which are more explicitly tied to the vocabulary of EFL textbooks and exams. Nation's Levels Test (1983) takes the same approach.

A second potential problem with the frequency model is that frequency is not the only factor which can influence whether words are learned. Part of speech may affect learning; nouns are usually learned more easily than verbs, which are more readily learned than adverbs. More concrete and imageable words are learned more easily than abstract words. Words which are similar to, borrowed from, or cognate to words in the first language tend to be easier to learn than those which are not. In principle, these other factors ought to affect the slope of this profile. If these other factors have little influence on learnability and the effect of frequency is very strong then the slope of the profile should be steep. Actually, it should be very steep on the left hand side since the most frequent words in a language tend to be very much more frequent than most other words. On the other hand, if frequency of occurrence is not a strong factor affecting learning, because it is overwhelmed by other factors, the slope of the profile should be shallow.

This relationship between frequency and learnability appears to be so self-evident that it is difficult to find a clear empirical demonstration of it in the literature. However, it is not hard to illustrate, at least for populations of learners, and to draw up a lexical profile reflecting the learners' lexical knowledge. Such a profile, drawn from all 227 learners at a school in Greece, ranging in ability from beginners to Cambridge First Certificate level, and created using *X-Lex* (Meara and Milton, 2003a) is shown in Figure 2. The mean score for each frequency level is shown and the resultant graph is remarkably similar to Meara's model in Figure 1. The expected slope from left to right exists demonstrating that the group, as a whole, has a greater know-

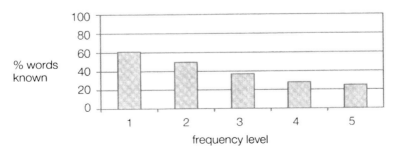

Figure 2   Mean scores for frequency bands

ledge of each succeeding band of greater frequency. It might be argued on the basis of this graph that the profile, which is not a straight line, is steeper to the left between bands 1 and 2 and flattens on the right between bands 4 and 5. This ought to indicate the salience of frequency of occurrence as an influence on the learnability of words. The more frequent a word is, the more likely it is to be learned, as a general rule, and other factors such as the part of speech or concreteness of the words, or the idiosyncrasies of the textbook, do not seem to reverse this trend. A Friedman Test on all of the results confirms the impression that the overall trend is very strong indeed in a population as a whole ($\chi^2 = 512.55$, asympt sig = .000). Very similar results and conclusions have been found among French foreign language learners and are reported by Richards and Malvern (this volume).

But languages are not learned by populations of course, they are learned by individuals. There are good reasons for thinking that individuals may not behave with the same ordered regularity that populations display. Some of the reasons for thinking that individuals may vary are based on the observation of individual profiles. A small study by Vassiliu (1994, reported in Milton and Vassiliu, 2000) notes a dip in some learners' profiles in the second thousand-word frequency band. This is tentatively attributed to a corresponding dip in level two vocabulary presented in the course books his learners used, and he called this feature *level two deficit*. The significance of this is that a test such as the Vocabulary Levels Test draws heavily on level two knowledge which, it seems, may give a misleading impression of overall ability in at least some learners. Subsequent work has suggested that there is indeed something very odd about the lexis particularly in the second thousand-word frequency band. A level two deficit profile is shown in Figure 3.

Meara and Milton (2003b: 5) note a more radical departure from the normal frequency-based profile. Some learners are observed with

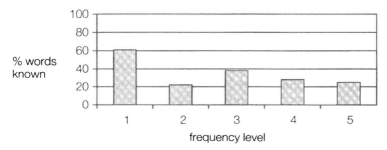

Figure 3   Level two deficit profile

good knowledge of infrequent words but a marked deficiency in knowledge of the highly frequent, structure words which are necessary to put them together to communicate. This produces a profile which is much lower on the left than would be the case in a normal profile and an example is shown in Figure 4. Meara and Milton call this sort of profile *structural deficit*. The significance of this is that a test such as the Eurocentres Vocabulary Size Test is auto-adaptive and relies on a small, initial sample of the most frequent lexis. If scores are low here it presumes that the learner knows even less of the infrequent lexis and does not test it. Such a test would appear likely to underestimate learners with profiles of this sort.

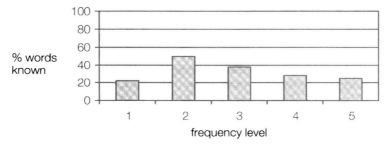

Figure 4   Structural deficit profile

Other reasons for thinking that individual profiles may vary are based on theory. Meara, Milton and Lorenzo-Dus (2001) suggest that learning style might influence the profile, with analytic learners able to acquire structure words (which also tend to be most frequent) easily while memory-based learners will find lexical vocabulary (which is less frequent but tends to be more concrete and imageable) more readily learnable. It might be reasoned that analytic learners should display normal profiles, where structural vocabulary predominates, while memorisers might display level two or structural deficit profiles.

This sort of approach might help explain an anomaly which Vassiliu could not account for. While some of his learners appeared to follow the content of the textbooks and acquire vocabulary with a level two deficit profile, other learners in the same class made up the deficiency in level two lexis and emerged with a normal profile. How could they do this if they were not exposed to the vocabulary? If these learners were strong analytically they might be expected to apply their rule-based systems in generating, bottom-up, their ideas in a foreign language. This approach would inevitably reveal gaps in knowledge, such as that in level two lexis, and these could be addressed by asking a teacher or looking in a dictionary. Such learners are giving themselves much more opportunity for learning outside the textbook. While this is a nice idea, we have no evidence to suggest whether this really is the case. And in the same way we really have no idea whether all learners behave the same way in the lexis they learn or whether they vary according to aptitude, learning style or level. But this question strikes at the heart of the construct validity of vocabulary size and level tests. If some students do not follow the frequency model of lexical learning then the tests based on this model may make poor estimates of their knowledge.

Frequency profiles and learner aptitude

In order to investigate this for this chapter I have examined the individual profiles generated by the 227 Greek learners described in Figure 2. For the purposes of categorisation I divided the learners according to their profiles as follows:

Normal profile $1 > 2 > 3$
Level two deficit $1 > 2 < 3$
Structural deficit $1 < 2 > 3$

Approximately 60% of learners displayed normal, frequency-based profiles, a further 25% level two deficit (L2D) profiles and approximately 10% structural deficit (SD) profiles. A very small proportion of the results defied classification by these rules. A breakdown of these results over the seven classes involved is shown in Figure 5.

The proportions of each type appear relatively stable over the levels and only appear to change in the two final classes and in particular in the FCE class. Almost certainly, this is the result of ceiling effects. Learners' knowledge of individual lexical levels appears to peak at

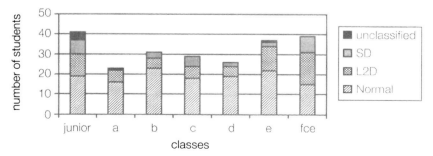

Figure 5 Distribution of profile types

around 85–90%, and not at 100% as expected, and in the highest class this peak has been reached in the most frequent bands. At this stage, a shift of a single mark can change the profile, something that does not happen in lower classes where the differences between frequency band scores are greater.

It might reasonably be questioned whether these profiles are stable, and therefore a reflection of some characteristic of the learner's vocabulary knowledge, or whether they are a result of some variation which the testing method generates. Reliability measures of vocabulary size and level tests (for example, by Adamopoulou, 2000) generally suggest that they are incredibly reliable by language testing standards. Test–retest correlations of 0.99 suggest that the profiles are unlikely to change. With the Greek learners in this particular study, 29 learners took the test twice (a different form each time) and the profiles produced were compared. The results showed that in each test there were 15 learners with normal profiles and 14 learners with level two deficit, but that there was some movement between these groups and this is shown in Figure 6.

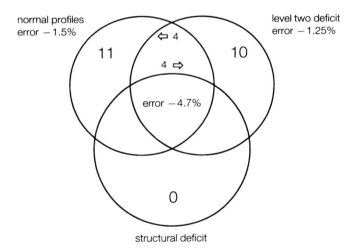

Figure 6   Movement between profiles

The majority of learners, 21 out of 29, retained stable profiles between tests. Eight learners, however, changed profile, four moving each way between normal and level two deficit profiles. The reason for profiles destabilising may lie in the guesswork which learners use, calculated as error figures (the percentage of false words identified as real words) which are also shown in Figure 6. Learners whose profiles remain consistent show very little error, approaching an average of only 1%, and must be very sure of their vocabulary knowledge since they guess hardly at all. Learners whose profiles change have much higher error rates, three or four times higher, and these errors, or rather the guesswork that produces them, may well be enough to destabilise the profiles. This observation lends additional weight, if it were needed, to this chapter's opening point that guesswork can seriously destabilise a test's results.

The first tentative conclusion to be drawn from this is that it seems possible that as many as a third of learners may depart in some way from the frequency model of vocabulary learning. Despite the strength of the frequency effect on learners as a population, it appears that there is some systematic variation among learners as individuals. In principle, this should challenge the validity of frequency-based lexical size tests.

It might be expected, if these different profiles are the product of the learners' varying aptitude, and in particular memory and analytic skills, that learners will display different scores on aptitude tests designed to evaluate just these qualities. If the theories of Meara, Milton and Lorenzo-Dus (2001) are correct then those with a normal profile should do comparatively well on tests of analytic ability while those with level two deficit profiles should score comparatively well on tests of memory. The 21 Greek learners with stable profiles were therefore also asked to take two tests from the Meara, Milton and Lorenzo-Dus (2001) range of aptitude tests. These were LAT_B, a paired associates learning task designed to test memory in language learning, and LAT_C, a language rule recognition task designed to test inductive and analytic language learning skills. The learners were grouped according to their profiles, eleven normal profiles and ten level two deficit, and their scores on these aptitude tests calculated. Mean scores are presented in Figure 7.

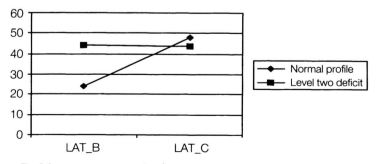

Figure 7   Mean scores on aptitude tests

Broadly, these results bear out Meara, Milton and Lorenzo-Dus' (2001) expectations. Learners with normal profiles score higher on the analytic skills test, LAT_C, than the learners with level two deficit, while learners with level two deficit score higher on the memory test, LAT_B, than those with normal profiles. The LAT range of aptitude tests have been normalised so it appears that the normal profile learners are much stronger in analytic skill than in memory, and this would support the idea that they are likely to be analytically orientated learners. The difference in their scores, and the difference compared to the level two deficit learners is very marked. The level two deficit learners score higher in memory than in analysis but the difference is much smaller and given that normalisation was not carried out on this age group it would probably be a mistake to read too much into the similarity of this group's aptitude scores. An ANOVA analysis of the results shows that there is a group effect and a test effect and, more importantly, a significant interaction between group and test. Even though these groups are very small, the results suggest there is a difference in aptitude between learners with the two different profiles. Results are shown in Figure 8.

Source	LATBC	Type III	df	Mean Square	F.	Sig.
LATBC	Linear	1248.200	1	1248.200	6.981	.018
LATBC*Style	Linear	1355.756	1	1355.756	7.583	.014
Error (LATBC)	Linear	2860.800	26	178.800		

Figure 8   Test statistics on aptitude test scores: within subjects contrasts

These results suggest that, as Meara, Milton and Lorenzo-Dus (2001) indicated, different learning strengths and styles really can influence the foreign language lexis that learners acquire in class. The frequency effect may not disappear from their profiles entirely, but learners may not always learn the vocabulary in the first two 1,000-word frequency bands with the ease and facility which the frequency model suggests they should. In these ranges, a learner's aptitude or style may help determine what is learned.

Conclusions

What then can be concluded from this, and how important to the validity of the vocabulary tests we use, is this observation concerning the effect of aptitude on lexical learning? To put this into perspective, one thing that should emerge from this chapter is that the frequency model appears to be a really very cogent model of learning as a whole. Notwithstanding these observations of individual variation it cannot be discarded. The frequency effect on vocabulary learning is very strong and this should not be lost. The individual variations observed here appear to affect only the most frequent 2,000 words and normal interaction between frequency and learning appears to assert itself again beyond these levels. On the face of it, therefore, vocabulary size and knowledge tests based on frequency retain very good construct validity. In this respect the frequency model they are based on is probably better than the models underlying many other widely used language tests.

Once this is said, however, the evidence, though still slight, supports the idea that individuals may vary in the vocabulary they learn according to learning style or particular aptitude strengths, and that this produces different frequency profiles. Analysis of Greek learners has supported the theoretical assumption made by Meara, Milton and Lorenzo-Dus (2001) that in addition to the normal frequency profile two other types of profile are identified. A level two deficit profile where the 2,000-word level is disproportionately low in comparison to the others, and a structural deficit profile where the 1,000-word level is disproportionately low. Students with level two deficit profiles appear strong in memory compared with students with normal profiles, who are stronger in analysis. About three or four in every ten students tested displayed these odd profiles.

This is an interesting finding but what is the implication for the validity of lexical size tests based on frequency? The remainder of the frequency profile remains generally frequency based so the impact on lexical size tests need not be so great if the methodology is not dependent on knowledge of the 2,000 most frequent words. Meara and Milton's (2003b) *X-Lex*, which tests each of the first five 1,000-word frequency bands separately, and then provides a score out of the 5,000 most frequent words, would appear unaffected. Its construct validity appears unchallenged by these findings.

Other tests are likely to be more affected. The Vocabulary Levels Test (Nation, 1983) relies for its estimation of ability quite heavily on knowledge of the second 1,000-word frequency band. Overall ability is inferred, in part, from this knowledge. Clearly learners with level two deficit are likely to perform disproportionately badly since an inference will be made that other levels will be low when this need not necessarily be the case. Other levels are tested, of course, and this will mitigate the effect of the underestimation. But it is a concern where as many as one in four may have profiles of this type.

Potentially the test most likely to be affected is the auto-adaptive test which Meara and Jones (1990) created for Eurocentres. This test makes an initial estimate of overall vocabulary size based on knowledge of the most frequent vocabulary levels, before testing in depth at the language level the initial test elements suggests. Where learners have disproportionately low knowledge of this frequent vocabulary, the later in-depth test is likely to be at the wrong level. The conclusion to be drawn from this chapter is that these frequent levels may not be the best predictors of overall lexical size and may underestimate in as many as one in three cases. Meara and Jones recognise that this is likely to be a particular problem with low-level learners and warn against this, but it is a concern.

3 Learners' response behaviour in Yes/No Vocabulary Tests

June Eyckmans, Hans Van de Velde,
Roeland van Hout and Frank Boers

Introduction

In the introductory chapter of this book, Nation briefly addresses the contradiction that poor scores on vocabulary tests are not always a reflection of poor knowledge. In fact, bad test scores can be the result of several factors, including some that fall outside the scope of the construct being tested. He mentions some of these factors: participants may not have taken the test seriously, they may have proceeded too quickly in answering the test items, they may have lacked test-taking strategies or misused them. Such problems are common to all tests and language tests are no exception. This chapter will look in more detail at one particular problem associated with the checklist style of testing which is very popular in vocabulary testing. While the format is a popular one, it is unusual in language testing in that it tries through the use of false words to make some of the strategies used by testees explicit and to quantify and compensate for them. It is assumed that learners have control over the strategies they use and can show a true version of their vocabulary knowledge if they choose to present it. It is also assumed that the compensation mechanisms used in these tests can appropriately compensate for strategies such as guessing, and this process may sometimes lead to the conclusion that the results which learners present do not represent their real knowledge, as in the Yes/No Vocabulary Size Test (Meara and Buxton, 1987).

This information would have been extremely useful for the teacher in the opening chapter who was trying to test student knowledge of the Academic Word List, and who derived a whole scheme of teaching on the basis of what turn out to be badly misleading data. The purpose of this chapter is to question how and why test-takers use strategies like guesswork, how varied they are in doing this, and to ask whether compensating for guesswork in the scores such tests present is really possible.

Other researchers have addressed the effect of extrinsic motivation on learners' attitudes to, and performance on, tests. Shohamy (2001) argues that the power of tests originates from their capability of causing a change in behaviour in the test-takers. She compares this phenomenon to the relationships observed in economic models where producers and consumers take steps to maximise their profits and refers to Bourdieu's model 'the economy of practice' (1999, cited in Shohamy, 2001). In this model Bourdieu explains that various situations, which may not be governed by strictly economic logic, may nonetheless conform to a logic that is economic in a broader sense because the individuals concerned are trying to gain some kind of capital (e.g. cultural or symbolic capital), or the increase of some kind of symbolic 'profit' (e.g. honour or prestige). Following this train of thought, Shohamy suggests that the test-takers' desire to maximise their test scores obeys an economic logic because higher scores will result in better grades or job opportunities and gains in terms of recognition by teachers, parents and peers (Shohamy, 2001: 105–6). Language learners who take objective-style tests, such as Yes/No vocabulary size tests, are particularly likely to follow an economic logic in their test-taking. The test format actually requires them to take decisions based on their confidence in their language knowledge, where this knowledge is partial and incomplete. If the stakes are high enough, there may be considerable motivation to gamble, and to try to outsmart the test's correction systems, in order to gain the prize of higher marks. Even the manner of test delivery, the computer format which forces a Yes/No answer even if the learner is undecided, may predispose learners to this type of behaviour.

Such factors can affect test performance and appear beyond the control of the test developer. However, Bachman and Palmer (1996) claim that the way test-takers perform on a language test is influenced to an important extent by the characteristics of the test itself. The characteristics of the language test will largely determine how performance on that test can be related to language use in non-test situations. In other words, the nature of a particular test task will determine the validity of the test and the inferences made on the basis of the scores it produces. Because of the need to make inferences on the basis of test performance, it is crucial to understand the test-taker's approach to the testing procedure, more specifically, his intention to fulfil the test requirements to the best of his abilities. Test developers should be aware of the dangers of negative affect creeping into participants' test experience (Boers, Demecheleer and Eyckmans, 2004) and of the fact that unclear or ambiguous tasks may produce biased response behaviour (Eyckmans, 2004). It might reasonably be asked, therefore, whether certain task types such as the Yes/No format actually precipitate problems in assessment where other tasks are more neutral, and whether Yes/No formats are less valid if we wish to make inferences about language use outside the test-taking situation.

In this chapter we will concentrate on the interaction between learner and task in the Yes/No Vocabulary Test. Experiments have shown that the data gathered with this test can be influenced by a response bias. This is a result of the interplay between the multitude of characteristics that determine the learner (cultural, psychological, sociological, etc.) and which constitute his attitude to the task, and the vocabulary knowledge that the Yes/No Test is supposed to be measuring (Beeckmans, Eyckmans, Janssens, Dufranne and Van de Velde, 2001; Eyckmans, 2004). In this chapter, therefore, the role of the computer interface as part of the test characteristics is considered. The influence of a computer-controlled interface design on the response behaviour of the participants is also investigated and is best illustrated through a practical experiment.

Learner attitude and the Yes/No Vocabulary Test

The validity of a test can be defined as the degree to which test scores accurately reflect the test-takers' various abilities. When test results turn out to reflect learner attitude rather than language skill, this may cast doubt on the effectiveness of certain test formats. A series of experiments with the Yes/No Vocabulary Test as part of a placement test for French-speaking learners of Dutch has cast doubt on the validity of this format, at least for this group of learners (Eyckmans, 2001; Eyckmans, 2004). In the past, the Yes/No Vocabulary Test has been used as a measure for receptive vocabulary size (Meara and Buxton, 1987; Meara and Jones, 1990; Meara, 1990; Meara, 1992). Currently, the DIALANG diagnostic language testing system uses the format as a vocabulary measure to inform the test-taker of his lexical ability in the target language with a view to selecting the appropriate level of language test. In the Yes/No Vocabulary Test, the participants have to indicate by means of a *Yes* or *No* response whether they know the meaning of words that are presented to them as isolated items in a list, or – in the DIALANG version of the format – whether the words exist in the target language or not. The task is complicated, at least for the testee, by the presence of pseudowords. Testees are penalised for identifying these false words as real.

The Yes/No task is often mistakenly compared with the task in a True/False test. In a True/False test, the presence of a possible bias towards one or the other of the two responses can be considered as being part of the task. In a True/False grammar test, for example, a participant who tends to use only simple structures and tries very hard not to make mistakes, would exhibit a bias in judging many items to be incorrect. One could argue that this bias is part of the task and is relevant to the competence that is being measured. On the other hand, in a Yes/No Vocabulary Test, the participant's task is closer to self-assessment than to a real language task. The bias can therefore only be attributed to factors which are beyond the competence of the participant.

In the several uses we have made of the Yes/No Vocabulary Test with French-speaking learners of Dutch in higher education, the data consistently revealed a considerable response bias undermining the test format's concurrent validity (Beeckmans et al., 2001; Eyckmans, 2000; Eyckmans, 2004). The participants in our experiments (altogether approximately 2,000) exhibited a preference for a *Yes* or *No* response independent of their actual vocabulary knowledge. This bias tainted the validity of the responses and consequently of the test results as a whole. The observed response bias was not a product of cognate effect, the close relationship between the learners' L1 and the target language (Van de Velde and Eyckmans, 2005). Instead, it appeared to be related to a complex interplay between the Yes/No task, the learners' profile and the particular testing context. The test's response bias is in fact caused by the element of self-assessment that is part of the test format. An individual's self-assessment here is heavily dependent on a decision criterion. However partial or rich a learner's knowledge of a particular word may be (word knowledge is not an all-or-nothing phenomenon), he has to choose between an unequivocal *Yes* or *No* response. When in doubt, the testee may lean towards either a *Yes* or a *No* response simply because of his response style (overestimation, underestimation, refraining from answering) or attitude (analogous to Bourdieu's 'economy of practice'). The Yes/No task makes such a strong appeal to learners' self-rating of language skills that it tempts some participants to overestimate their knowledge, and this is penalised in the Yes/No testing system. Moreover, research into self-assessment has demonstrated that the reliability of learners' self-assessments can be affected by their experience of the skill that is being assessed, which seems to indicate that learners resort to recollections of their general proficiency in order to make their judgements (Ross, 1998).

Thus, in a study with a similar student population, Janssens (1999) found her students failed to estimate their vocabulary knowledge accurately. Her experiment was designed to test whether the students were able to use contextual clues to infer the meaning of words they did not know. First, the participants were presented with a list of target words and were asked to give the French translation (a). Then, the participants received a short text containing the target words and were asked to underline the words they did not know (b). Finally, they got the text plus the target words and were asked to translate the words once again (c). Comparing (b) and (c) provides a means of evaluating students' self-assessment. Most students (69%) had a tendency to overestimate their vocabulary knowledge and there were large individual differences in their self-evaluation which were not due to their differences in language competence.

Regarding the Yes/No Vocabulary Test specifically, it is shown that the presence of a response bias artificially enhances the reliability of test data (Beeckmans et al., 2001; Eyckmans, 2004) and Fitzpatrick (this volume) has noted that this test generally produces extremely high reliability coefficients. As a consequence, test users risk placing too much confidence in tests which, even though reliable, actually measure a different construct than the one aimed for and may therefore lack the desired validity. There are two ways of dealing with the response bias issue. One would be to eliminate the bias from the data through the use of a particular correction formula. The several correction formulae that have been proposed in the literature for marking the test use the number of *Yes*-responses to pseudo-words (so-called *false alarms*) as a means to reduce the score of *Yes*-responses to words (so-called *Hits*) in order to arrive at a reliable estimate of the participant's vocabulary size. The way in which this reduction is executed differs from one formula to the next (Huibregtse and Admiraal, 1999; Beeckmans et al., 2001) but this issue only becomes problematic in the case of high rates of *false alarm*-responses, because then the different formulae yield divergent test scores.

Another way of dealing with the problem would be to better disambiguate the task and to make it independent of attitudes that might lead to biased responses. The fact that the Yes/No task seems to elicit different kinds of response behaviour in different participants has major consequences for the marking of the test and its psychometric qualities. It is clear that this needs to be avoided. Unfortunately, learner attitude is hard to control in test administration. It may depend on cultural or meta-cognitive variables as well as on the testing context (high- versus low-stakes tests). Therefore, it is important for the test developer to exert as much control as possible on the way the testee proceeds in taking the test so that variability between testees can only be attributed to knowledge of the tested construct and not to preconceptions or attitudes.

In Eyckmans (2004) it was concluded that in order to re-establish the validity of the Yes/No format, ways had to be found to reduce or eliminate the response bias observed in the participants. As the *false alarm* rate is essentially the surface phenomenon through which a response bias is revealed, the described experiments were aimed at a reduction of the *false alarm* rate. One of the hypotheses was that the response behaviour in the Yes/No Vocabulary Test might be influenced by the task description and that clearer instructions would result in a different proportion of *hits* and *false alarms*. This hypothesis was confirmed. The false alarm rate decreased significantly when the instructions emphasised that the students were to refrain from ticking words in the list if they were not absolutely sure that they knew their meaning. Unfortunately, this did not lead to a higher concurrent validity at least when compared with an L1 translation test of the words the testees claimed to know the meaning of. The learners made a very poor job of translating the words they had ticked in the Yes/No vocabulary test. Although it can reasonably be argued that translating words is a productive task and thus significantly different from the passive recognition which is tested in the Yes/No task, it can be assumed that asking the participants to provide L1 equivalents of target language words is the most unequivocal way of verifying recognition knowledge. The problematic nature of assessing concurrent validity is something that Fitzpatrick addresses more directly later in this volume. Nonetheless, it appears that influencing participants' response behaviour through better instructions and directions does not automatically result in a more valid measure. Another way of intervening in the way a test-taker approaches and completes a test task is through the design of the computer interface.

The computer interface as part of the test characteristics

It is clear that the use of computers has numerous advantages for language testing. Test compilation and construction are facilitated, the problem of deciphering student handwriting is eliminated and test scores or exam results can be provided instantly. The basic item types for discrete vocabulary testing (checklist, multiple-choice, matching, blank-filling) are very attractive for computerised presentation, and context-independent items in particular lend themselves well to computer-adaptive testing.

Apart from the fact that computers have a great potential to contribute to language test construction and assessment, it is important to acknowledge the influence the computerised design may have on the characteristics of a particular test. Gervais (1997) argues that the accuracy of a computer-based test versus a traditional paper-and-pencil test can be considered by addressing the advantages of a computer-delivered test in terms of accessibility and speed of results on the one hand, and possible disadvantages in terms of bias against those with no computer familiarity or with negative attitudes to computers on the other hand. However, the specific design of a computer interface may exert much larger effects. It is our view that one should go beyond the advantages the computer offers in terms of speed and ease of test correction, and also exploit the computer's possibilities to gain more control over the testing situation. Through computer programming, time limits per item can be built in, the possibility of omitted responses can be ruled out, test-takers can be denied an overview of the test, etc. All these factors may affect the individual's test performance. Therefore, they also have to be considered as part of the characteristics of the test task. In view of the multitude of factors (individual characteristics of test-takers, changes in the test-takers' physical or mental condition during the test administration, etc.) that may impede or complicate the already difficult relationship between the testee's test performance and the testee's actual knowledge or skill, controlling the test-task characteristics by design seems imperative. A good interface design should reduce the possibility of construct-irrelevant variance, which may threaten the inferences that may be drawn from test scores (Fulcher, 2003a). The central question we will deal with in this chapter is whether a computer-based test can offer any added value over a paper-and-pencil test in the particular case of the Yes/No Vocabulary Test.

When designing a computerised version of a paper-and-pencil test two approaches seem feasible: one can mimic the paper-and-pencil format as closely as possible or one can make the most of the computer's advantages to control the test characteristics. Within the DIALANG assessment frame the first option has been taken. From the point of view of computer design, the DIALANG Yes/No Vocabulary Test resembles the paper-and-pencil Yes/No tests. All the items are presented on the screen in a list, the test-taker chooses in what order to respond to the items, responses can be altered and there is no time limit involved in taking the test. The only control that is built in and that clearly distinguishes the test from a paper-and-pencil version from a structural perspective is the fact that the test-taker is forced to respond to all items before quitting the test. This is a control measure that is taken with a view to correcting the test and it guarantees the exclusion of omitted responses. In short, it turns the test into a forced-decision task. However, there are other ways in which the computer can furnish a more controlled environment for the Yes/No Vocabulary Test:

1 When programming a computer-delivered Yes/No test, sequential operations can be preferred over the traditional presentation of items in a list. Presenting the items on the computer screen one by one is of greater importance than one would think because it changes the test experience drastically. Firstly, testees do not have an overview of the complete test, which is the case in the traditional 'list-presentation' where all the items are presented in front of the test-taker. Secondly, they do not know how many items are still to come and, in the case of the Yes/No test, may not remember how many of them they have already rejected. Finally, they cannot alter the choices they have already made and they cannot ponder their choice by deciding to leave a particular item unanswered and to go back to it when they have skimmed through the remaining items. Any of these might influence the testees' response pattern.

2 A computer application can be designed to present the items to the different test-takers in a random order, in order to prevent sequence effects, i.e. differences due to fatigue or boredom when responding to the last items of the test. This is hard to do with a paper and pencil test since one can only work with a limited set of fixed orders.

3 Regarding the problem of omitted responses, two approaches seem possible in a computerised version of the test. Either the test is designed to elicit a response for each item, which means the test-taker will not get a test result without having responded to all test items (i.e. an 'omitted response' category is ruled out), or the test allows for omitting responses (test-takers can leave an item unanswered and move on to the next one) but the computer records when this happens.

4 Computer programming allows the imposition of a time limit per item. A time limit can serve several goals but the most important one is that it leads to more uniformity because the time variable no longer comes into play. It makes the test more unequivocal for all test-takers.

5 The task description can be repeated on each screen in order to remind the test-takers of the exact nature of the decision they are expected to make. This is likely to trigger more consistent decision behaviour.

It might be expected that the Yes/No Vocabulary Test's construction may be better dealt with in a specifically designed computer application because of the more controlled environment it could provide. We can hypothesise, therefore, that this more controlled environment would result in a less biased response behaviour by the testees and consequently in a decreased *false alarm* rate.

Testing the computer interface

The influence of the computer interface on the particpants' test performance was investigated by comparing two computer applications (A and B) of the Yes/No Vocabulary Test. After the participants had taken the computerised Yes/No Vocabulary Test, they were asked to translate the words of the Yes/No test so that some measure of the validity of their Yes/No responses could be gained. The focus of the experiment was on the role and the influence of these different computer test designs on: (1) the *false alarm* rate, (2) the correlation between the performance on words and on pseudowords (which serves as an indication of a response bias), and (3) the external validation of the Yes/No responses in both cases.

The participants were French-speaking university students of Economics and Business Administration at the Université Libre de Bruxelles following Dutch language courses at lower intermediate level. Two groups (a total of 125 participants) were given a computerised Yes/No Vocabulary Test in order to evaluate their knowledge of core vocabulary in Dutch.

A Yes/No Vocabulary Test was constructed that consisted of 60 words and 40 pseudowords. The test sample was a random selection of words from *Woorden in Context* (Dieltjens et al., 1995; Dieltjens et al., 1997), a standard work of Dutch core vocabulary that contains 3,700 Dutch words selected on the basis of frequency and usefulness. The random selection was modified along the following constraints:

1 The test sample was restricted to nouns and verbs on the assumption that these grammatical categories generally carry stronger lexical meaning than, for instance, adverbs or prepositions, and should therefore be easier to recognise when encountered in isolation.

2 Cognates were not included in the test material. Although previous item analyses (Meara, Lightbown and Halter, 1994; Eyckmans, 2004) had shown that cognates were not responsible for the overestimation revealed by test-takers, it could be argued that the mere presence of cognates in the test material could have elicited an uncertain response behaviour in the test-takers which might lead them to overestimate their vocabulary knowledge when confronted with non-cognate words and pseudowords.

The computerised Yes/No Vocabulary Tests

The tests that were constructed for this experiment differed only in their computer interface design. Computer application A was designed to resemble the paper-and-pencil version of the Yes/No test and had the following characteristics:

- All the items of the test were presented on the screen in a list allowing a complete overview of the test items. If the testee wanted to, he could count the total number of presented items.
- The item order was the same for all testees.
- The participants could scroll up and down the list and they could change their responses as often as they liked. When confronted with a test that consists of a set of items, participants may want to count the number of times they have responded *No* in proportion to the total number of test items, and they may consequently wish to change their responses.
- No time limit was imposed, but the participants' individual test-taking times were recorded by the computer. They could not end the test unless all items had been answered. As a consequence there were no omitted responses to be dealt with in the data analysis.
- The instruction for computer application A was as follows: *Indiquez les mots dans la liste dont vous connaissez la signification. Attention: Certains mots repris dans la liste n'existent pas en néerlandais!* (Mark the words in the list that you know the meaning of. Beware: the list also contains words that do not exist in Dutch.)

Computer application B was designed to make the most of the computer's potential to provide a controlled environment. The ways in which this control was exerted are listed below:

- The test items were presented to the testees sequentially: the words appeared on the screen one by one. This aspect allows the test developer more control of the test-taker's response pattern: the testee has no knowledge of the total number of items in the test, and it is practically impossible to keep tally of the number of items one has responded *No* to. Responding to particularly difficult items cannot be postponed until later and decisions cannot be altered in retrospect.
- The items were presented in a different and random order to each participant.
- Two buttons were created on the screen: one with the text 'je connais ce mot' (I know this word) and one with the text 'je ne

connais pas ce mot' (I do not know this word). With every item, these buttons re-appeared and the testees had to click one of them.

- There was no time limit. On the one hand, a time limit per screen seemed attractive because it could be argued that it should not take these participants long to identify known core vocabulary, and a time limit might prevent them from dwelling on their knowledge of the items. On the other hand, the pressure of having to respond within a time constraint could lead to biased responses. As the main aim of the experiment was reducing the response bias, we did not impose a time limit.

- The possibility of omitting responses was excluded by designing the computer programme in such a way that testees could not skip items. This turned the test into a forced-decision task.

- The instruction for computer application B read: *Cliquez sur le bouton JA si vous connaissez la signification du mot qui apparaîtra à l'écran. Cliquez sur le bouton NEE si vous ne connaissez pas la signification du mot. Attention: Certains mots repris dans la liste n'existent pas en néerlandais!* (You will be presented with a set of words. Click the JA button if you know the meaning of the presented word, click the NEE button if you do not know the meaning of the presented word. Beware: the set also includes words that do not exist in Dutch.) The instruction was repeated with each new screen because we hoped that this would reinforce the nature of the decision task, which in turn might result in a more consistent decision behaviour.

- Special care was taken to avoid double jeopardy (inadvertently evaluating not only language but also computer expertise). Before starting the test, the testees were given a warm-up session in order to familiarise themselves with the computer application.

The computerised translation task

After they had finished the Yes/No Vocabulary Test, the participants were presented with the 60 existing Dutch words of the Yes/No Vocabulary Test they had just completed and were asked to provide a translation for each item in their mother tongue. We considered a translation task the most unequivocal way of verifying the validity of the participants' *Yes* responses to words in the Yes/No Vocabulary Test because:

1 it constitutes an external criterion in which a response bias cannot intervene;

2 the similarity in content permits the avoidance of a lack of correlation between the two assessments, test and criterion, due to sampling problems;
3 it is less time-consuming than interviewing the participants individually;
4 we assumed the translation task to measure a well-defined construct: the extent to which the participants are able to provide an L1 translation of L2 words that belong to the core vocabulary of Dutch.

We turned the computer correction into a kind of human-assisted scoring because we considered all the given responses ourselves first before feeding the computer the correction key of which responses to accept and which to reject. This human-assisted scoring scheme was most lenient in that it accepted all possible translations and allowed grammatical as well as spelling or typing mistakes.

Test results

Table 1 illustrates that the mean scores for the word-items (51.14 for computer application A and 52.69 for computer application B) were high but the mean scores for the pseudoword-items were low (30.64 for Computer Application A and 30.31 for Computer Application B). The reliabilities of the pseudowords are very similar to those of the

Table 1　Mean scores, standard deviations, test reliabilities and correlations between performances on word versus pseudoword items of the Yes/No Vocabulary Test for Computer Application A and Computer Application B

Computer Application	[Words/60]				Correlation Words/Pseudo
	mean	SD	%	reliability	
A (*n* = 64)	51.14	5.39	85.23	.789	
B (*n* = 61)	52.69	4.34	87.82	.719	
	[Pseudowords/40]				
	mean	SD	%	reliability	
A (*n* = 64)	30.64	4.83	76.60	.779	− .345*
B (*n* = 61)	30.31	4.16	75.78	.696	− .005

Note: The reliabilities are calculated with Cronbach's alpha. Significant correlations are marked with * (*p* < .05), ** (*p* < .01) and *** (*p* < .001).

real words. This indicates that there seems to be a systematicity to how the pseudowords function in the test.

The correlation between the measure of the performances on words and the measure of performances on pseudowords was negative for computer application A ($r = -.345^*$). For computer application B there was no correlation between the measure of the performance on words and the measure of the performance on pseudowords ($r = -.005$, not significant). In previous experiments (Eyckmans, 2004), high false alarm rates were always accompanied by a negative correlation between the ability to identify words and the ability to reject pseudowords. The presence of a negative correlation may be seen as an indication of the presence of a systematic response bias in the data, the definition of response bias being that participants express a preference for one particular response alternative when taking the test. Our interpretation is that only the assumption of a bias can reasonably account for this systematic negative correlation. A difference in discriminability between the two item categories or the fact that the two item classes measure substantially different skills could result in a decrease in the correlation but it could not render it negative. The existence of a bias, however, would automatically lead to a negative correlation, for the bias has the particularity that it works in opposite directions at the same time. An individual bias towards *Yes* responses will produce an increase in the partial score for the words together with a decrease in the partial score for the pseudowords, and vice versa. Although we found no evidence of a negative correlation between the performances on word-items and those on pseudoword-items in the data of computer application B, this does not exclude a possible presence of a response bias, for the raw data were characterised by a low score on the pseudoword-items, which means we were again confronted with a high false alarm rate. The reason why the overestimation by the test-takers did not translate into a systematic negative correlation might be found in the sequential aspect of computer application B (where the items were presented one after another and participants could not skip them and return to them later), which might have prevented the participants from keeping their decision criterion stable throughout the test.

The false alarm rates were high (see Figure 1) and exceeded the rates we had obtained in previous experiments (average false alarm rate of about 20%). An investigation of the matrices revealed that this false alarm rate was accompanied by a substantial hit rate (85.2% and 87.8%). It seems that the exclusion of cognates in the test material had not prevented the participants from overestimating

Response alternative
Computer Application A
Yes   No

Response alternative
Computer Application B
Yes   No

Item alternative

		Yes	No		Yes	No
Word		Hit 85.2%	Miss 14.8%		Hit 87.8%	Miss 12.2%
Pseudoword		False alarm 23.4%	Correct rejection 76.6%		False alarm 24.2%	Correct rejection 75.8%

Figure 1   The item-response matrices of the Yes/No Vocabulary Tests for Computer Applications A and B. Percentages are calculated within each item alternative

their vocabulary knowledge blatantly. With an average of 24.2% false alarms the test-takers of computer application B did not obtain a lower false alarm rate than the test-takers of computer application A (23.4% false alarms).

Table 2 illustrates that the mean raw scores (number of hits) were severely reduced by the correction formulae as a consequence of the high rate of false alarms.

The test reliability of the translation task (Table 3) was calculated with Cronbach's alpha and amounted to .867 for computer application A ($n = 64$) and .865 for computer application B ($n = 61$). With an average score of 32/60 the participants of computer application B

Table 2   Results on the Yes/No Vocabulary Tests with the different methods of scoring. The raw score is the number of hits and the corrected scores are based either on the all-or-nothing model (cfg) or on the continuous model (Isdt and Hcfb)

Computer Application	Formula	Test score /60 mean	SD	%
A ($n = 64$)	Raw (hits)	51.14	5.39	85.23
	cfg	48.56	6.57	80.93
	Isdt	37.93	6.91	63.22
	Hcfb	39.03	7.10	65.05
B ($n = 61$)	Raw (hits)	52.69	4.34	87.82
	cfg	50.19	6.04	83.65
	Isdt	38.83	7.18	64.72
	Hcfb	39.96	7.56	66.60

Table 3 Descriptive statistics of the results on the translation task

Computer Application	Mean /60	Translation score SD	Reliability
A (*n* = 64)	27.91	7.85	.867
B (*n* = 61)	31.77	7.93	.865

appeared to be slightly stronger in vocabulary than the participants of Computer Application A who obtained an average score of 28/60. The discrepancies between the scores on the translation task and those on the Yes/No Test were substantial.

This raised the question as to what may have caused the participants to accept so many items in the Yes/No Test.

The correlations between the results on the Yes/No Vocabulary Test and the Translation Test (Table 4) were relatively low for Computer Application A (*r* = .663 [Raw]; *r* = .737 [cfg]; *r* = .693 [Isdt]; *r* = .741 [Hcfb]) as well as for Computer Application B (*r* = .704 [Raw]; *r* = .731 [cfg]; *r* = .677 [Isdt]; *r* = .719 [Hcfb]). It should be noted that concurrent validity is usually based on the correlation between two measures differing in their formats *and* their content. The lack of reliability which is linked to inferential factors is then of major importance. In our case, things were different because we created the opportunity of using formats with the same content, thus avoiding the inferential problems. This also implies that, in our case, the correlation should be very high in order to obtain good evidence of concurrent validity since the negative effect of the lack of reliability due to the inference factor is ruled out. With the exception of the correlation between the raw Yes/No scores (number of hits)

Table 4 Correlation between the results on the Yes/No Vocabulary Test and the results on the Translation Test

Computer Application	Correlation Yes/No test and Translation Yes/No formula	Correlation with Translation
A (*n* = 64)	Raw	.663
	Cfg	.737
	Isdt	.693
	Hcfb	.741
B (*n* = 61)	Raw	.704
	Cfg	.731
	Isdt	.677
	Hcfb	.719

and the translation scores, the correlations were weaker for computer application B than for computer application A. This means that the validity of the Yes/No Test that was administered under the experimental condition was not superior to the one that mimicked the paper-and-pencil version of the test.

An item analysis was carried out in which the responses to words in the Yes/No Test for both computer applications were matched with the translations that were given for these items. Table 5 reflects the four possible patterns that resulted from these matches. Of the two possible responses to words in the Yes/No Test (*Yes* and *No*), the participants could have rendered either a correct or an incorrect translation of the item in the translation task.

Table 5   The four possible patterns that result from the match between the responses to words in the Yes/No Vocabulary Test and the translation task for Computer applications A and B

	Responses to words in the Yes/No Test		Translated words	
	Response	%	Correct %	Incorrect %
Computer Application A	Yes	85	53	47
	No	15	12	88
Computer Application B	Yes	83	52	48
	No	17	13	87

Almost half of the word-items that evoked a *Yes* response in the Yes/No Test were translated incorrectly. One interpretation of this is that it confirms earlier suspicions about the amount of trust that can be placed in the *hit* responses of the Yes/No Test. Poor self-assessment by the participants seemed to run through both computer applications. Possible explanations of this effect, and how different tests access word knowledge are discussed by Fitzpatrick in Chapter 6.

Conclusion

Contrary to our expectations, the controlled environment of Computer Application B did not have the desired influence on the participants' response behaviour. Although the raw data were not characterised by a negative correlation between the performance on word-items and the performance on pseudoword-items in Computer Application B, the false alarm rate was not reduced. The controlled environment of Computer Application B did not prompt the testees to respond more carefully or more accurately to the instructions. Concurrent validity was rather weak and not higher than in the control condition: the correlations between the Yes/No Vocabulary Test and the translation task were unsatisfactory, which is not surprising given the high false alarm rate. In short, the sequentially programmed computer Yes/No Test did not offer any added value in this investigation. None of the control measures that were taken seem to have contributed to the validity of the participants' responses and hence the validity of the test. Finally, it was again demonstrated that excluding cognates from the test sample does not improve the quality of the test. In situations where there is no confusion caused by the lexical resemblance between the participants' mother tongue and the target language, overestimation remains high. These findings provide some confirmation for the view that the response bias functions independently of lexical skills or linguistic factors.

The reported experiment centred on the hypothesis that a controlled computer design might make the testees' responses more valid because it would prevent them from tailoring their response behaviour to certain characteristics of the test. A controlled computer application might hinder the testees' tendency to develop the kind of test-taking expertise through which they try to manipulate the test in order to obtain a better test score. Regrettably, the controlled computer application did not lead to unbiased responses: quite the contrary. It is possible that when confronted with a succession of isolated 'words' in Computer Application B, the testees decided to be on the safe side and developed an even stronger bias for the *Yes* response than the testees of Computer Application A.

Influencing test-takers' response behaviour by manipulating certain variables of the Yes/No Vocabulary Test is undoubtedly possible, but these variables do not overcome or counterbalance the inherent problem of the format, namely that two dimensions are measured at the same time: the vocabulary size of the participants and their own estimation of their vocabulary knowledge. The fact that the bias lies hidden in the Yes/No format of the text itself may be too strong an element to be counterbalanced by test design. The Yes/No format is too susceptible to the interference of construct-external variables: the interaction between the effects the pseudo-words may exert on learners, the dichotomous character of the Yes/No decision process and the possibility of socio-cultural interference undermines the test's construct validity. Therefore, derivative formats that avoid the ambivalence of the Yes/No task and reduce the undesirable variability between test-takers by restraining their response styles should be developed. In this perspective the Recognition Based Vocabulary Test (Eyckmans, 2004) – a test in which testees are presented with 60 pairs of words and pseudowords and are asked to distinguish the real word in the item-pair – could prove to be a valuable alternative.

For future language testing research it is clear that we should investigate the nature and the scope of the tasks we present to test-takers and we should be aware of how these tasks may interact with the characteristics of different individuals and with the testing context. Considering the inscrutable nature of language testing, gaining as much control as possible over the processes and strategies that learners engage in when responding to test items, or trying to minimise the likelihood that tasks could interact with the characteristics of individuals, seems imperative.

PART III:
THE UNIT OF ASSESSMENT AND MULTIPLE VOCABULARY MEASURES

4 Validity and threats to the validity of vocabulary measurement

Brian Richards and David Malvern

Introduction

In the first chapter of this volume, Paul Nation draws our attention to six factors that are potential threats to the validity of language assessment. By way of introduction to this chapter we will briefly consider three of these before concentrating on issues connected with 'multiple measures' and 'the unit of counting' in more detail. We will omit 'testing vocabulary in use', but not because we do not think it is important. More naturalistic approaches to language testing including aspects of normal language use are advocated in many areas of applied linguistics (see Porter, 1997, on second language oral testing; Wells, 1985, on early first language assessment; Holmes and Singh, 1996, on vocabulary in aphasia; Bucks, Singh, Cuerdon and Wilcock, 2000, on analysing lexical performance in dementia patients). Issues that touch on this will be addressed under 'multiple measures'.

All three remaining factors discussed by Nation – frequency lists, learner attitude, and first and second language formats – strike a chord with our own concerns related to research, language teaching, and the education of teachers. In the past, we have been sceptical about the use of word-frequency lists in second language assessment (Malvern, Richards, Chipere and Durán, 2004). At lower and even intermediate levels, exposure to vocabulary can be too limited and too heavily biased towards the lexical idiosyncrasies of teachers and textbooks for native speaker norms to be a reliable metric. Recently, however, we have been forced to think again. As part of an investigation into learner strategy training funded by the Economic and Social Research Council (RES 000 23 0324) we recently piloted the French version of *X-Lex* (Meara and Milton, 2003a). *X-Lex* is a computerised Yes/No vocabulary test (Meara and Buxton, 1987) aimed at 'low-level intermediate students'. The French file is based on Baudot's (1992) frequency count and the 'real' words are divided into five frequency bands (1K to 5K). Our colleague Helen Bradley tried out the test on twelve Year 12 students at a local grammar school to see whether the level of difficulty was suited to school students who were in only their sixth year of French language study. We paid particular attention to the scores in each frequency band to see whether the participants really did find the rarer words more difficult.

In spite of our scepticism, the results were a highly convincing demonstration that this was the case. In addition to 20 non-words, students were tested on 20 words from each frequency band and their average scores on these declined steadily from 19.50 on the highest frequency words though 15.00, 13.50, 12.08, to 10.00 on the rarest group of words. Curve estimation shows that these reductions are equally well fitted by a linear or logarithmic function and that, not only are they statistically significant for the group as a whole, but for 10 out of 12 individuals. Clearly for these students at this age and of this second language experience, word frequency is a factor to which they are sensitive as suggested in Chapter 2. This is despite their contact with native speakers and the authentic L2 linguistic environment being limited.

With regard to the issue of first language versus second language test formats referred to by Nation, this can sometimes be seen as illustrating the tensions between different forms of validity. In the mid-1990s the General Certificate of Secondary Education (GCSE) in England, a set of national examinations taken by students at the age of 16, moved away from first language test formats in modern foreign languages. Changing the rubrics into the second language affected all four skills, but, as would be expected, the wording of questions in the second language had the greatest effect on the tests of listening and reading comprehension (see Page, 1993; School Curriculum and Assessment Authority, 1994; Woods and Neather, 1994; Neather, Woods, Rodriguez, Davis and Dunne, 1995; Powell, Barnes and Graham, 1996). The reasons for this change appeared to be greater authenticity of tasks, raising the status of the target language, raising the status of the examination, and, most importantly, encouraging positive washback effects on classroom teaching, namely greater use of the target language by both teachers and students. In spite of these noble aims, however, the move was controversial and has remained so, with particular concerns about weaker students and those with special needs such as visual impairment (Suzanne Graham, personal communication, 11/5/04), and there has been much debate about what the listening examination, for instance, is testing. Subsequently, the amount of second language in the rubrics has been reduced, especially for speaking and writing tasks. In this context, the tensions between face validity, content validity and '*consequential validity* – the extent to which the test has the consequences it should have' (Alderson, 2002: 17) become particularly apparent.

Like Nation, we are also particularly worried about learner attitude. In terms of reliability, this comes under Norris and Ortega's (2003) heading of 'potentially unpredictable sources of error' (p. 741) that include 'idiosyncrasies of participants, such as interest, attention and motivation' (p. 740). In oral tests, learner attitude is likely to interact with the age, gender and personality of the interlocutor and the test-taker's familiarity with him or her (see, for example, Porter, 1997). Dörnyei and Kormos (2000) show that the quantity of speech elicited in an oral argumentation task is positively related to students' self-confidence and attitude towards their language course. Kormos and Dörnyei are reported to have obtained a negative correlation between lexical richness and anxiety and to have evidence of the importance of attitude to the task for accuracy (Ágnes and Kormos, 2004). This suggests an important relationship between the face validity of a task or test and the attitude and motivation of test-takers, something that has been suggested as a reason for problems with the C-test (Alderson, 2002).

As researchers, we are aware of the potential influence of variation in participant co-operation on the reliability of results. This has been well documented for early first language testing with two-year-olds (Richards, 1990). What is of greater concern, however, is the effect on students taking tests and examinations that affect life chances. In our analysis of authentic French oral examination tapes from students taking their GCSE at 16 years (Malvern and Richards, 2002), it is clear that some candidates are under-performing despite the importance of this rite of passage. One candidate (code W20) who had been judged by his teacher to be worthy of entry to the *higher* rather than the *basic* level of the examination still only managed to say 41 words (21 different words) in what was meant to be a five-minute oral interview, compared with the teacher-examiner's 266 words (81 different words). His mean length of utterance was 2.2 words compared with 5.44 (excluding backchannels) for the teacher, but even this tends to flatter him because some conversational turns that had to be omitted from the calculation consisted of non-linguistic grunting noises. Even more surprising was the candidate's failure to answer the very first question, 'Comment t'appelles-tu?' resulting in the teacher's prompt, 'Tu t'appelles Colin, n'est-ce pas?' When one considers that this student had been learning French for five years with four lessons per week and had received intensive practice in preparation for the oral test, this hardly represents an optimum performance.

Multiple measures

Although we have recently spoken of a 'unified approach' to measurement (Malvern and Richards, 2004), this should not be taken to mean, as some have assumed, that we think that a single index can represent either competence or performance in relation to vocabulary, or, for that matter, any other linguistic domain. Our 'unified approach' entails a common theoretical position that underpins more than one measure. Our starting point was the problems associated with measuring lexical diversity, and the solution lay in mathematically modelling the falling relationship between the Type–Token Ratio (TTR) and the number of tokens in a language sample. This procedure is implemented through a computer program called *vocd* that outputs a vocabulary diversity measure, D. Essentially, *vocd* plots the Type–Token Ratio against increasing numbers of tokens in a language sample and compares this empirically derived curve to the theoretical curves represented by an equation that has D as a parameter. D is adjusted in the equation until it provides the best fit with the particular curve obtained from the transcript. Higher curves arise from greater lexical diversity. Higher values of D fit higher curves and therefore stand for higher diversity (McKee, Malvern and Richards, 2000).

In a further development, we applied the same underlying model to the assessment of lexical style by enabling comparisons to be made between the diversity of different word classes. Such comparisons may be required in areas such as language pathology where, for example, a ratio of the diversity of nouns or verbs to other word categories can be informative, particularly when comparisons are made with a typically developing population (see Stokes and Fletcher, 2000). Similar measures are also applied to spontaneous speech samples in the study of different styles of early lexical development (for example, Bates, Bretherton and Snyder, 1988) and vocabulary composition (Pine, Lieven and Rowland, 1996), and recently to cross-linguistic investigations into the extent of a 'noun bias' in early vocabulary learning (Gentner, 1982). Typically, measurement has been carried out either by counting the raw number of different words in each class, or by calculating TTRs for each, or computing Type-*Type* Ratios such as Noun Types/(Noun Types + Verb Types) (Tardif, Gelman and Xu, 1999). All three approaches are flawed if the number of word tokens in each word class, and across subjects is not standardised. Our solution is based on modelling the introduction of new word types of each word class into a language sample of increasing token size (Malvern et al., 2004). This results in descending curves of TTR against tokens for each word class. Dividing one curve by the other yields a Type–Type-Ratio-against-tokens curve which has a limiting value that can be estimated from the diversity values for each word class by the simple relationship of $\sqrt{D_1 / D_2}$.

Finally, as will be shown below in our discussion of the unit of counting, by applying these same modelling procedures to different lexical units and comparing the resulting D values we can obtain an index of morphological development that reflects productivity (Malvern et al., 2004). It can be seen, therefore, that a panoply of measures addressing a broad spectrum of research questions can have a common thread binding them together in a consistent set of theoretical relationships – in this case the mathematical model under-pinning the calculation of D. There is thus no conflict between a 'unified approach' and the use of multiple measures.

Elsewhere we have likened the search for the perfect measure of vocabulary richness that seems to be implicit in much of the litera-ture, to a quest for the Holy Grail (Malvern et al., 2004). Interest-ingly, and unknown to us at the time, Alderson (2002: 22) also argues for multiple methods using a Holy Grail metaphor in his refutation of the universal validity of the C-test (Klein-Braley and Raatz, 1984). Multiple measures are useful for the purpose of triangulation (Chaudron, 2003), but primarily to avoid 'construct underrepresentation' (Norris and Ortega, 2003). With regard to vocabulary, it is widely accepted that knowledge is multidimensional and that, in the past, a preoccupation with vocabulary size has left depth of knowledge a neglected area. A number of models and assessment schemata exist that attempt to take account of compre-hension and production and different facets of depth of under-standing such as collocational knowledge, precision of meaning, and organisation of the lexicon (Wesche and Paribakht, 1996; Henriksen, 1999; Bogaards, 2000; Qian and Schedl, 2004). Wesche and Paribakht's (1996) Vocabulary Knowledge Scale is probably the best-known assessment instrument of levels of knowledge.

As far as first language development is concerned, the relationship between measures of comprehension and production is sometimes surprisingly weak. Using the infant version of the MacArthur Com-municative Development Inventories, a vocabulary checklist filled in by parents that assesses both receptive and productive vocabulary, Fenson et al. (1994) obtained a correlation of .53 between the comprehension and production scores of 659 children once age had been partialled out. They argue that even this 'relatively modest association' (p. 64) is an exaggeration of the relationship between the two because children vary so much in the gap between spoken and receptive vocabulary size. Children at the 90th percentile for production, for example, who have a receptive vocabulary of over 200 words, have a spoken vocabulary that may be only slightly smaller. At the other end of the scale, however, 36 children (6.2%) with a receptive vocabulary of 50 words had no words reported in production and some children with 200 words in comprehension also had no reported spoken words at all. These discrepancies are explained by individual differences in learning style such as imitativeness and degree of caution (Fenson et al., 1994: 64). The complex relationships between comprehension and production have been further explored by Harris, Yeeles, Chasin and Oakley (1995) and by Goldfield (2002) who studied variation in the time lag between comprehension and the onset of production for individual words, the gap being considerably greater for verbs than for nouns – infants produced 19.6% of the nouns they comprehended but only 4.4% of verbs. It is relevant here that our measure of lexical diversity, D, essentially an index of productive vocabulary *deployment*, has failed to correlate with tests of vocabulary comprehension when applied to the spoken language of preschool children even though it is consistently and significantly associated with age and other measures of language production (Richards and Malvern, 2004; Durán, Malvern, Richards and Chipere, 2004). In light of the above, therefore, it is clear that a single measure of early vocabulary gives an incomplete picture of developmental processes.

In the case of vocabulary *richness* we have also supported a multiple measure approach, endorsing Read's (2000) four-dimensional model of lexical variation, lexical sophistication, lexical density and number of errors (pp. 200–5), seeing these as interrelated but complementary sources of information. For example, Meara and Bell (2001) argue in favour of a measure that takes word frequency into account (an extrinsic measure) rather than those that simply depend on counting types and tokens within the text (intrinsic measures) on the grounds that this tells us more about the second language user's lexical resources. We would take the view, however, that these two kinds of measure are complementary – the former tells us about access to, and deployment of, more rare, more difficult, more precise vocabulary, possibly appropriate for more advanced registers, while the other tells us about access to a wide range of vocabulary and, by inference, its skilful use. Of course, it goes without saying that these two types of measure are related. After all, you cannot continue varying vocabulary indefinitely without adding rare words once a basic lexicon has been exhausted. In addition, both can be expected to correlate with word length. Biber (1988) sees both lexical diversity and word length as measures of lexical *specificity* that are weakly but significantly correlated ($r = .365$) in his own research. Word length, however, is also related to word frequency – more frequent words tend to be shorter (Zipf, 1949) and often have more general meanings. We would therefore expect weak but significant associations among these three variables, but it might be expected that the correlation between word length and rarity would be stronger than between diversity and word length.

We explored the interrelationships between diversity, rarity and word length in a study of 918 samples of children's narrative writing carried out by Ngoni Chipere (Malvern et al., 2004). To indicate lexical diversity we used our measure, *D*. Word length was the mean number of alphabetic characters in a word; and Meara and Bell's (2001) *P-Lex* software was used to provide an index of rarer, more difficult words. As predicted, there is a significant, relatively weak correlation between lexical diversity and rarity ($r = .423$) and a stronger association between rarity and word length ($r = .566$). What we did not predict, on the other hand, was that the strongest relationship would be between word length and lexical diversity ($r = .678$) and that if word length is partialled out of the correlation between diversity and rarity, it falls almost to zero ($r = .064$). On reflection, however, these results may not be so surprising. The relationship between word length and rarity is an imperfect one that is carried to some extent by the difference between the average length of content words and that of frequently repeated function words. Texts with a high word length may have a high proportion of content words, and content words are repeated less often than function words. Thus, texts with a high lexical *density* are likely to score highly on diversity but not necessarily on rarity. An additional measure of lexical density would have helped to tease apart these interrelationships.

The unit of counting

In first language acquisition, the development of computer software such as SALT (Systematic Analysis of Language Transcripts) (Miller and Chapman, 1993) and CLAN (Computerised Language Analysis) (MacWhinney, 2000a) has opened up new avenues for language development researchers that are now becoming more available to those working in bilingualism and second language acquisition (see Marsden, Myles, Rule and Mitchell, 2003). For example, when combined with CHAT (Codes for the Human Analysis of Transcripts) (MacWhinney, 2000a), a sophisticated transcription and coding system, CLAN becomes a powerful and flexible tool that allows researchers to conduct analyses according to their own operational definitions of what counts as a word and what counts as a different word. The validity of these definitions will, of course, depend on the purpose of the investigation, the precise research questions, and the age and language stage of the participants. A study of vocabulary development at one age, for example, might treat *can't*, *don't* and *won't* as single morphemes, whereas later on they would more likely be considered as two. The use of longer and more complex 'chunks' is even more problematic. Richards (1990) showed that among two- to three-year-olds, tag questions appeared to vary from functioning as a single lexical unit (/inIt/, /enIt/) to being fully analysed. The latter appeared in children who were able to match the auxiliary in the matrix clause with the correct auxiliary in the tag and demonstrated productive usage of negation, inversion, pronoun substitution and ellipsis elsewhere. Between these extremes one child in particular showed evidence of *partial* analysis – the correct application of a battery of complex tags in their correct contexts but without the necessary understanding of the auxiliary verb system to construct them himself.

Similar decisions have to be made about the status of onomato- poeia such as animal noises that might need to be filtered out of transcripts at an early age, but which would be treated as nominals if used consistently for labelling a homogeneous class of referents. In cross-linguistic research there are considerable difficulties in finding a theoretically consistent definition of a word (see, for example, Berman and Verhoeven, 2002). Naturally, such issues are neither confined to vocabulary measurement, nor to first language acquisition research. How to count morphemes or words and utterances in the calculation of mean length of utterance (MLU), a much used index of early language made popular by Brown (1973), has been a matter of some debate (Wells, 1985; Hickey, 1991). In the second language field there has been a revival of interest in what are variously referred to as prefabricated phrases, unanalysed chunks, frozen phrases, formulae, rote-learned phrases (Weinert, 1995), particularly with the recogni- tion of the extent to which many foreign language teachers explicitly encourage the rote learning of chunks (Mitchell and Martin, 1997). These concerns imply not only that the unit of counting should be consistent with the purpose of the analysis overall, as stated by Nation, but also that, where possible, individualised coding is more appropriate than a 'one analysis for all subjects' approach.

As noted above, computers give the researcher immediate access to fast, powerful, flexible and replicable analyses that, in the past, would have entailed days or even weeks of laborious sorting and counting that was susceptible to clerical errors. The other side of the coin is that, just like powerful statistical packages that carry out sophisticated analyses of data that may not fit their assumptions, they may be open to abuse. This can be a particular worry when data collected and transcribed for one purpose are used for another.

In order to investigate whether the effect of changing the unit of counting really makes an appreciable difference, we measured the lexical diversity of spoken language from 29 children at two ages, 30 and 36 months, by carefully editing their transcripts in a way that tailored the unit of analysis to different theoretical assumptions. The transcripts were from the Bristol Corpus, collected by Wells (1985) as part of a normative study of language development in preschool children, and were obtained in CHAT format from the CHILDES (Child Language Data Exchange System) database (MacWhinney, 2000b). Each transcript was run through the *vocd* program, which is part of the CLAN software, producing values of D to represent the lexical diversity of the child's speech.

The five versions of the transcripts were as follows.

Version 1: The child's utterances were processed from the unedited files at their face value. All transcribed sounds that were preceded and followed by a space or an utterance terminator were automatically treated as a word by the software. Different orthographic representations˙ were automatically counted as different words. The result of this process will be referred to as $D_{unedited}$.

Version 2: First, self-repetitions and self-corrections that had been coded in the transcripts were eliminated from the analysis using the appropriate filter. Reducing repetition in this way should increase D values. Second, word lists were output from each transcript and doubtful words were checked against their context. An 'exclude file' was built of invalid items. These consisted of laughter, pause markers, onomatopoeia that had no referential value, and some exclamations including cries of pain or surprise. Third, phonetic variants of the same word (for example, *me book* versus *my book*) were given CHAT codes so that they could be treated as the same word type. This would have the effect of reducing D values, particularly for children for whom the same word had been transcribed in several different ways. These results are referred to as D_{edited}.

Version 3: First, all transcripts were re-coded for repetitions and self-corrections as these had been found to be unreliable in the original. Second, the procedures for building the exclude file and coding phonetic variants were repeated by a second coder and corrections made. Third, some spelling inconsistencies in the original transcripts were corrected. Fourth, homographs (for example, *may* as a modal verb versus the month of *May*) were disambiguated. The last two procedures would tend to increase D values. These results are referred to as $D_{inflected}$.

Version 4: Boundaries between noun and verb stems and their inflections were marked so that they could be removed by an appropriate switch, and the analysis carried out on word stems only. Clearly, for children who are using inflected forms, this has the effect of reducing D values. The three previous versions have treated *run*, *runs*, and *running* as different word types, which confounds lexical diversity with the development of inflectional morphology. These results are referred to as D_{stems}.

Version 5: Irregular forms (*ran*, *went*, *feet*) were coded such that the lemma would be processed. This will further depress D values. These results are referred to as D_{lemmas}.

The five versions represent a progression from the relatively 'quick and dirty' analysis of Version 1 through successive refinements and more reliable coding relating to what counts as a word at all, and what is a different word, information that is often skipped over in published research reports. A valid choice between Versions 4 and 5 may well depend on the researcher's view of the storage and mental processing of regular and irregular verbs (see Pinker, 1999).

Having produced the five measures the next step is to compare them by examining their inter-correlations. These are presented for each age in Table 1.

All correlations are over .900 and range from .930 to .998. It is notable that the weakest correlations are between the Ds for Versions 1–3, those that differ most in relation to excluding non-words, editing the transcripts and improving reliability. By contrast, the strongest correlations, all over .990, are between Versions 3–5, that is, those that differ solely on whether the unit of analysis is inflected forms, word stems or lemmas. In other words, in this case it appears to be the basic work of transcript coding and file preparation, rather than the theoretical appropriateness of the measure, that makes the greatest difference.

Table 1   Pearson inter-correlations between the lexical diversity measure, *D*, obtained from five versions of transcripts of the same spontaneous speech samples (*p* values all less than .001)

Version	1	2	3	4	5	
Age 30 months (*n* = 29)						
1		.957	.934	.942	.945	
2		–	.932	.933	.939	
3			–	.997	.993	
4				–	.998	
5					–	
Age 36 months (*n* = 29)						
1		.983	.930	.937	.933	
2		–	.949	.956	.953	
3			–	.996	.994	
4				–	.995	
5					–	

With such a high set of correlations, some might argue that the five versions are essentially measuring the same thing and that we all might just as well save ourselves a lot of trouble and stick to the 'quick and dirty' method. There are three very good reasons, however, for not taking this view. Firstly, careful preparation of data eliminates sources of error and improves the reliability of the scores obtained. As Thompson (1998: 36) points out, 'Score reliability is one of the several study features that impact detected effects. Score measurement errors always attenuate computed effects to some degree.' Secondly, even a high correlation between two measures can conceal substantial changes in the rank order of children. For example, one child, Stella, at 30 months is ranked 2nd and 3rd on Versions 1 and 2, but only 12th, 11th and 10th respectively on Versions 3–5. In any context where judgements are to be made about individuals, therefore, it is particularly important that we bear in mind that validity is not an inherent property of a measure or test but of the way it is applied (Norris and Ortega, 2003: 739).

Thirdly, because in the formula for Pearson correlations the values for each variable are converted to standard scores (Ferguson, 1981), correlation coefficients do not take into account the magnitude of scores on one variable compared with those on the other. As noted by Bland and Altman (1986: 307) in the context of clinical assessment, '*r* measures the strength of a relation between two variables, not the agreement between them.' This is the reason why care should be taken when using correlation coefficients as an indicator of reliability:

> If the second [parallel form] ... of the [language] test gave each subject exactly 10 marks (or 50 marks) more than the first version, the correlation would be 1, and the reliability would be apparently perfect, though the marks for each subject are quite different on the two applications of the test.
>
> (Woods, Fletcher and Hughes, 1986: 217)

This is illustrated by the mean scores, ranges and standard deviations of D for the five versions displayed in Table 2. There is a progressive and sizeable drop in mean values from Version 1 to Version 5, with all possible comparisons between means being statistically significant on t-tests at each age. The implication is that scores obtained from different researchers working on different projects cannot be compared with any confidence unless we are sure of their exact procedures. In addition, an inspection of the ranges reinforces the point made above about the impact on some individual children. This is illustrated by the effect on the maximum values: a drop of 30 in the D values from Version 1 to Version 5 at 36 months.

Table 2   Descriptive statistics for the lexical diversity measure, D, obtained from five versions of the transcripts of the same spontaneous speech samples ($n = 29$)

Version	Mean		Range		SD	
	30 months	36 months	30 months	36 months	30 months	36 months
1	53.81	63.09	9.63–91.05	21.85–96.85	22.82	19.00
2	46.66	55.61	3.53–82.79	13.87–81.98	20.93	17.18
3	43.63	50.18	4.03–79.52	13.69–74.63	18.40	14.72
4	41.53	47.83	4.05–69.67	13.26–69.95	16.93	13.97
5	40.32	45.88	4.04–65.67	13.17–66.39	16.09	12.81

It is worth noting that Versions 3 to 5 offer differing degrees of lemmatisation, and, while it is D_{stems} from Version 4 that can be regarded as having the highest construct validity as a measure of early vocabulary deployment, a comparison between the scores on this and $D_{inflected}$ from Version 3 will give us useful additional information about a child's development. In a recent longitudinal study of the children in the Bristol Corpus (Malvern et al., 2004; Durán et al., 2004), we have observed that between the ages of 18 months and five years there is a consistent and statistically significant upward trend in lexical diversity for all three versions (Versions 3–5). The differences between them are small at 18 and 21 months but after this, the gaps at each age point widen. Why should this be? If, for simplicity, we confine the discussion to the difference between the *D*s for Versions 3 and 4 ($D_{inflected} - D_{stems}$) we can see that the difference is due to the use of inflectional morphology. At the younger ages children use few, if any, inflections. Therefore, the difference between a diversity measure based on stems and one that treats different inflected forms as different words will hardly be discernible. As children learn to apply more inflections to more word stems, however, the gaps will be larger.

This phenomenon has an obvious application in the assessment of children's morphological development. Furthermore, whereas other measures such as the mean number of inflections per word stem or the percentage of inclusion of morphemes in obligatory contexts are based on frequencies of occurrence, a measure that consists of the difference score ($D_{inflected} - D_{stems}$), that is, between Versions 3 and 4, would tap a combination of the range or diversity of inflections and the range or diversity of the stems to which they are applied. It can therefore be interpreted as reflecting productivity (cf. Stokes and Fletcher, 2000, on 'collocational diversity'). We refer to this index as Inflectional Diversity and have found that for 38 American English-speaking children between 27 and 33 months it correlates significantly with age ($r = .405$) and strongly and significantly with mean length of utterance ($r = .733$) and inflections per utterance ($r = .846$) (Richards and Malvern, 2004). With the Bristol Corpus, it correlates significantly and strongly to moderately strongly at nearly all ages with inflections per utterance. As one might expect, correlations with other language measures such as the Bristol Language Development Scales, though often significant, are weaker and less consistent (see Malvern et al., 2004). An analysis of data from Spanish-speaking children at comparable ages (Malvern et al., 2004) shows considerably higher Inflectional Diversity values than for English at all points beyond 21 months, which is exactly what one would expect from a language with a more complex system of inflections. Additionally, the Spanish values continue to rise beyond 36 months, the point at which they tend to plateau for the Bristol children. This suggests that Inflectional Diversity might be particularly useful as a developmental measure for languages that have a rich inflectional morphology.

Conclusion

We endorse all the concerns expressed by Nation in Chapter 1 and, like him, we find learner attitude to be the most intractable, and we do so in our roles both as teachers and teacher educators as well as researchers. The effect of this factor is unpredictable and, as Nation points out, an area over which we can have little control. Perhaps the most we can do is to improve motivation by increasing face validity and carry out carefully conducted pilot studies on equivalent population samples.

We also come down firmly in favour of multiple assessments. As we have demonstrated in our own work, multiple measures can be derived from a coherent theoretical model. The choice of measures needs to be theoretically motivated to have good construct validity in relation to the contexts, purposes, and research questions to which they are applied. What is to be avoided is unnecessary formal assessment, which would be unethical, and the use of an unprincipled battery of measures purporting to represent a similar construct followed by a selective interpretation of statistically significant results and retrospective theorising.

In our examination of the effects of varying the unit of counting, we found that high correlations between the lexical diversity of different versions of the same transcripts masked substantial consequences for the scores of at least some of the individuals who supplied the data. They also concealed significant and large differences between the mean values of D for each version. For this demonstration we chose to use our measure, D. The same kind of result would, without doubt, be obtained from other language measures and particularly those based on counts of types and tokens of vocabulary. Thus, the general point we are making is not about a particular measure but about principles of reliability and validity in language measurement that relate to careful selection of the unit of analysis.

5 Comparing measures of lexical richness

Roeland van Hout and Anne Vermeer

Introduction: lexical richness measures

This chapter is intended to build upon the previous chapter's consideration of the way we try to measure and assess the nature of the productive lexicon by looking at these measures in more detail. It will address in particular the concern that measures which aim to reveal the richness of the lexicon used to produce a text, suffer generally from reliability and/or validity problems. In this chapter, therefore, we intend to discuss these problems and then explore the possibility of combining three elements that seem to work relatively successfully: (a) lexical (frequency) layers, (b) alternative type–token functions, and (c) (re)sampling procedures.

Several lexical richness measures are being used in research on language acquisition, the most popular one being the Type–Token Ratio. This measure is provided, for instance, by CLAN (Computerised Language Analysis Program), which comprises the analytic tools for data formatted according to the CHAT (Codes for Human Analysis of Transcripts) guidelines. Both CLAN and CHAT belong to CHILDES (Child Language Data Exchange System), the successful databank on (first) language acquisition (cf. MacWhinney, 2000a and b). The Type–Token Ratio is calculated for data files containing transcribed utterances. In language acquisition research it often means transcriptions of spontaneous speech, including unguided narratives, guided retellings or speech elicited by a series of successive pictures.

Plain Type–Token Ratios can produce erratic outcomes, especially when the numbers of tokens vary substantially between the texts to be compared, as we will show (again) below. Alternatives have been suggested, like Guiraud's Index and *vocd*, measures which assume another functional relationship between the number of types and tokens. In addition, *vocd* uses random (re)sampling of a lexical distribution to estimate the richness parameter. *Vocd* is nowadays available in CLAN. An overview of the most important lexical measures is given in Table 1.

Table 1   Terminology and lexical richness measures

Lexical measure	Label	Formula
Number of words	Tokens	N
Number of different words	Types	V
Number of words occurring once	V_1	V_1
Type–Token Ratio	TTR	V/N
Indice de richesse	Guiraud	$V/\sqrt{N}$
Herdan's Index	Log TTR	$\log V / \log N$
Uber's Index	Uber	$(\log N)^2/(\log N - \log V)$
Vocd	D	$TTR = [D/N][(1+2N/D)^{1/2} - 1]$
Zipf's Z		
Yule's K		

More information on the measures of Zipf and Yule mentioned in Table 1 can be found in Baayen (2001). They are relevant for larger sample sizes, larger than what is common in acquisition research. In this contribution we will focus in particular on V, TTR, Guiraud and D. Another and different contribution to the discussion about lexical richness comes from measures that distinguish different (frequency) levels in the lexicon and which take these layers into account in estimating vocabulary richness. This layered approach will be discussed in a separate section in this chapter.

The reason for discussing different lexical measures is to get a better grip on what lexical measures can tell us. Does a higher outcome really reflect a richer underlying lexicon? Can we be certain and happy about the values produced by lexical measures? Which measures are reliable and valid? This chapter will start, therefore, with a discussion on the relationship between the number of types and tokens on the basis of concrete samples with different token sizes. This exercise shows the problematic character of the Type–Token Ratio. We will explain how changes might improve the lexical richness measure. We will present results from Dutch learners for a series of lexical measures including Malvern and Richards's *vocd**. We will then turn to computer simulations, based on the 'random urn' model, but also including properties related to human lexicons. We include several types of lexicon and extra attention is paid to the

---

* *Vocd* is the command in CLAN for the computation of D (see also the editors' introduction).

role of sample size. Next, we will consider how the inclusion of lexical frequency information may improve lexical richness measures. Finally, we evaluate the possibility of combining three elements that seem to work relatively successfully when separate: (a) the distinction of lexical (frequency) layers; (b) the use of alternative functions of the number of types in relation to the number of tokens; (c) the application of (re)sampling procedures (as is done in *vocd*, but applied to other measures, too).

The lexical constant and linearising transformations

The TTR produces a specific constant outcome if the relationship between the numbers of types and tokens is linear. Linear relationships have straightforward mathematical properties which is the reason why they are preferred in regression analysis: outliers can be detected, interpolation and extrapolation are straightforward, and the whole analytic machinery of (linear) regression analysis can be used for expressing and interpreting the relationship(s). It is common practice in statistical analyses to straighten non-linear curves, by linearising transformations. More general information about such transformations is given in Rietveld and van Hout (1993).

The way the linearity assumption works in linear regression analysis can be illustrated by an example of the relationship between types and tokens in a concrete text. The text chosen consists of the first three chapters of Genesis (King James Bible). The number of words or tokens is 2,241, whereas the number of types (the number of different words) is 376. Let us suppose we want to investigate the relationship between the number of tokens (= N) and the number of types (= V). In order to investigate this relationship, samples of different sizes (running from 100 to 1,000 tokens) were drawn. For each specific number of tokens (see Table 2) five random samples (with replacement) were drawn. For every sample the number of different word types was calculated. The mean number of types found over the five random samples for a specific number of tokens is given in Table 2. By taking the mean number of types the amount of the standard error (sampling error) is redressed.

The relationship between the number of types and the number of tokens can be visualised by making a graph as shown in Figure 1. The number of types (V) increases much more slowly than the number of tokens (N). The curvilinear track shows that there is no straightforward linear relationship between the number of types and tokens. For 100 tokens the number of types is 58; for 1,000 words it is not 580, but 261.

Table 2   Number of tokens (= N) and types (= V) obtained by random sampling (with replacement) of the first three parts of Genesis; the number of types is the mean value of five random samples

Number of tokens (= N)	Number of types (=V)
100	58
200	97
300	133
400	155
500	184
600	199
700	214
800	236
900	245
1000	261

Nevertheless, applying linear regression to the data given in Table 2 seems to lead to fairly satisfying results at first sight. The regression coefficients b_0 and b_1 are given in Table 3, as well as the correlation (= r) between the predicted and the observed scores, which is extremely high: .98. However, there are two reasons for rejecting this result. Further, the solution makes no sense, because it implies that a sample of 0 or 1 tokens will give 59 types (see the value of b_0 in Table 3). Secondly, the residuals are not randomly distributed. For the

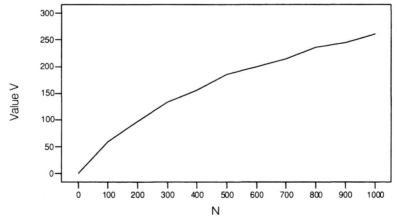

Figure 1   Number of tokens (= N) versus the number types (= V) obtained by random sampling (with replacement) of the first three parts of Genesis

Table 3 Results for regression of number of types (= V) on (1) number of
tokens (= N), (2) square root number of tokens, (3) logarithm
number of tokens, and (4) logarithm number of types and
number of tokens; all parameters b_0 and b_1 are significant

Measure	Dependent	Independent	r	b_0	b_1
TTR	V	N	.98225	59.2000	.2164
Guirand	V	$\sqrt{N}$	.99854	-32.9891	9.3994
*	V	log N	.99047	-372.9031	207.4955
Herdan	log V	log N	.99637	.4974	.6462

* This is another plausible measure as yet unnamed in the literature.

relevance of the distribution of residuals, we refer to Rietveld and
van Hout (1993).

In order to obtain better results, transformations can be applied to
make the curve a straight line. The results are given in Table 3 as
well. The table gives the highest r for the square root.

One may think that we are exaggerating by calculating the
transformations as given in Table 3. However, these transformations
directly correspond to the measures found in the literature on lexical
richness. Three of them are given in Table 4. The three measures in
Table 4 do not contain a constant (= b_0), an important aspect that we
do not discuss here. All three measures yield a biased distribution of
the error distribution. None of the models really performs satisfactorily, but Guiraud's Index seems to be the best one.

Table 4 Measures on lexical richness in relation to their linear form

Measure	Formula	linear form (types dependent)
Type–Token Ratio	V/N	$V = b_1 N$
Guiraud's Index	$V/\sqrt{N}$	$V = b_1\sqrt{N}$
Herdan's Index	log V/log N	$\log V = b_1 \log N$

Table 3 shows that of all measures the Type–Token Ratio performs
least satisfactorily (this conclusion is corroborated by other diag-
nostics; see Rietveld and van Hout 1993), this is an interesting fact as
this index is still widely applied (for instance in research on language
acquisition, cf. for an overview, Richards, 1987). A high r signifies an
important relationship. It does not imply, however, that the right
underlying model has been found. In addition, the example with the
number of types and tokens shows that finding the right model for
the relationship between variables is not a trivial matter.

Empirical results

The measures mentioned in Table 1 do not always reveal the desired differences in lexical richness and, in longitudinal studies, an increase in vocabulary growth. We will give some examples from studies we carried out, mainly on Dutch as a second or first language, among both adults and children.

The first example is a longitudinal study on 32 Turkish and Moroccan children, aged between 6 and 9, learning Dutch as a second language very rapidly (Vermeer, 1986). These learners provided examples of spontaneous speech and data from other language tasks, at six intervals over some two and half years, between grades 1 and 3. In each data set positive and significant (p < .01) correlations were found between the vocabulary task and the Guiraud's Index (r between .49 and .64), but all correlations between the vocabulary task and the TTR turned out to be negative (r between −.37 and −.04). The results are shown in Table 5. Thus, at each moment in time, children with high scores on the vocabulary task tended also to have higher scores on Guiraud's Index.

Table 5 Correlations between spontaneous speech measures and the vocabulary task (Vermeer, 1986, *n* = 32, Dutch L2-children in 6 moments over 2.5 years (**= *p* < .01)

	Time 1	Time 2	Time 3	Time 4	Time 5	Time 6
TTR	−.33	−.28	−.37	−.21	−.20	−.04
Guiraud's Index	.64**	.59**	.57**	.49**	.49**	.53**
Herdan's Index	−.13	−.12	−.22	−.11	−.03	−.13

In the scattergrams, the TTR tended to have a 'U-shaped curve' (cf. Plunkett and Marchman, 1991): a low as well as a high score on the TTR corresponded to a high score on the vocabulary task, whereas an intermediate TTR corresponded to a low score on the task. The acquisition and use of (frequent) function words by the more proficient children may have caused this effect. Notwithstanding these changes, none of the different lexical measures turned out to increase over time. This negative longitudinal effect is shown in Table 6.

The restriction to about 200 types per sample apparently contributes over time to the negative effect of the lexical measures, whereas the increasing number of tokens seems to point to an increase in utterance length. The drop is particularly obvious in the TTR measure. With increasing proficiency, we would have expected an

Table 6   Means of lexical measures of 32 Dutch L2-children, 6 moments
of measurements over 2.5 years (200 utterances for each child in
each moment of measurement)

	N types	N tokens	Guiraud's Index	TTR	Herdan's Index
Time 1	246	691	9.40	.372	.85
Time 2	212	593	8.77	.376	.84
Time 3	232	646	9.17	.377	.85
Time 4	221	623	8.93	.379	.85
Time 5	253	691	8.87	.361	.84
Time 6	249	841	8.64	.302	.82

increase in number of types as well as tokens. We do not know why
Guiraud's Index, the TTR and Herdan's Index decrease with increasing language proficiency, be it the proportion of function words,
the longer utterances the children use, or the different topics that
were discussed at different times. Orlov (1982: 215, cited in Baayen,
1989: 81) points out that, for increasing N, Guiraud's Index will first
increase, then reach a maximum, after which it steadily decreases.

Our second data set derives from Broeder, Extra and van Hout's
(1987; 1993) study of lexical richness in 20 adult L2-speakers from
six different L1 sources and five different L2 targets. These subjects
provided data three times at nine-monthly intervals. The scores on
the lexical measures tended to remain equal (Guiraud's Index), or
even to decrease rather than increase over time (TTR), as is shown in
Table 7. For instance, 10 of the 20 informants scored lower for TTR
in the final data set than they did on the first data set. It should be
noted that the kind of language activity had a significant effect on the
outcomes: TTR as well as Guiraud's Index are higher in free conversation then in film retelling. This can be seen again in Table 7, a

Table 7   Mean scores for 20 adult L2-informants (Broeder, Extra and
van Hout, 1987) (nine-monthly time intervals)

	Film retelling			Free conversation		
	Time 1	Time 2	Time 3	Time 1	Time 2	Time 3
Tokens	607.65	790.65	888.65	917.15	917.35	1118.95
Types	141.65	182.25	208.20	176.90	177.05	205.80
Guiraud's Index	5.89	6.42	6.90	6.61	6.71	7.19
TTR	.27	.24	.24	.32	.35	.28

result that can be explained by the many different topics which may occur in free conversation.

The data in Table 7 illustrate the fact that, as proficiency develops, the number of both tokens and types increase, and the type–token-based lexical measures fluctuate depending on the kind of activity and text length. Nevertheless, Guiraud's Index produces the most acceptable results.

The outcomes of different lexical measures seem to depend to a great extent on the way in which the relationship between types and tokens varies as proficiency develops. If the number of types produced develops unpredictably in relation to the number of tokens produced, as proficiency increases, then a stable measure cannot be found. If there is a linear relation between the increases in the number of types and tokens (produced during a certain activity) over time, the TTR, for example, will have a constant value, and no development will be measured. In a curvilinear relationship, where the number of tokens increases relatively faster than the types, the TTR will decrease in value. However, depending on the stage of acquisition, an irregular pattern is also possible. Imagine a learner having just acquired the function words *a* and *the* at a certain stage of acquisition. Only these two types will account for a strong increase in the number of tokens, because *a* and *the* are very frequent. The denominator (N variants) outnumbers the numerator (V variants), producing a *de*creasing curve, although it is clear that the learner has made progress in language acquisition by learning those function words. Quite possibly, this effect may explain the results seen in Tables 5, 6 and 7. All of these calculations might be helped, it would seem, if a distinction were made between function and content words. Richards (1987: 207) has attempted this but such a distinction did not lead to better and more reliable results for the lexical measures he investigated.

In addition to distinguishing between function and content words, distinctions in word frequency might also influence the analysis. The first 1,000 most frequently used words of a language (which may also include many function words) are comparatively very frequent compared with all other words. This is known as Zipf's Law (frequency multiplied by rank has a constant value), and graphically displayed as a hyperbola (cf. Alekseev, 1984). Both increasing length of sentences and variance in word frequency make any measure based on a relationship between types and tokens in a growing vocabulary very complicated. Malvern and Richards (1997; 2000; 2002; McKee, Malvern and Richards, 2000; Malvern, Richards, Chipere and Durán, 2004) address this problem by use of mathematical modelling to overcome the influence of variable text length. They calculate the probability of a new vocabulary item being introduced into longer and longer samples of the text. Their measure is calculated in two steps. First, a curve of the TTR against tokens is produced by randomly sampling words from the text. Next, the software (*vocd*) finds the best fit between this empirical curve and theoretical curves calculated from the model by adjusting the value of a parameter. This parameter, D, is currently a standard CLAN program of the CHILDES project (MacWhinney, 2000a and b). According to the CLAN manual (paragraph 5.40) this measure D 'has been shown to be superior to previous measures in both avoiding the inherent flaw in raw TTR with varying sample sizes and in discriminating across a wide range of language learners'. But this does not mean that the results it produces always correlate with other measures of language proficiency.

Jarvis (2002) shows that the parameter D provides accurate curve-fitting models of lexical diversity. His data include written narrative descriptions of a silent film by 140 Finnish-speaking and 70 Swedish-speaking learners of English, and an additional group of 66 native English speakers. However, D does not always discriminate very well between groups with obvious differences in vocabulary. For instance, Finnish 7th graders and Swedish 9th graders, both with four years of ESL education, and Finnish 9th graders with six years of ESL education, all have higher scores for D than 7th grade native English speakers. The results are presented in Table 8.

Table 8 Means per group, based on Jarvis' (2002: 68) Table 2

	Learner groups ($n = 35$, for each learner group)						Native Speakers ($n = 22$, each group)		
	F5	F7	F9a	F9b	S7	S9	E5	E7	E9
Tokens	140.91	172.71	230.46	244.83	222.34	275.00	196.86	285.77	217.14
Types	56.91	69.14	87.83	86.09	75.57	98.63	77.32	100.45	87.05
TTR	.44	.43	.43	.37	.36	.37	.45	.37	.43
D	22.02	25.64	29.36	23.02	18.55	26.62	27.68	24.69	29.36

F = Finnish ESL speakers, S = Swedish ESL speakers,
E = native speakers of English

Moreover, with respect to the relationship between the lexical measures on the one hand, and holistic quality ratings by teachers on the other, Jarvis (2002: 77, Table 6) found significant correlations for only two out of nine groups. For the number of types, all but one group had high and significant correlations with the ratings. With respect to the scores of the ESL learners on a vocabulary test, only three of the six groups had significant correlations between test scores and the lexical measure D (and for the number of types all but one). So, in Jarvis' data, the lexical measure D does not discriminate between groups with obvious differences in vocabulary, and shows only low concurrent validity.

Malvern and Richards (2002) find 27 French L2 learning students to have a lower D than their teachers (44.9 versus 56.9), and this is possibly due to the examination situation in which the teachers tried to rephrase questions, and to elicit answers wherever students experienced difficulty. With respect to concurrent validity, they report low correlations between D on the one hand, and teacher ratings and examination results on the other. Guiraud's Index, or often simply the number of types, apparently performs better according to most studies. Whatever it is that D can tell us about lexical richness and the qualities of vocabulary in a text, it appears that an individual text may tell us very little about a learner's productive vocabulary knowledge or general language level. Difficulties may lie therefore, not only in establishing stable and reliable measures of lexical richness, but also in establishing a workable construct of how vocabulary and other language knowledge can manifest itself in the qualities of a text. The issue of test validity, and particularly the appropriateness of concurrent validity in all ciurcumstances, is dealt with in Chapter 6.

Modelling and sampling lexicons: the 'urn' model

How can we show in a more concrete way how sampling a lexicon works? A promising approach is to use computers to simulate lexicons and drawing samples. In this section we try to simulate specific properties of 'human' lexicons, and we start with the simplest definition of a lexicon. A lexicon can be defined as an arbitrary set of lexical elements, each lexical element having an equal chance of being selected. The lexicon might be thought of as an enormous urn containing lexical elements. The simplest situation (and the most trivial one) is a lexicon of a certain size ($=\Omega$) in which all elements ($=$ word types or lemmas, v_1, to v_Ω) have an equal chance of being selected. Given a number of withdrawals ($=$ number of tokens $=$ N), the expected number of different elements in the sample ($=$ number of types $=$ V) can be calculated with the formula: $V = \Omega \left(1 - (1 - 1/\Omega)^N\right)$.

What steps can be taken to give such a lexicon better human language properties? A distinction can be made between two lexical levels or categories, the category of content words and the category of function words, in fact between a group of frequently occurring words and a group of infrequently occurring words. This can be done by assigning function words a higher chance of being selected. Table 9 shows the expected TTRs for withdrawals of 500 and 1,000 words for three lexicons of increasing size, and in proportion and probability of occurrence of function words (these also increase). Words within a category have an equal chance of being selected. The table also gives the expected TTRs for 500 and 1,000 drawings.

Table 9   Three hypothetical lexicons having two categories of lexical items: frequent ones ('function words') and infrequent ones ('content words')

	Lexicon A	Lexicon B	Lexicon C
Size of lexicon	750	1,000	1,250
Proportion of function words	.100	.150	.200
Proportion of content words	.900	.850	.800
Probability of function words	.150	.250	.400
Probability of content words	.850	.750	.600
TTR 500 words	.726	.776	.794
TTR 1,000 words	.549	.620	.651

The size of the three lexicons in Table 9 increases from 750 to 1,250 (a growth rate of 67%). The proportion of function words increases as well as their probability as a category. Because of the increase of function words and their increasing weight, the differences in TTR remain minimal, especially when the samples are small. The TTR discriminates poorly between the three hypothetical lexicons.

The complicated relationship between the number of types observed or expected and the properties of the lexicon becomes even more conspicuous in another example. Again, three lexicons are involved, all three having the same size: 1,000 types. In Lexicon 1, all types have an equal chance of being selected. Lexicon 2 includes a category of function words with a higher chance of being selected (their proportion is .10; their total probability of occurrence is .40). In comparison to Lexicon 2, Lexicon 3 has some properties that make it more like a human lexicon. Within the group of function words, the chance of being selected varies for the types. A probability function was applied by which a small group of types had a relatively high chance of being selected and by which a larger group of types had a relatively low chance of being selected. The proportion of function words is .20, their probability of being selected is .40. Within the class of content words each type has the same probability of being selected. The chances change, however, with each selection. The probability of the type selected is increased for the next selection (this is consistent with the finding that content words once used tend to re-occur). In addition, the probabilities of the types adjacent to the type selected are increased (adjacency being defined in terms of the case numbers of the types). It applies to 20 types to the left and 20 types to the right of the type selected; the probability is increased by a probability function. This is consistent with the finding that types belonging to the semantic domain of the topic discussed have an increased chance of being selected. The consequence is that the selection of words is marked by a high degree of dependence, a circumstance that corresponds to the use of real words by real speakers. However, the expected number of types can no longer be calculated by formulas. They have to be obtained by simulating selections on a computer.

Table 10 Properties of three different lexicons

	Lexicon 1	Lexicon 2	Lexicon 3
Size of lexicon	1,000	1,000	1,000
Proportion of function words	.000	.100	.200
Proportion of content words	1.000	.900	.800
Probability of function words	.000	.400	.400
Probability of content words	1.000	.600	.600
Dependent sampling	–	–	+

Samples were drawn from each of the three lexicons in a random way. The sample size varied between 100 and 1,000 drawings. For each sample size 10 samples were selected and their mean results are given in Table 11. In interpreting the results in Table 11, it is important to bear in mind that the three lexicons are equally rich: all three contain 1,000 types.

Table 11 shows that the outcomes for the three lexicons differ considerably and systematically. Lexicon 1 produces the highest numbers of types. Lexicon 3 produces the lowest numbers of types. If very large samples had been drawn, the differences between the lexicons would decrease and even disappear, because large samples would exhaust the whole lexicon. The numbers of types in Table 11 are represented graphically in Figure 2.

Another interesting effect of the properties of a lexicon is the resulting reliability. Not only do the numbers of types sampled

Table 11 Mean number of types (10 samples) for varying sample sizes
for three equally rich though different lexicons (see Table 10)

N (tokens)	Lexicon 1	Lexicon 2	Lexicon 3
100	95.2	91.2	73.9
200	181.4	167.7	120.9
300	259.3	233.3	167.7
400	329.8	290.7	203.7
500	393.6	341.8	228.9
600	451.4	387.9	257.4
700	503.6	429.8	269.8
800	550.9	468.2	302.4
900	593.6	503.6	335.3
1,000	632.3	536.3	377.2

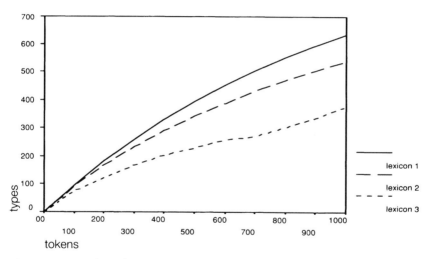

Figure 2 Number of types versus number of tokens for the different
sample sizes of the three lexicons of Table 11

change, but the confidence intervals change as well. The 95%
confidence intervals observed for the three lexicons on the basis of
ten samples of 1,000 tokens each are given in Table 12.

Table 12 shows that the confidence interval of the third lexicon is
about six times as large as the intervals for the other two lexicons.
This result is not encouraging. It implies that the reliability of lexical
measures is fairly low and that a lot of unwanted fluctuations enter
the measurements, especially in the case of small samples, and, in

Table 12   Confidence intervals for the three lexicons on the basis of
10 samples of 1,000 tokens

	V	Standard error	Confidence interval 95%
Lexicon 1	629.3	2.399	623.88 – 634.72
Lexicon 2	579.6	2.257	534.50 – 544.70
Lexicon 3	377.2	13.296	347.15 – 407.25

addition, especially when the lexicon possesses realistic, human-like properties.

Lexical Frequency Profiles

A major concern with type/token-based measures is that they do not take into account the *frequency* of a word. Whether a word is frequent or not, these type/token-based measures simply count how many types and tokens appear in the data. Since the frequency of a word is related to acquisition order (see, among others, Kibby, 1977; Nation, 1990: 77; Huttenlocher et al., 1991; Brown, 1993: 277; Vermeer, 2001), a more valid measure of lexical richness might be to relate the words in spontaneous speech data to their frequency (or frequency classes) in a corpus, such as that of Francis and Kučera (1982). This is comparable to a procedure in the Lexical Frequency Profile (LFP) (Laufer and Nation, 1995, Meara and Milton, 2003a,b) for written texts, in which four levels are distinguished, or the measure *AG* (Advanced Guiraud, Treffers-Daller and van Hout, 1999; Daller, van Hout and Treffers-Daller, 2003) for spoken texts, in which two frequency levels are distinguished. Moreover, a measure of lexical richness, based on a frequency list, makes possible an indication of absolute vocabulary size, in the same way as is done by extrapolating scores on some vocabulary tests (cf. the Vocabulary Levels Test, Laufer and Nation, 1999). In the next section, we will analyse the outcomes of such a lexical measure, the Measure of Lexical Richness (MLR) (Vermeer, 2004b), based on the relative frequency of words as they occur in daily language input.

To establish a frequency-based measure of lexical richness, we distinguished nine categories of frequency classes (we will call them voclists) based on the geometric means of the frequencies: the geometric mean covers aspects of both word frequency and variation between different corpora, see van Hout and Vermeer (1992) in Schrooten and Vermeer's word list (1994). In this word list (see Table 13) nearly two million words (tokens) were collected in schools

(Kindergarten and grades 1 to 6), yielding a total of 26,000 lemmas – from both oral and written language input in primary education: teachers' instructions, picture books, readers, and from language, arithmetic and social studies textbooks.

Table 13   Word lists on the basis of Schrooten and Vermeer (1994). Number of tokens, lemmas, and token coverage on each frequency level

Frequency levels	Tokens per voclist	Lemmas per voclist	Token coverage	Cumulative lemmas	Cumulative coverage
Voclist 1	1669651	1000	85.3	1000	85.3
Voclist 2	117031	1000	6.0	2000	91.3
Voclist 3	51222	1000	2.6	3000	93.9
Voclist 4	29718	1000	1.5	4000	95.4
Voclist 5	19196	1000	1.0	5000	96.4
Voclist 6	19002	1500	1.0	6500	97.4
Voclist 7	13348	1613	0.7	8113	98.1
Voclist 8	20340	4577	1.0	12690	99.1
Voclist 9	18470	13890	0.9	26580	100.0
Total	1957978	26580			

As can be seen in the third column of Table 13, the first voclist consists of the 1,000 lemmas that have the highest (geometric) mean of frequency, in other words, the thousand most frequent words in daily input in elementary school. The second voclist consists of the 1,000 lemmas that follow, etc. voclists 6 and 7 consist of about 1,500–1,600 lemmas, voclist 8 has about 4,500 lemmas, and the ninth voclist more than 13,000 lemmas. The first 1,000 lemmas in the first voclist account for no less than 85.3% of the tokens in the entire corpus, as can be seen in the fourth column, the second voclist with 1,000 lemmas covers 6% of the corpus. In line with Zipf's Law, only a few lemmas are very frequent, whereas the 13,000 least frequent words account for less than 1% of all tokens in the corpus.

To calculate the MLR, the relative distribution of the token coverage in the Schrooten and Vermeer corpus in the fourth column is taken as a 'model'. In other words, if the relative distribution of the words of an analysed text over the nine voclists is the same as those in the fourth column in Table 13, then the MLR score is considered to match with a vocabulary of about 26,000 words. If a person uses relatively more words from the first four voclists, then his score is lower. If someone with a very low vocabulary uses words from the first voclist only, his MLR score is 1 (indicating a vocabulary size of about 1,000 words). The MLR score is calculated by adding up each quotient of the text coverage of the transcript of the child's speech, and the 'model' coverage of Schrooten and Vermeer (1994) ('Token coverage' in Table 13) of each voclist, 1–9.

The MLR formula is as follows: MLR = q1 + 1/1.25*q2 + 1/1.75 *q3 + 1/2*q4 + 1/3*q5 + 1/4*q6*(1.5) + 1/4*q7*(1.6) + 1/6*q8* (4.6) + 1/9*q9*(13.8), in which q1–q9 = quotient of text coverage of the transcript of the child's speech and 'model' coverage of Schrooten and Vermeer ('Token coverage' in Table 13) in that voclist (1–9).

Each quotient is multiplied by the number of lemmas (and divided by 1,000) in that voclist (1–9), as indicated in column 3 in Table 13. Voclists 2 and higher have a weighted multiplication factor in the denominator to compensate for the fact that most transcripts under investigation do not have two million, but only about 1,000 tokens. A huge corpus has relatively more hapaxes, and relatively higher coverage percentages in the lower frequency ranges. The multiplication factor in the denominator ranges from 1.25 in voclist 2 to nine in voclist 9. This formula is explainable, but on the other hand far from elegant. For the time being, we are only interested in the power of the frequency approach in making calculations of lexical richness more reliable and useful. In Table 14 a concrete example of the calculation of the MLR score of a transcript (spontaneous speech of a child) is given.

Because the MLR score is related to the Schrooten and Vermeer corpus, it can give, like an extrapolated score on a vocabulary test

Table 14 Concrete example of the calculation of the MLR score of one text

voclist	tokens/%	'model'	(cov %/(model*weight))*nlemmas/1,000	
1	832/89.5	85.3	(max/85.3) * 1,000/1,000	1.00
2	43/4.6	6.0	(4.6/(6.0*1.25)) * 1,000/1,000	0.61
3	11/1.2	2.6	(1.2/(2.6*1.75)) * 1,000/1,000	0.26
4	7/0.8	1.5	(0.8/(1.5*2)) * 1,000/1,000	0.27
5	6/0.6	1.0	(0.6/(1.0*3)) * 1,000/1,000	0.20
6	15/1.6	1.0	(1.6/(1.0*4)) * 1,500/1,000	0.60
7	4/0.4	0.7	(0.4/(0.7*4)) * 1,600/1,000	0.23
8	6/0.6	1.0	(0.6/(1.0*6)) * 4,600/1,000	0.46
9	6/0.6	0.9	(0.6/(0.9*9)) * 13,800/1,000	1.02
not in the lists	41		MLR-score total	4.65
total	930		indicated productive vocabulary size	4,650

related to a dictionary, an indication of a person's vocabulary size. Thus, a total score of 2 indicates a vocabulary size of about 2,000 words, a score of 5 indicates a vocabulary size of about 5,000 words. In Table 14, the child in question has an indicated productive vocabulary of about 4,650 words.

How good is the MLR? To find out, we compared the outcomes of this frequency-based measure with other type/token-based lexical measures, such as Guiraud's Index and *vocd*, and with receptive and productive vocabulary tasks. We wanted to investigate which measures differentiate best between groups with obvious differences in vocabulary, which lexical measures correlate best with performances on vocabulary tasks, and to what extent they are independent of the number of types and text length.

Spontaneous speech data were gathered from and language tasks administered to 16 Dutch native speakers, and 16 ethnic minority children with Dutch as a second language. All children had their primary socialisation in the Netherlands, and were at school in grade 2 (mean age 7.11, sd. 0.7). For each child, a corpus of 150 to 200 T-units was transcribed. The following variables were counted: the number of utterances, tokens, types and lemmas, on the basis of which Mean Length of Utterance (MLU) and Guiraud's Index were calculated. In addition to these, the *vocd* program in CHILDES calculated *D*, of which the '*D*_optimum average' was taken. For the frequency-based lexical measure, two kinds of MLR were calculated. MLR1 was based on the first, most frequent meaning of a word in the lists, regardless of the speaker's intended meaning. Thus, for MLR1, if a child uses the word *bank*, we counted the most frequent meaning of *bank* in the lists. However, of course, the intended meaning of a word is not necessarily the same as the most frequent one in the lists. For instance, in one example, the child meant a financial *bank* whereas the most frequent meaning according to the lists is *couch* (in Dutch the word *bank* has these two meanings). Then, to obtain a count for MLR2, using the speakers' intended meanings, we carried out a disambiguation-by-hand for the entire corpus. A computer program (based on a modified version of VocabProfile, see Nation and Heatley, 2002) matches the words in the corpus with those in the nine frequency classes of Schrooten and Vermeer's word list (1994, see Table 13).

In addition to collecting spontaneous speech data, we evaluated the children's vocabulary by using a receptive vocabulary and a definition task. In the Receptive Vocabulary Task (*n* items = 96), the child had to point to one picture (out of four), which was the correct referent of an orally presented word, as in the Peabody Picture

Vocabulary Test. In the Definition Task (*n* items = 45), the child had to explain or describe the meaning of a given word.

In Table 15, the means and standard deviations of the different measures are displayed, for the Dutch native speakers and the children for whom Dutch was a second language (the means and standard deviations differ slightly from those given in Vermeer, 2004a, because the data presented here are re-analysed in CHAT). In the last column, t-values show whether the scores of these two groups differed significantly or not. On the two vocabulary tasks, the Dutch L1 and L2 children obtained significantly different scores. Of the type/token-based measures of lexical richness, only Guiraud's Index showed significant ($t = -2.37$, Sig $t = .024$) differences between the two groups. The number of types and the number of lemmas showed a tendency to significance. *Vocd*, however, does not discriminate between Dutch L1 and L2 children. The mean scores of *D* are quite high (73 and 75) as compared to the ones Jarvis obtained (scores of *D* between 18 and 29 in Table 8). The number of tokens and types in his data, however, were less than a quarter compared to those in Table 15.

MLR2 (based on the correct meaning of a word in the context), discriminated significantly ($t = -2.48$, Sig $t = .019$) between the two groups. The score of MLR1, based on the first, sometimes not intended, meaning of a word, discriminated almost significantly ($t = -1.953$, Sig $t = .060$). For the Dutch L1 children, the score on MLR2 was somewhat higher than on MLR1, because they also used more infrequent meanings of words, which is clear only after disambiguation of the text. The score of the Dutch L2 children on MLR2 was somewhat lower than MLR1, because some words, in particular the names of children (e.g. 'Koen', which, as an infrequently used adjective means *brave*; or 'Bob', which can also mean *sledge*), were counted as words before disambiguation (in MLR1), whereas all proper names were left out in MLR2. Therefore, the MLR2 score seems to offer a number of advantages over TTR and *vocd*-based measures as a test of lexical richness and, potentially, an indicator of productive vocabulary knowledge. Including frequency information in the calculation can be argued to improve the calculation because it includes an important feature of real language and language use. A second benefit appears to be that it allows us to measure a feature of lexical production in limited texts which we can relate to overall lexical knowledge and performance. MLR2 successfully discriminates between two groups with obvious differences in vocabulary in Dutch. Of the measures which do not include this frequency information, only Guiraud's Index performs in a comparable way.

Table 15 Means and standard deviations for Dutch L1 (DL1) and Dutch L2 (DL2) speakers

	Dutch L1 (n = 16)		Dutch L2 (n = 16)		DL1 vs DL2
	Mean	sd	Mean	sd	t-test, df = 30 t/Sig t
Utterances	197.4	46.3	184.6	54.2	−.72/.480
MLU	5.9	0.96	5.4	0.83	−1.52/.140
Tokens (N)	1133.0	329.9	984.3	378.3	−1.19/.245
Types (V)	330.9	61.4	285.3	77.4	−1.83/.078
TTR	0.30	0.05	0.30	0.04	.10/.919
Lemmas	314.1	58.2	272.3	65.3	−1.91/.065
Guiraud (V/√N)	9.88	0.88	9.13	0.92	−2.37/.024
Vocd	75.17	12.04	72.84	11.48	−.56/.579
MLR1	3.62	0.73	3.17	0.57	−1.95/.060
MLR2	3.75	0.97	3.04	0.60	−2.48/.019
Definition Task	25.8	5.6	14.8	3.4	−6.73/.000
Rec. Voc. Task	83.2	12.7	63.4	10.5	−4.78/.000

In Table 16, correlations between different lexical measures and vocabulary tasks are displayed for all the children ($n = 32$). As can be seen, of the type/token-based measures of lexical richness, only Guiraud's Index shows significant correlations with the Receptive Vocabulary Task ($r = .49$, $p < .01$) and the Definition Task ($r = .40$, $p < .05$). Guiraud's Index and the number of tokens, types and lemmas also have high and significant correlations with mean length of utterances and number of utterances, showing their dependency on syntactical abilities and text length. *Vocd* shows low, non-significant correlations with both the Receptive Vocabulary Task and the Definition Task. It only has a significant correlation with the number of types ($r = .42$, $p < .05$). High and significant correlations are found between both MLR scores and the Definition Task (for MLR1, $r = .61$, and for MLR2, $r = .71$, both $p < .01$) and the Receptive Vocabulary Task (for MLR1, $r = .45$, and for MLR2, $r = .50$, both $p < .01$), showing the concurrent validity of the MLR. The correlations of both MLR scores with the number of tokens, and the number of utterances and mean length of utterances are all very low ($r = .05$, $.03$; $.05$, $−.03$; $.03$, $.08$), indicating that the MLR is independent of text length or syntactical abilities.

Extrapolation of the mean scores of the Receptive Vocabulary Task shows an indicated vocabulary size of 5,020 words for Dutch L1 children, and 4,040 words for Dutch L2 children. The MLR2-based sizes of productive vocabulary (associated with spontaneous

Table 16 Correlations between different lexical measures (all children, $n = 32$, ** $= p < .01$, * $= p < .05$, $t = p < .06$)

	MLR1	MLR2	Type	Token	Lemma	TTR	Guiraud's Index	Def	RecV	MLU	N utterances
Vocd	.18	.11	.42*	.23	.43*	.06	.61**	.12	.09	−.14	.25
MLR1		.92**	.23	.05	.24	.07	.41*	.61**	.45**	.03	.05
MLR2			.17	.03	.18	.04	.30	.71**	.50**	.08	−.03
Type				.93**	.98**	−.63**	.81**	.28	.35 t	.41*	.68**
Token					.90**	−.84**	.54**	.17	.20	.43**	.76**
Lemma						−.63**	.79**	.25	.34 t	.48**	.71**
TTR							−.07	.02	−.04	−.42*	−.73**
Guiraud's Index								.40*	.49**	.22	.35 t
Def. Task									.67**	.20	−.01
RecVoc Task										.20	.17
MLU											.09

speech data, and thus, vocabulary use) are about 1,000 words lower: 3,750 words for Dutch L1 children, and 3,040 words for Dutch L2 children.

Another way to show how lexical frequency classes and their richness measures are related to vocabulary knowledge is presented in Figure 3. Within each lexical category (voclist 1 to 9), four measures – number of tokens, number of lemmas, Guiraud's Index and the TTR – were computed. All calculations were based on the lexical distinctions made by the procedures for computing MLR2. The outcomes of the four measures within the voclists were correlated to the results on the Vocabulary Definition Task.

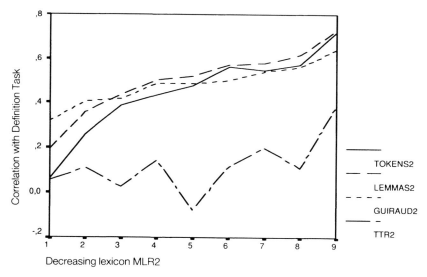

Figure 3 Correlations for lexical classes (voclist 1 to 9) according to the MLR2 procedure and the Vocabulary Definition Task for decreasing lexicon sizes based on voclist categories

Both tokens, lemmas and Guiraud's Index show increasing correlations in Figure 3 while, in contrast, the TTR produces shifting and low correlations. Figure 3 seems to tell us that infrequent words may be able to tell us more about lexical richness than frequent words, but not apparently when calculations use a TTR format. The results confirm what Daller, van Hout and Treffers-Daller (2003) concluded: a distinction should be made between words or lemmas on the basis of their class, as basic or advanced vocabulary. The pattern in Figure 3 is even more conclusive in showing that finer distinctions produce better measurements. Further research is required to determine if we can profit better from this consistent pattern. We need more data and more evaluative studies.

Conclusions and recommendations

Lexical richness measures aim to reveal the richness of lexis used in a given text or sample of speech, with the intention also of discovering the richness of the lexicon which produced the text or sample of speech. But all kinds of measures turn out to have reliability and/or validity problems. Malvern and Richards (2002, see also Malvern et al., 2004) have attempted a mathematical answer to the question of calculating lexical richness itself. But such measures still perform unsatisfactorily in concurrent validations and, however good they may be as calculations they do not as yet seem able to tell us all that we would like to know about the quality of the lexicon which produced the text they are measuring. The data we presented in this chapter on pp. 98 and 112 indicate that Guiraud's Index is often a better transformation, at least from the perspective of concurrent validity. It suggests that taking a square root is a happy medium between doing nothing to the number of tokens (TTR) and applying too strong a transformation (as in Herdan's logarithm) that levels out all relevant differences.

Our computer simulations on pp. 104–6 evidenced the reliability problem of human-like lexicons, as regards function and content words, and with dependencies in the sampling process. The simulations contribute to understanding the reliability problems we seem to have with many lexical measures, with the implication that it is hard to overcome the large error range typical of small sample sizes. On the other hand, they reveal that the frequency factor could be helpful in improving lexical richness measures. This also became clear in the research on lexical richness by Daller, van Hout and Treffers-Daller (2003): good results on the basis of a distinction between a basic and an advanced vocabulary class, in combination with Guiraud's Index.

In this chapter we have presented a more detailed analysis of frequency classes and the results were promising for the two new lexical measures we used. We looked at the contribution of different lexical layers to the (cor)relation with a vocabulary task, and a systematic effect came out where more infrequent layers produce higher correlations. We will pursue this line of research to find out how we may combine weighting frequency layers with a Guiraud-like transformation. To do so, we need to prepare and analyse more data, which is a laborious task. We also want to investigate whether repeated sampling of a given text or speech data may improve the reliability of a frequency-based lexical measure.

Another relevant conclusion is that computer simulations can help us to understand how richness measures are related to underlying lexicons and their properties and how these properties have an impact on sampling processes, i.e. lexical production. These simulations should be made more intelligent, reflecting human lexicons and language production. Empirical data can help us in this respect, too. To distinguish frequency levels or other lexical strata we need larger corpora. Lexical measures need empirical anchoring. Pure mathematical definitions of lexical richness do not suffice and it brings us to the conclusion that we need very large corpora (the basis of current research in corpus linguistics) to better inform our study of small ones (the basis of current research in many language acquisition studies).

6 Productive vocabulary tests and the search for concurrent validity

Tess Fitzpatrick

Introduction

The question this chapter raises is whether it is always possible to collect useful validity information for new vocabulary tests which claim to target specific aspects of knowledge. The difficulties entailed in collecting such information may help explain why some tests emerge into general use before such data is available. The quest for objective measuring tools which can quantify lexical knowledge has spawned a plethora of L2 vocabulary tests. Several of these are mentioned elsewhere in this volume, for example the Vocabulary Levels Test (Nation, 1983), the Lexical Frequency Profile (Laufer and Nation, 1995), *P-Lex* (Meara and Bell, 2001), *X-Lex* (Meara and Milton, 2003b), and various applications of Type–Token Ratios (TTR) (for example Arnaud, 1984; Laufer, 1991). The practical nature of tests such as these – they tend to be relatively quick to administer and mark, and produce a numerical score – makes them extremely attractive to EFL teachers who are often required to assess the proficiency or progress of large numbers of students. As a consequence of this, we often see tests being used to make judgements about the language level of non-native speakers and/or about the lexical richness of a text (see the concerns of van Hout and Vermeer (Chapter 5), this volume) before we have conclusive proof that the tests themselves produce reliable and valid results.

One test which has been pressed into use prematurely in this way is the *Lex-30* test of productive vocabulary. Meara and Fitzpatrick (2000) described the design of the *Lex-30* test, and reported that a pilot experiment had indicated a degree of reliability and concurrent validity, but concluded that 'there are, of course, a number of outstanding issues concerning the reliability and validity of the *Lex-30* methodology' (p. 28). Before these outstanding issues could be addressed, though, the test had been adopted for use in a number of investigative projects (including Jiménez Catalán and Moreno Espinosa, 2004). Read observes of the Vocabulary Levels Test: 'given the widespread use and influence of the test, there has been surprisingly little research until recently to establish its validity' (Read, 2000: 120), and the same problems seem to be surfacing in connection with *Lex-30*. Vocabulary measures are not only used in the field of second language testing. Malvern and Richards (1997: 59) list 'stylistics, forensic linguistics, studies of emotional disorders, schizophrenia, stress and anxiety' as areas to which measures of lexical diversity such as Type–Token Ratios have been applied. Their recent studies, though (1997, and Richards and Malvern, Chapter 4, this volume) demonstrate that there are still problematic elements to the application of TTR measures (for example, sample size). As they point out (Malvern and Richards, 2004), the implications of this for legal convictions which have depended heavily on TTR-based evidence are alarming.

It is a matter of some concern, then, both within and outside the field of second language testing, that assessment tools which are still being developed, and whose validity and/or reliability are still in question, are used so widely in a number of fundamental decision-making processes.

It is certainly not the case that studies introducing and discussing new vocabulary measures ignore issues of reliability and/or validity. Pilot tests invariably address these issues, but the extent to which this is done, and the judgement of what constitutes 'reliable' and 'valid' vary enormously. Of the two, 'reliability' is perhaps the more straightforward to identify. Whether we are using test-retest or split-half methods, reliability measures do not require the complicating inclusion of a second variable in the form of the collateral tests often used to measure concurrent validity, or the interviews and questionnaires needed to assess face validity or content validity. Perhaps it is this fact which prompts Lado (1961) to demand that a reliability coefficient of at least .9 is required before tests of vocabulary, structure and reading comprehension can be considered 'reliable' (he allows a slightly lower coefficient for listening and speaking tests). When we look at the reliability coefficients quoted for some of the vocabulary tests mentioned above, though, we find .88 for the Levels Test and .82 for the Controlled Levels Test (Laufer, 1998), .65 for *P-Lex* (Meara and Bell, 2001), and .84 for the *Lex-30* test (Meara and Fitzpatrick, 2000). None of these tests has reached Lado's target of .9, and yet their authors all describe the tests as 'reliable'. It seems, then, that despite Lado's prescriptive reliability threshold of .9, this concept is often measured according to more subjective, or flexible, criteria.

Similarly varied claims are frequently made about the validity of test tools. For example, Laufer and Nation conclude that the Lexical Frequency Profile Tool 'has been shown to be a . . . valid measure of lexical use in writing' (1995: 319). This claim for validity is based on the fact that the 'infrequent items' and 'University Word List' elements of the LFP produce significant correlations of between .6 and .8 with the Vocabulary Levels Test (Nation, 1983). Meara and Bell (2001) are encouraged by correlations of .339 ($p = .017$) and .565 ($p < .001$) between their *P-Lex* measure and the Levels Test. The use of concurrent validity studies and the reporting of correlations with other test measures imply that there is a strength of correlation which, if demonstrated, will indicate that a new test is 'valid'. However, as Hughes points out, 'Whether or not a particular level of agreement is regarded as satisfactory will depend upon the purpose of the test and the importance of the decisions that are to be made on the basis of it' (Hughes, 1989: 24). This perhaps explains why the studies quoted above vary so much in their acceptance of what a 'satisfactory' correlation figure might be.

It is probably the very fact that concurrent, or criterion-related, validity seems to be a quantifiable concept, in that it can be expressed numerically, that makes it not only the most widely used validity tool in the studies mentioned above, but also 'undoubtedly the most commonly used in language testing' (Bachman, 1990: 248). Construct and content validity of tests are equally deserving of attention (Hughes, 1989), but can only be expressed in a qualitative (in the case of construct validity), or contextualised (in the case of content validity) way. Concurrent validity, though, as Bachman tells us, can be tested by 'examining correlations among various measures of a given ability' (Bachman, 1990: 248), in other words, by comparing subjects' performance on the target test with their performance on a second test which claims to measure the same ability. The study described below investigates the concurrent validity of a test of productive vocabulary, using the sort of collateral data which Bachman describes.

Background

This chapter will describe an attempt to gain information about the validity of one of the tests mentioned above: *Lex-30* (Meara and Fitzpatrick, 2000). *Lex-30* was designed in response to a number of perceived problems with existing vocabulary tests. Most tests focus on receptive rather than productive vocabulary, as this kind of knowledge is more straightforward to elicit. Those which do attempt to evaluate productive vocabulary knowledge tend to rely on the production of lengthy texts (for example Lexical Frequency Profile, TTR measures) and/or are extremely context-dependent (for example the Productive Levels Test (Laufer and Nation, 1999)). *Lex-30* aims to combine the conceptual advantages of a context-independent test of 'free productive knowledge' (Laufer, 1998) with the scoring and administrative advantages of a quantifiable measuring tool. The test comprises a word association task, in which subjects are presented with a list of 30 stimulus words and are required to produce three or four responses to each of these stimuli. There is no predetermined set of response target words for the subject to produce, and in this way, *Lex-30* resembles a free productive task. However, the stimulus words tend to impose some constraints on the responses, and *Lex-30* thus shares some of the characteristics of context-limited productive tests. Word association tasks typically elicit vocabulary which is varied and only minimally constrained by context.

All of the items produced by a subject in response to the stimulus words form a corpus which is then processed, and a mark is awarded for every infrequent word a subject has produced. In this test, an infrequent word is defined as one which falls outside the first 1,000-word frequency band (Nation, 1984). The *Lex-30* score represents the number of infrequent words produced, expressed as a percentage of the total number of responses given by that subject. In order for the test to focus on productive knowledge, to differentiate as much as possible between subjects, and to encourage subjects to produce infrequent words, the stimulus words have been chosen to meet the following criteria:

- All the stimulus words are highly frequent; they are taken from Nation's first 1,000-word list (Nation, 1984). This minimises any employment or measurement of receptive knowledge.
- None of the stimulus words typically elicits a single, dominant primary response. The formal criterion adopted here was that the most frequent response to the stimulus words, as reported in the Edinburgh Associative Thesaurus (Kiss, Armstrong and Milroy, 1973), should not exceed 25% of the reported responses. In this way, stimulus words like *black* or *dog*, which typically elicit a very narrow range of responses, were avoided, and stimulus words which typically generate a wide variety of different responses were selected.
- Each of the stimulus words typically generates responses which are not common words. The formal criterion here was that at least half of the most common responses given by native speakers were not included in Nation's first 1,000-word list (Nation, 1984). In

this way, the stimulus words give the subject a reasonable opportunity to generate a wide range of response words.

An example of a completed *Lex-30* test (paper and pencil version) can be seen in Figure 1.

Name: anonymous	Date: dd / mm / yy

Look at the words below. Next to each word, write down any other words that it makes you think of. Write down as many as you can (more than 3, if possible). It doesn't matter if the connections between the word and your words are not obvious; simply write down words as you think of them.

1 attack .... war, castle, guns, armour
2 board .... plane, wood, airport, boarding pass
3 close .... lock, avenue, finish, end
4 cloth .... material, table, design
5 dig .... bury, spade, garden, soil, earth, digger
6 dirty .... disgusting, clean, grubby, soiled
7 disease .... infection, hospital, doctor, health
8 experience ...... adventure, travel, terrible
9 fruit .... apple, vegetable, pie
10 furniture ...... table, chair, bed
11 habit .... smoking, singing, nagging
12 hold .... grip, hang on, cling
13 hope .... expect, optimistic, pessimistic
14 kick .... football, ground, goal, footballer
15 map .... country, roads, way, location
16 obey .... disobey, children, mum and dad, school rules
17 pot .... kitchen, vegetables, cook, roast
18 potato .... salad, roast, boiled, baked, chips
19 real .... true, sincere, really
20 rest .... pause, sleep, music
21 rice .... pudding, fried, pasta
22 science .... technical, physics, chemistry
23 seat .... bench, sit, sofa
24 spell .... grammar, test, bell
25 substance ...... material, chemical, poisonous
26 stupid .... dumb, silly, brains
27 television ...... tv, cupboard, video, armchair, relax
28 tooth .... ache, dentist, drill, filling, injection
29 trade .... commerce, bank, exchange, money
30 window .... house, glass, broken, pane

Figure 1   Example of a completed *Lex-30* test

As noted above, *Lex-30* was introduced as a test with a certain amount of potential as a means of measuring productive vocabulary, but with issues of validity still needing to be resolved. In line with other researchers in this field and with Bachman's comments (see above), we describe here the use of collateral measures to explore the concurrent validity of *Lex-30*, comparing subjects' performances on the *Lex-30* test with their performances on two other tests of productive vocabulary. The two other tests, which are described in detail below, are the Controlled Productive version of the Levels Test (Laufer and Nation, 1999), and a straightforward translation task from L1 to L2.

It is intended that the results of this analysis will enable us to draw useful conclusions about the validity of the *Lex-30* test, and indeed about the nature and value of concurrent validity measures.

Experiment tools

Two tests of productive vocabulary were used in this analysis as tools to assess the validity of *Lex-30*. It should be noted that the tests are similar to those used by Eyckmans et al. (Chapter 3 in this volume) in just such an attempt to assess the concurrent validity of Yes/No tests. There are few standardised and well-researched tests in this field, and we inevitably go back to the same tests in establishing base-line data to compare with new test formats.

The Productive Levels Test

For the purposes of this paper, Laufer and Nation's vocabulary-size test of controlled productive ability (1999) will be referred to as the Productive Levels Test. This test, like *Lex-30*, evaluates vocabulary knowledge with reference to word-frequency bands. Eighteen target words are selected from each frequency band, and are embedded in a contextually unambiguous sentence. The first few letters of the target word are given in order to eliminate other semantically possible answers, and subjects are required to complete the target word. The vocabulary knowledge displayed in the completion of this test is productive in that the subject has to be able to write – produce – the word rather than recognise it. It is controlled in that the subject is prompted to produce a predetermined target word, whereas in freer productive vocabulary tasks such as composition writing or oral presentation, or indeed *Lex-30*, there is no compulsion to produce specific words.

The study described here, like Laufer and Nation's original study, tested five frequency bands: the 2,000-, 3,000- and 5,000-word levels, the University Word List level and the 10,000 level. Laufer and Nation suggest a number of ways in which this test might be scored, but in their 1999 study, scores are calculated simply by counting the number of correct answers given at each level and adding them together. This is the method used here, with subjects being awarded one point for each correct answer. Spelling errors and errors of morphology (what Laufer and Nation call 'grammatical errors') were not penalised. If subjects made the wrong word choice, or omitted to answer the question at all, they scored 0. The highest possible score was 90 (5 levels × 18 words).

The translation test

The second validation tool used is a straightforward translation task from the subjects' L1; in this case, Chinese. The Chinese (Mandarin) translations of 60 words were given to subjects for them to translate back into English. In order to standardise the selection of words, and so that target items of varying 'difficulty' were included, 20 of the English target words from Nation's first 1,000-word frequency list, 20 from the second 1,000 and 20 from the third 1,000 were randomly selected. To minimise the effects of synonyms and homonyms, the initial letter of each target word was given. In the scoring of the test, subjects were awarded a point for every target word produced, regardless of the accuracy of spelling.

Clearly this is a task of productive vocabulary ability, and whereas words produced in the Productive Levels Test might have been dependent on understanding of context, the translation task is context-free. Like the Productive Levels Test, though, it is a controlled test, with predetermined target words.

Lex-30, *the Productive Levels Test and the translation test: shared characteristics*

The Productive Levels Test and the translation test were selected as tests of concurrent validity because they share certain characteristics with *Lex-30*:

- All three tests work on the premise that vocabulary can be measured – i.e. that we can, to an extent, quantify the number of words a subject has in their L2, and that this number is somehow meaningful in terms of overall proficiency.
- All three are tests of productive rather than receptive vocabulary,

requiring subjects to write down words which are prompted in various ways (we should note here that the Productive Levels Test does require subjects to engage receptive skills too, to an extent).

- The three tests are similarly administered: all three are paper and pen tests taking 15–60 minutes to complete.
- The use of frequency bands is central to the design of all three tests; the Productive Levels Test focuses on subjects' knowledge of words at five different word bands, and the translation test on the 1,000–3,000-word bands, and *Lex-30* awards points for words produced from outside the 1,000 level.
- All three are tests exclusively of vocabulary; syntactical knowledge is not tested.

According to the concept of criterion-relatedness (Bachman, 1990), if the *Lex-30* test is valid, subjects' performance on it will correlate strongly with their performance on the other two tests. This is clearly based on the assumption that the three tests address the same 'ability'; which in this case is the ability to produce, in response to a cue, L2 words which represent various word-frequency bands.

Method

Fifty-five Chinese learners of English were used as test subjects. The subjects were all undertaking a preparatory 'pre-sessional' programme of English language improvement classes in preparation for entry to university in Britain. Their class teachers rated them from intermediate level to advanced, which normally means that they could be expected to know most of the target words in the translation test and the first two to three levels of the Productive Levels Test, and all of the cue words in the *Lex-30* test.

The tests were administered during two class sessions, with subjects first completing the *Lex-30* test task. For this study the paper and pen version of the *Lex-30* test was used, as it was administratively appropriate, and allowed subjects 15 minutes to complete the test. After completing the *Lex-30* task, in the same class session subjects completed the translation task. In the following day's class, subjects were given the Productive Levels Test.

Results

Table 1 shows the mean scores and standard deviations for the three tests. The standard deviations are broadly comparable across the three tests, and indicate that each test produced a good spread of scores.

Table 1   Lex-30, translation and Productive Levels Test scores

	N	Mean	Sd
Lex-30	55	27	11.99
Translation test	55	32	12.59
Productive Levels Test	55	17	10.55

Comparisons were then made between subjects' performance on each test in order to establish the relationships between these three vocabulary measurement tools. Table 2 shows that there are significant correlations between all three tests, and a particularly strong relationship between performance on the Productive Levels Test and the translation test. However, the set of correlations indicates that a subject scoring high on any one of these tests is also likely to be a high scorer on the other two.

Table 2   Correlations between test scores

	Productive Levels Test	Translation test
Lex-30	.504 ($p < .01$)	.651 ($p < .01$)
Productive Levels		.843 ($p < .01$)

What can these results tell us?

Three important issues arise from the results of this experiment. The first of these relates specifically to the qualities of the *Lex-30* test tool, and the degree to which it can, in the light of such an analysis, be considered valid. The second issue is to do with the value of concurrent validity measures in the general field of language testing, and the third is to do with the usefulness of the construct of productive vocabulary.

The above description of experimental tools lists a number of characteristics shared by the three tests which might lead us to expect high correlations between subjects' performance in them. However, while the results of this experiment show a strong correlation between the translation test and the Productive Levels Test, there is a more modest correlation between these two tests and *Lex-30*. This suggests that either the tests are in fact measuring different things, or that the tests vary in their degree of accuracy.

The accuracy of the tests is extremely difficult to comment on. *Lex-30* is a relatively new measuring tool, but initial experiments (Meara and Fitzpatrick, 2000; Fitzpatrick and Meara, 2004), including a split-half reliability test and concurrent validity test using a receptive vocabulary measure, indicate that it is a reasonably robust testing tool. Although the Productive Levels Test is seen as a controversial tool by a number of researchers (Meara and Fitzpatrick, 2000; Meara and Bell, 2001) in terms of its format and its underlying premise, it too has displayed a degree of validity and reliability (Laufer, 1998; Laufer and Nation, 1999; Read, 2000). Translation tests have long been accepted in the classroom as tools for assessing specific vocabulary knowledge. The target words in the test used here were from the first 3,000 in Nation's lists, and from our subjects' scores these seem to have been appropriate to their language level (only two subjects scored the top mark of 60, and the spread of other marks was fairly even). Our discussion of how accurately the three tests measure the ability in question, productive vocabulary, is in danger of becoming a circular one. Bachman observes that:

> Frequently, evidence for the validity of the criterion itself is that it is correlated with other tests, or other indicators of the ability, which simply extends the assumption of validity to these other criteria, leading to an endless spiral of concurrent relatedness.   (Bachman, 1990: 249)

If there was no significant correlation between *Lex-30* and other tests of productive ability, we might be justified in declaring the test to be 'invalid'. Significant, but moderate, correlations require more complex interpretation.

Superficially, the strong correlation between the Productive Levels Test and the translation test seems to indicate that both tests succeed in measuring productive vocabulary knowledge accurately; subjects perform similarly on each test. However, if we investigate the features of these two tests more closely, we can find another explanation for the strong correlation between them. The Productive Levels Test presents questions in blocks of 18, beginning with the block of questions targeting the 2,000-word level, and getting progressively more difficult. All subjects, as we might predict, scored higher on the 2,000-level than on subsequent levels. In fact, when we compare the number of correct answers produced at the 2,000- and 3,000-levels with those produced at more difficult levels, we see a huge difference in performance. On average, subjects produced 14 correct answers at the 2,000- and 3,000-word levels, and only three correct answers at the other three levels. In fact, half the subjects did not answer any questions correctly in these three less frequent bands. This means that the Productive Levels Test scores reflected to a very large extent – exclusively in many cases – subjects' knowledge of the first 3,000 words. The translation test, of course, tested knowledge of target words taken from the first 3,000-word frequency bands. It is likely that this makes a considerable contribution to the high correlation between the two tests; in effect, both were focusing on the knowledge of the same 3,000 words.

The *Lex-30* test, on the other hand, takes into consideration, and awards marks for, any words from outside the first 1,000. By requiring subjects to produce words spontaneously rather than prompting them to produce pre-selected target words, the *Lex-30* test can give credit for knowledge of all infrequent words, no matter which frequency band they are categorised in. We know from previous investigations (Meara and Fitzpatrick, 2000) that the *Lex-30* scores consist mostly of words from the third thousand and beyond, with some contribution from the second thousand band. The *Lex-30* system of word retrieval, together with the *Lex-30* scoring system, will inevitably assess a different area of the subjects' lexical knowledge from that accessed by the translation and Productive Levels Tests, which, as we have see, focus on the first 3,000 words. Moreover, the Productive Levels Test assesses, for example, knowledge of the 10,000-word band – which represents 5,000 words – by selecting just 18 target words for testing (a sample of less than 0.4%). The *Lex-30* test, on the other hand, does not operate according to predetermined target words, but will give a subject credit for any words produced from that 10,000-word band (or indeed from any band other than the first thousand). It is demonstrated in Milton's chapter in this volume (Chapter 2) that the relationship between the scores on tests of different levels is simple only in as much as learners are likely to know less at each level of succeeding infrequency; knowledge of one level is unlikely to predict knowledge of any other level very precisely because of ceiling effects in the more frequent bands. Since *Lex-30* differentiates only between very frequent words (the first 1,000-band) and others, a high correlation with scores on the tests which use finer band distinctions is perhaps unlikely.

I suggest, therefore, that these differences and similarities in the design and scoring of these three tests can explain the fact that the correlation between the Productive Levels Test and the translation test is stronger than the correlation between either of those and the *Lex-30* test. However, the fact that subjects perform rather differently on these three tests, which initially appear not only to share so many design characteristics, but also to be built on the same fundamental construct – productive vocabulary knowledge, leads us to question the value of concurrent validity measures. Bachman, we remember, encourages us to examine 'correlations among various measures of a given ability' (1990). We now have to consider that our three tests might not have been measuring the same 'given ability'; we have to focus more clearly on those aspects of vocabulary knowledge which are actually being measured by these tests and this involves considering factors in addition to the frequency of the lexis being tested.

Our initial expectation of high correlations between the tests was based on the assumption that all three tests are eliciting information about the same kind of vocabulary knowledge in the same way. We now need to examine whether this is in fact the case, and we will approach this question in two ways.

Firstly, we can look at the ways in which the different tests access the lexicon. Figure 2 illustrates this by presenting three models of activation, representing the *Lex-30* test, the translation test and the Productive Levels Test. These models attempt to represent the ways in which the various tests activate, or stimulate, the production of target items. If we think of each test as having 'activation properties', we see that the Productive Levels Test, which asks subjects to complete target words in a sentence context, has three activation properties: L2 semantic stimulus, L2 orthographic stimulus and L2 collocational stimulus. The translation test, which gives subjects a word in the L1 for translation, and provides the first letter of the target words, has two activation properties: the L1 semantic stimulus and the L2 orthographic stimulus. *Lex-30*, the word association task, has one activation property: the L2 semantic stimulus.

The fact that the three tests activate knowledge in such different ways surely indicates that the quality of knowledge required to produce a response might differ from test to test. The chance of producing a word in response to the three cues provided by the Productive Levels Test, for example, might be higher than the chance of producing it in response to the single cue provided by the *Lex-30* test. This in itself does not necessarily explain the lack of a strong correlation between tests, but we can extend our observations to consider whether different types of learner might perform better on one test than another (Skehan, 1989: 35–6). An analytical learner, for example, might perform better on the Productive Levels Test, which allows them to work out possible responses from contextual as well as orthographic cues, whereas a memory-based learner might perform better on the translation test, which relies on a knowledge of L1–L2 word pairs.

The second way of approaching the question of whether the three tests measure similar aspects of knowledge is to examine the tests in the light of models and categorisations of lexical knowledge which

Translation Test:

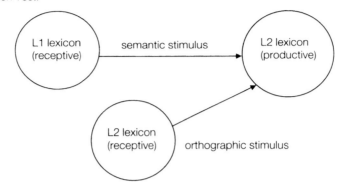

Productive Levels Test:

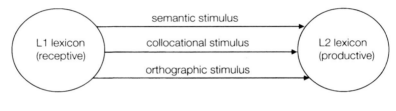

Lex-30:

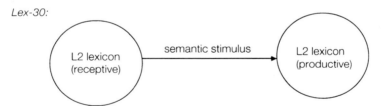

Figure 2   Models of activation for the three tests

have been proposed by various researchers, and to identify to what extent our three tests address knowledge as defined by these models. Nation's list of aspects of word knowledge (1990) illustrates the complexity of this lexical knowledge, but uses a clear system of categorisation to do so, distinguishing between receptive and productive knowledge, and dividing each of these into eight sub-categories. This enables us to match our three tests against 16 theoretical categories of knowledge, and to identify which categories each test addresses. Table 3 shows which categories of knowledge are addressed by each of the three tests.

Table 3 Aspects of word knowledge (adapted from Nation, 1990) tested by the translation test (T), the Productive version of the Levels Test (P), and *Lex-30* (L)

Aspect of word knowledge (R = receptive, P = productive)			T	P	L
Form: spoken form	R	what does the word sound like?			
	P	How is the word pronounced?			
Form: written form	R	What does the word look like?			
	P	How is the word written and spelled?	✓	✓	✓
Position: grammatical position	R	In what patterns does the word occur?		✓	
	P	In what patterns must we use the word?		✓	
Position: collocations	R	What words or types of words can be expected before or after the word?		✓	
	P	What words or types of words must we use with this word?			
Function: frequency	R	How common is the word?			
	P	How often should the word be used?			
Function: appropriateness	R	Where would we expect to meet this word?			
	P	Where can this word be used?		✓	
Meaning: concept	R	What does the word mean?			
	P	What word should be used to express this meaning?	✓	✓	✓
Meaning: associations	R	What other words does this word make us think of?			
	P	What other words could we use instead of this one?			✓

The table indicates that, although each of the three tests claims to test productive vocabulary, in fact they all test different aspects of this, and the Productive Levels Test addresses aspects of receptive vocabulary too. This attention to the multi-faceted nature of vocabulary knowledge might at least partly explain the apparently contradictory results which Eyckmans et al. (Chapter 3, this volume) record for a Yes/No test and a translation task which target the same lexical items. The Yes/No test only addresses Nation's question 'What does the word look like?' whereas the translation task asks 'What does the word mean?'

It seems, then, that we should be at least as concerned with the construct validity of a new test tool as with its concurrent validity. Bachman concludes that 'only the process of construct validation can provide this evidential basis of validity. In the absence of evidence from construct validation, the examination of concurrent relevance either becomes circular or eventually appeals to 'real life' or 'natural' or 'normal' language use as a criterion' (Bachman, 1990: 249). Read, too, considers concurrent validity measures to be somewhat outdated and inaccurate, and claims that 'construct validation of tests ... [is] the most fundamental kind of research that language testers undertake' (2000: 95). In the case of the tests described in this study, the underlying construct would appear to be 'productive vocabulary'. In accepting productive vocabulary as a construct, though, we are making two major assumptions about the nature of lexical knowledge.

Firstly, we are assuming that there is a straightforward relationship between productive and receptive vocabulary knowledge. However, the two concepts have been variously described as occupying a continuum (Melka, 1997), being the products of word connections (Meara, 1997), being related to depth of word knowledge (Wesche and Paribakht, 1996), or themselves having subsets such as the free and controlled productive vocabulary proposed by Laufer (1998). An examination of the literature in this field reveals that many of the studies which use the concept of productive vocabulary are closely linked with the design of vocabulary tests, which encourages us to be wary that the construct is not an artificial one springing from a desire to find attractive and efficient ways of testing.

We must be equally cautious about the second assumption underlying the construct of productive vocabulary. A test which is labelled 'productive vocabulary', as we saw in the analysis illustrated in Table 3 above, will inevitably address only a selection of aspects of productive knowledge, and might, incidentally, test some aspects of receptive knowledge too. The multidimensional nature of vocabulary knowledge prompts Richards and Malvern (Chapter 4, this volume, p. 92) to favour multiple assessments where 'the choice of measures [has] good construct validity in relation to the contexts, purposes and research questions to which they are applied'. It is important to recognise that any practical attempt to measure a construct which is as multi-faceted and slippery as productive vocabulary will only succeed if there is a clear awareness of which facets of that construct are being addressed. In this sense, 'productive vocabulary' can be a misleading label.

Our exploration of the ways in which the tests access lexical knowledge, and of the aspects of lexical knowledge which they actually address, seems to offer a very plausible explanation for the lack of a strong correlation between the tests.

Conclusions

The study reported here encourages us to question the value of concurrent validity studies in the field of L2 vocabulary testing. The experiment described above lends credence to Bachman's warning of the 'endless spiral of concurrent relatedness' (1990: 249). We will never find a standardised, reliable, valid test of the exact linguistic ability we wish to measure (otherwise, why would we need to design a new one?), so our instrument of choice for concurrent validation is a hypothetical one. A meaningful relationship between performance on a new test and performance on a similar test which has been previously used with some success is certainly an indication that our new test has a degree of validity, but is not conclusive enough for that test to be used as a basis for serious decision-making.

The conclusions drawn from this study, then, encourage us to consider indications of concurrent validity as a mere starting point in the quest for test validation; a close examination of the constructs on which the test is based will be necessary before any real claims of validity can be made. On this basis, the concurrent correlation figures quoted in our introduction, relating to *P-Lex*, the Levels Test and the Productive Levels Test, can only be taken as indications of the potential validity of these tests. An exhaustive investigation into the constructs of these measures (as has been, and is still being, conducted in relation to TTR, for example) should be conducted before these tests are adopted unquestioningly by teachers and other decision-makers.

Perhaps the most interesting conclusion to emerge from this study is that in our anxiety to produce more accurate and efficient measures of lexical knowledge, we are in danger of missing some really interesting insights which existing tests of vocabulary knowledge, and comparison of learners' performance in these tests, can offer us. These include information about the ways in which different learners might access lexical knowledge, as indicated in Figure 3 above, information about the threshold at which receptively known items start to be used actively, the effect of different L1s on test performance and the relationship between aspects of word knowledge at different stages of learner development.

Rather than perpetuating the inevitably endless search for the 'best' test of productive (or, for that matter, receptive) vocabulary, then, perhaps we should pay closer attention to the constructs on which some of our more reliable and valid existing tests are based, and use these to improve both our understanding of the L2 lexicon, and the quality of any decisions which we base on test performance.

7 Exploring measures of vocabulary richness in semi-spontaneous French speech

A quest for the Holy Grail?

Françoise Tidball and Jeanine Treffers-Daller

Introduction

Mastering the vocabulary of a language is one of the key tasks facing children who are acquiring their L1 and learners of foreign or second languages (Laufer, 1994; Vermeer, 1997; Verhallen and Schoonen, 1998). Speakers continue to learn new words well into adulthood (Hall, Paus and Smith, 1993), even when the acquisition of the grammar has been completed, for example when they enter higher education as young adults, or when they start a new job which has its own professional register, or when they learn new words that are being coined for new inventions. It would be difficult for any speaker (native or non-native) to claim that they 'know' the vocabulary of a particular language, first of all because it is difficult to say how many words there are in a language (Hall et al., 1993). Second, adult native speakers differ widely from each other with respect to the number of words they know or use on a daily basis, as this is dependent on a range of factors, such as educational background, the need to use a particular language at work, reading habits, and so on. It is also very difficult to define how many words one must know in order to begin a university course, for example (Hazenberg and Hulstijn, 1996).

Because of the importance of vocabulary for the everyday lives of speakers in general, and because vocabulary knowledge is one of the major predictors of school success (Verhallen and Schoonen, 1998), researchers are interested in developing reliable and valid vocabulary measures. Malvern, Richards, Chipere and Durán (2004) give an excellent overview of the wide range of research fields in which such measures can be applied: they include forensic linguistics, stylistics, clinical linguistics and L1 and L2 research, to name but a few general fields.

It remains very difficult to assess precisely the breadth and depth of vocabulary knowledge and use of language users. In recent years, important advances have been made in particular in the study of lexical richness, i.e. the assessment of the diversity and the rarity of vocabulary used in speech or writing. While most researchers agree that vocabulary is a key component of language, there is far less agreement on how knowledge and use of the lexicon by L1 or L2 learners are to be measured. In addition, the constructs that are being investigated and the operationalisation of lexical richness differ from study to study, which makes it difficult to compare the results of different investigations. It is for this reason that Malvern et al. (2004: 15) call for valid and reliable measures of lexical diversity that can be used in different research contexts. We agree with Malvern et al. that finding a single measure that suits all purposes is somewhat similar to the search for the Holy Grail. Lexical richness is a multi-faceted concept and therefore different researchers may wish to focus on different aspects, because they are more suitable for the purpose of the investigation or the data that need to be assessed. In this study we hope to contribute to the discussion around the measurement of lexical richness by trying out a number of measures on a corpus of semi-spontaneous speech of L2 learners and native speakers of French. We do not think that one measure is intrinsically 'better' than another, because different measures tap into different aspects of vocabulary knowledge and use. It is still interesting to apply different measures to the same data set as this will further our understanding of the nature of the differences in vocabulary knowledge and use among learners and native speakers of a language.

The objectives of the current investigation are three-fold. First, we aim to explore the effectiveness of different measures of lexical richness in discriminating between different groups of learners and native speakers of French. This is relevant because very few researchers have tried out their measures on French, and one of the measures recently proposed in the literature, the Advanced Guiraud, has only been tested on English (see Daller and Huijuan Xue (Chapter 8); Daller and Phelan (Chapter 13), this volume), German and Turkish (Daller, van Hout and Treffers-Daller, 2003). French differs from English in that there are far more inflections on verbs, nouns and adjectives, as well as different forms for articles, demonstratives and pronouns, which poses interesting challenges for definitions of types and tokens and thus for measures of lexical richness that are based on the distinction between these two. Trying out measures over a range of languages is important in particular for studies which involve cross-linguistic comparisons of lexical richness, as it is still not well understood how we can compare measurements of lexical richness in highly agglutinating languages with those in inflectional languages. While the current study does not involve such comparisons, applying measures to a wide range of languages can help to develop a fuller understanding of cross-linguistic differences in vocabulary measurement.

Second, we want to contribute to the development of quantitative measures that take into account qualitative aspects of vocabulary knowledge and use, as we believe that measures that make a distinction between basic and non-basic words according to well-defined criteria can usefully complement those that are solely based on counts of types and tokens. We do appreciate the observation of Malvern et al. (2004: 124) that 'The proportion of words that are rare is [therefore] a function of the number of different words, which in turn is a function of the number of tokens.' As diversity and rarity are interrelated, Ménard (1983; in Malvern et al., 2004: 124) found a strong correlation between the number of different words and the proportion of rare words in texts of a standardised length. Still, Ménard points out that it is useful to measure rarity over and above diversity, as it offers additional information about a given data set.

Third, we aim to explore the usefulness of the *Français Fondamental Premier Degré* (FF1) in defining a basic vocabulary of French. As this list was developed on the basis of oral data, but with a supplement of data from written sources, it is potentially a good starting point for a definition of a basic vocabulary list that can be used as a criterion to distinguish between basic and more advanced words.

The data that are being used in this study are oral picture descriptions from students of French, who were enrolled on a Languages degree at the University of the West of England, Bristol, at the moment of recording and a control group of native speakers of French who followed a course in English as a Foreign Language at the same institution and a group of Erasmus students from France. In addition a C-test is used to assess the students' overall proficiency in French. The C-test is also used to investigate the criterion-related validity of the different measures.

We will begin this chapter with a brief overview of the measures and the hypotheses we are testing in this study. We present the methodology we followed to collect, transcribe and analyse the data. Finally, we present one result, a discussion of the results and our final conclusion.

Literature background and research questions

Over the past few years, several researchers have come up with new measures of lexical richness as an alternative to the Type–Token Ratio (TTR), which is well known to be flawed because of its extreme dependency on text length (Arnaud, 1984; Richards, 1987; van Hout and Vermeer, 1988; Tweedie and Baayen, 1998; Jarvis, 2002). In this section we will only give a very brief overview of a number of the measures, as a full discussion of all alternatives is beyond the scope of this chapter, and most of these are presented in more detail in the editors' introduction (this volume). Some of the new indices or parameters measure lexical diversity or lexical variation, i.e. 'the range or variety of vocabulary, traditionally conceptualised as the number of different words (word types) used in a text or transcript' (Malvern et al., 2004: 192). An example of a measure of lexical diversity is the *D*-measure (from now on *D*) developed by Malvern and Richards in 1997. *D* is the single parameter for a function that models the falling TTR curve (see Daller and Huijuan Xue in Chapter 8 of this volume for a fuller description). Other indices measure lexical sophistication, which Read (2000: 200) defines as the selection of low frequency words that are appropriate to the topic and style of the writing, but which is often used to refer to the proportion of words that are rare (Malvern et al., 2004: 192). An example of such a measure is the *P-Lex* software that Meara and Bell developed in 2001. This software calculates a parameter called lambda for the (Poisson) distribution of rare words.

The current project is a follow-up study on Daller et al. (2003) who proposed a new index of lexical richness, the Advanced Guiraud (AG), which aims at measuring both diversity and rarity. This measure is derived from the traditional Guiraud Index (types/√tokens). Instead of focusing on all types, the measure is calculated by counting the number of advanced types per informant and these are shared by the square root of the total number of tokens:

$$AG = \text{advanced types}/\sqrt{\text{tokens}}$$

Daller et al. (2003) showed this measure to be far more effective at discriminating between the language proficiency of different groups of bilinguals than the basic diversity measures TTR and Guiraud. For this purpose we needed to operationalise the notion of basic vocabulary for French. As the FF1 is being used as a basic vocabulary for teaching purposes, we have assumed that it would form a potential starting point for a definition of basic vocabulary (but see pp. 144–7 for more details). Clearly, the effectiveness of this measure depends entirely on a valid operationalisation of the basic vocabulary. If the choice of words in the basic vocabulary is flawed for some reason, the Advanced Guiraud cannot measure informants' vocabulary richness correctly. We will come back to this point at the end of this paper.

As D was not included among the measures that were investigated in Daller et al. (2003), we thought that comparing its effectiveness with that of Advanced Guiraud would be a valuable addition to the discussion (see also Daller and Huijuan Xue, and Daller and Phelan, Chapters 8 and 13 in this volume for a similar comparison on English data). Malvern et al. (2004) present convincing evidence that D is a reliable and valid measure of vocabulary richness, and that it can be applied to a wide variety of language data. We are also interested in exploring a version of D which discriminates between basic and advanced words, as we consider this distinction to be a key aspect of vocabulary knowledge. In this context, it may be interesting to note that Malvern et al. (2004: 134) also point to the possibility of using D to develop an index of the diversity of rare words and this chapter hopes to contribute to the development of this index.

Our original intention was to compare the diversity of the advanced words with that of the basic words, by calculating the ratio of D (advanced words) and D (basic). This turned out to be impossible for most informants in our corpus, because D can only be calculated on a minimum of 50 words, and the number of advanced tokens for many speakers was lower than 50. Instead we calculated D separately for basic words (as all speakers produced at least 50 basic tokens) and for all words. For the purposes of our investigation, we used a slightly altered version of the Limiting Relative Diversity (LRD) measure, as proposed by Malvern et al. (2004). The LRD is a type–type ratio that was originally developed to enable researchers to study the ratio of nouns over verbs. It can be used for transcripts of different sizes, but is not a function of text length (Malvern et al., 2004: 148). The original version of the LRD is as follows:

$$\text{LRD} = \sqrt{D(\text{verbs})/D(\text{nouns})}$$

The measure we used was derived from the above:[1]

$$\text{LRD(basic/all)} = 1 - \sqrt{D(\text{basic})/D(\text{all})}$$

For the LRD(basic/all) it is crucial to ensure that the distinction between basic and advanced words is based on valid criteria (see

---

[1] We are grateful to David Malvern and Brian Richards for their advice regarding the calculation of this new measure.

above in the presentation of the Advanced Guiraud). As we are interested in comparing the effectiveness of different measures of lexical richness we have used the same criteria to distinguish basic and advanced words for the LRD(basic/all) and the Advanced Guiraud.

In our analysis we do not include the TTR, because it is well known that the latter is flawed. The TTR is still widely used, for example, by researchers who work on language impairment (Holmes and Singh, 1996; Cole, Truman and Vanderstoep, 1999), and therefore comparisons between TTR and other measures can still be relevant, if only to demonstrate the drawbacks of using TTR. As the Guiraud Index in its original form has been shown to be clearly better than TTR (Daller et al., 2003), we have decided to include it as well. This will also give us an interesting point of comparison with the Advanced Guiraud, which was derived from the Guiraud Index.

This contribution would not be complete without an analysis of the performance of all measures in relation to an external criterion such as a measure of general language proficiency. For the purposes of this investigation we have developed a French C-test which is deemed to measure general language proficiency. The C-test principle was originally developed by Klein-Braley (1997) and further tested and applied to different languages by a large number of researchers. A good overview of the work done on the C-test can be found in Grotjahn (1995) and some more recent references can be found in Daller and Phelan in Chapter 13 of this volume. The C-test we developed turned out to be highly reliable (Cronbach's alpha .965). We are confident that this is a useful external criterion against which the different measures can be validated, although we are aware of potential drawbacks of the C-test principle, for example in relation to its face validity (Jafarpur, 1995).

In this project we set out to answer the following two research questions:

- Is the index of diversity of rare words that we introduce here, the LRD(basic/all), able to discriminate between two groups of learners of French and a group of native speakers?
- Can the *Français Fondamental Premier Degré* be used as the basis for an operationalisation of the notion of basic French vocabulary? Does it need to be modernised and adapted to the task set?

Method

Subjects

The subjects were students of French enrolled on a Languages degree at the University of the West of England (UWE), Bristol, and a control group of native French speakers. The learners of French included 24 first-year students (all with an 'A' level in French) and 16 final-year students – the latter had all undertaken a one-semester or one-year placement in France the previous year. The native speaker group consisted of ten Erasmus students spending one academic year at UWE and 13 students in their first year at a French Business School following a three-month course in English as a Foreign Language.

All students who took part in the study were asked to fill in a questionnaire giving information on their background and their experience of learning French and other foreign languages. On the basis of the information given in the questionnaire, it was later decided to exclude three first-year students from the study: one of them came from a French-speaking country and gave French as his mother tongue; another was a German national who had worked in France for one year prior to enrolling on the degree course. The third student was a German national who had lived in France for a year at the age of five, had attended a nursery school, spoke fluent French at the time and had kept in contact with the language since then. The questionnaire confirmed that all three were indeed atypical of the group and we felt that their inclusion in the study would compromise the validity of our results. One other student in the group was also a German national but whose experience of learning French was similar to that of the British students. He was therefore not excluded from the study.

Among the 21 remaining first-years, 11 had studied or could speak another foreign language beside French, and 4 knew two other foreign languages. The mean age for this group was 19.2. In the final-year group, 10 out of the 16 students had studied or could speak another foreign language and 3 students knew two other languages. One student was a Spanish national who had been living and studying in England for five years. The mean age for this group was 22.3. For the 23 native speakers, the mean age was 20.4. Altogether there were 60 informants, with three different levels of proficiency, identified in the study as Level 1 (first-years), Level 3 (third-years) and native speakers.

Data collection

The data were collected at UWE during the last week of October and the beginning of November 2003, with the exception of the native speakers on the EFL course, who arrived in January 2004 and from whom data were collected in February. All students undertook the same task under the same conditions: they were asked to record their description of two picture stories presented as cartoon strips of six pictures each (Plauen, 1996 [1952]). We chose to give them two picture stories to ensure that enough tokens were collected for each informant. Students were told they could take as much time as they needed to look at the pictures and decide what the two stories were, but they were not allowed to make notes. They were free to tell the stories in any way they wished and there was no time limit, but they were instructed not to stop the tape until they had completed both stories. The recordings took place in individual booths in the Interpreting laboratory at UWE, with no intervention from a tutor. The total number of tokens in the corpus is 20,340; the total number of types 932. The questionnaire mentioned above was filled in during the same session.

Each participant also completed a French C-test under controlled conditions during a language class within the same period. The test consisted of six short texts (average 88 words) on a variety of topics (see Appendix 1). From the second sentence onwards in each text, the second half of every second word was deleted and students had to provide the missing half (these are the underlined segments in the passages in Appendix 1). There were 20 blanks in each of the six texts, giving a maximum score of 120, which was then converted to a percentage. As lexical competence is needed to complete the C-test successfully, we would expect native speakers to achieve the highest scores, and Level 3 learners to do significantly better than Level 1 learners.

Transcription of the corpus

All oral data were transcribed and coded in CHAT (Codes for the Human Analysis of Transcripts), the standard transcription format for the Child Language Data Exchange System (CHILDES) (Mac-Whinney, 2000a,b) and analysed using the Computerised Language Analysis program (CLAN).

Transcribing French oral data presents a number of challenges: the transcription of verb forms which are indistinguishable in the spoken language but have different written forms (*aller* 'to go'/*allé* 'gone'/

allait 'went') poses a problem, especially when they are used inaccurately by the learner (*il jeté* 'he thrown'?). Inflected forms of a noun or an adjective will appear as different words (*petit/petite/petits/petites* 'little'), where they would count as a single type in languages with few inflections such as English. Furthermore, unclear pronunciation can lead to spelling variations and inconsistencies between different transcribers (*un/une* 'a' – article, *premier/première* 'first', *joue/jeu* 'plays' – 'to play' 3rd pers. sing./'game'). Clearly some standardisation was essential in order to be able to conduct a valid analysis of lexical richness and it was necessary first of all to decide what we would count as a token and what would constitute a type.

The following methodology was adopted: all inflected verb forms were counted as one word type (*jette* 'throws', *jeté* 'thrown', *jetait* 'threw' were counted as one type) and reduced to their root form (*jeter* 'to throw'). An interesting comparison between different versions of the same measure (*D*) using three different definitions of a word type (inflected form, stem form and root form) is provided by Malvern and Richards (2004). We considered that the choice of the root form for our own analysis would give us a more reliable measure as it eliminated the inconsistencies relating to the transcription of inflected forms highlighted above. Furthermore, the root form of verbs only is used in the FF1 list and, finally, all inflected forms could easily be changed to their root form in one operation using the text replacement program in CLAN (*chstring*). Similarly, morphological variants of nouns and adjectives and the different forms of articles, pronouns and demonstratives were also counted as one word type e.g. *le/la/l'/les* ('the' article) = one type, *son/sa/ses* ('his/her' possessive adjectives) = one type, *tout/toute/tous/toutes* ('all' indefinite adjective) = one type. Compound words or expressions which were listed as a single item in FF1 (*c'est-à-dire* 'that is to say', *bien sûr* 'of course', *à l'extérieur* 'outside', *tout le monde* 'everyone', reflexive verbs – *se lever* 'to get up', *se battre* 'to fight', etc.) were also counted as one type. All forms to be replaced were listed in an ASCII text file and the *chstring* program applied to all transcripts. The *freq* program was then run on all edited transcripts and the word lists checked for any inconsistencies still remaining.

It is to be noted that no distinction was made in this study in the grammatical functions of a word (e.g. *que* 'whom, which' relative pronoun and *que* 'that' conjunction) nor did we take account of grammatical inaccuracies (e.g. *il ne lui aime pas* 'he does not like to him') as our study is concerned with vocabulary and not grammatical aspects of language.

Furthermore the transcripts contained various markers of spoken language (hesitations, exclamations, repetitions), as well as other items which, if included in our analysis, would adversely affect the validity of our findings. Thus English words, non-existent words (e.g. *noticer*), hesitation markers and other non-words were excluded using CHAT symbols; retracings (repetitions with or without correction), which in some cases grossly inflated the number of tokens, were coded and excluded using the +r6 command in *vocd* and in *freq*. An example of a transcript with all the root forms and codes for retracings is given in Appendix 2.

Basic vocabulary

Le Français Fondamental Premier Degré (FF1), which we are using in our study as a starting point for distinguishing between basic and more advanced vocabulary, is a basic vocabulary list established by G. Gougenheim, Michéa, Rivenc and Sauvageot in 1956 from an oral corpus of 312,135 words collected in 163 recorded conversations and interviews. From the 7,995 different words in the corpus, those with a frequency of 29 or higher (just under 1/10,000) were selected. Gougenheim et al. recognised however that some common words, especially 'concrete' words – e.g. *une fourchette* 'a fork' – did not appear in the list, although they could be considered as basic vocabulary (a young child would know *une fourchette*), because they belonged to a specific context and therefore had a lower frequency. Thus, to the criterion of frequency was added that of 'availability' (*disponibilité*), describing words commonly known by all native speakers and which can be easily recalled if the context requires it. Written surveys were carried out on a number of different topics and the most frequently mentioned words were added to the general frequency list. After a number of other amendments based on the judgement of a commission of experts, a final list of 1,445 words was established.

Le Français Fondamental Premier Degré is the only vocabulary list based largely on an oral corpus and although there are more recent frequency lists, these are all based on written, mostly literary corpora. *Le Trésor de la Langue Française* (TLF), considered one of the most important, is based on a corpus of 90 million words, 70 million of which are taken from 18th- to 20th-century literary texts. Frequency lists are dependent on the corpus on which they are based and differences will invariably be found between them. Comparisons of the first 1,000 words of three existing frequency lists elaborated from French literary corpora (*TLF* 1971, Juilland, Brodin and Davidovitch, 1970, and Engwall, 1984) showed that they had 80%

of words in common, whereas FF1 had 65% in common with *TLF* (Picoche, 1993).

We are of course aware of the fact that FF1 was established in the late 1950s. It therefore contains words which are now dated and unlikely to be found in today's context (*charrue* 'plough', *moisson* 'harvest', *foin* 'hay' and *tracteur* 'tractor' are clearly evocative of post-war rural France). Out of the 1,445 words in FF1 these are however, a small minority.

With due caution regarding its shortcomings, we considered that FF1 would provide a valid starting point for our purpose: it is the only list based on oral data, many vocabulary lists used in the teaching of French today (as a foreign language and mother tongue) make use of it and it is still found as a reference in most recent studies on vocabulary.

After scrutinising all the lists produced by *freq*, we decided to add to FF1 20 words which were either context specific (e.g. *banque* 'bank', *parc* 'park', *prison* 'prison') and without which the stories could not be told, or which, in our judgement, can be considered as basic, such as *situation* 'situation', *normal* 'normal', *chic* 'stylish, smart', *rapidement* 'fast' (see Appendix 3 for the full list). Not including these words in the basic list would have given our students credit for using a larger number of advanced types. We consider these amendments are justified given the criterion of availability described above, the fact that the FF1 Commission considered it suitable to add to later editions items which it had rejected in the first edition (Gougenheim, Michéa, Rivenc and Sauvageot, 1964: 202) and that such adaptation of existing lists when deemed suitable for a purpose is commonly practised (Picoche, 2001).

Calculation of Advanced Guiraud and LRD(basic/all)

For the computation of the Advanced Guiraud, we counted the number of advanced types with the help of CLAN by compiling a file which contained all the basic words that formed our basic vocabulary list (ff1.cut). As the words in this file are all root forms we ensured that all inflected forms in the texts were replaced by the corresponding root forms as well (see p. 141 for more details). Subsequently we ran *freq* twice: first of all using the +r6 switch to exclude all repetitions and all retracings (*freq* +r6 filename). This gave us the total number of types and tokens per file. After that, we ran *freq* with a parameter that allowed it to leave out the advanced words (*freq* +r6 +s@ff1.cut filename). This gave us the total number of basic types and basic tokens per file. The number of advanced types was calculated by subtracting the total number of basic types from the total number of types. We took great care to check whether any misspellings or inflected words had been overlooked by *freq* and adapted the transcripts accordingly. Subsequently, the Advanced Guiraud was computed with SPSS.

We calculated the LRD(basic/all) by constructing a file that contained all the advanced types. These were extracted from the files with the help of *freq* by putting a parameter on *freq* that enabled it to ignore the words that were not in FF1.cut (*freq* –s@ff1.cut filename). We then compiled an exclude file which contained all these advanced words and ran *vocd* with a parameter that made it skip the advanced words (*vocd* +r6 –s@exclude filename).

Results

In this section we will first describe the differences between the groups' general language proficiency, as measured with the C-test, and present a descriptive overview of the types and the tokens produced by the three groups.

The C-test results

Figure 1 shows the performance of the three groups on the C-test: the first-year students obtain the lowest scores, the third-year students an intermediate score, and the native speakers the highest scores. The differences between the three groups are significant (ANOVA, F (df 2,57) = 106.409. $p < .001$. A Tukey post hoc analysis demonstrates that all three groups are different from each other ($p < .001$). These excellent results give us a good starting point for the analysis of the comic strip descriptions, as we would expect valid measures of vocabulary richness to be able to discriminate between groups that are so clearly different from each other on a measure of general language proficiency.

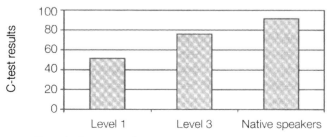

Figure 1   French C-test results (group means)

Tokens, types and advanced types

As one could have expected, the Level 1 students produced fewer tokens than the two other groups, and this difference is significant (ANOVA, $F = 5.65$ (*df* 2,57), $p = .006$). A post-hoc analyis reveals however that the differences between Level 1 and Level 3 students are only marginally significant ($p = .047$) and the differences between Level 3 students and native speakers are not significant. A simple count of tokens is thus not enough to gauge the differences between the groups. The results for the types are very similar to those for the tokens. While an ANOVA shows that the overall differences between the groups are significant ($F = 16.87$, *df* 2,57), $p < .001$), the differences between Level 3 students and native speakers are not significant.

For advanced types, the situation is slightly different. Figure 2 shows how the groups differ from each other in their use of advanced types. An ANOVA ($F = 17.18$; $df = 2,57$, $p < .001$) demonstrates that the overall differences are significant, but it is interesting to note that the Level 1 and the Level 3 students do not differ significantly from each other in their use of advanced types.

As the number of types per informant is a function of the number of tokens, it is not useful to make raw comparisons between the (advanced) types produced by each group: we clearly need more sophisticated measures, such as those presented on pp. 136–8. Below we will discuss the results obtained after applying these measures to our data.

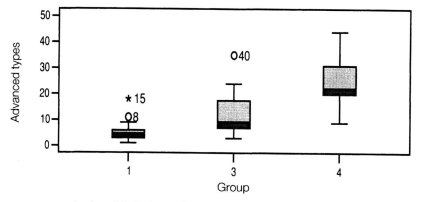

1 = Level 1 students, 3 = Level 3 students; 4 = Native speakers

Figure 2   Advanced types (group means)

The different measures of vocabulary richness

Table 1 demonstrates that the three groups differ from each other in predictable ways on all measures of vocabulary richness.

Table 1   Mean scores on different measures of vocabulary
diversity/richness per group

	D	Guiraud Index	Advanced Guiraud	LRD (basic/all)
Level 1	18.78	4.30	.33	.04
Level 3	26.46	5.25	.65	.06
Native speakers	34.87	6.27	1.37	.13

The D values are relatively low in comparison with those found for students and teachers in French proficiency interviews (Malvern and Richards, 2004: 104). In Malvern and Richards' study the 27 students obtained a mean score of 56.9 whereas the D for the teachers (probably because they were over-accommodating to the students) was 44.9. The lower scores of our students and the native speakers is clearly due to the fact that we calculated root forms, whereas in Malvern and Richards' study inflected forms were counted as different forms.

An Analysis of Variance reveals that all measures demonstrate that there are significant differences between the groups, which is not surprising given the large differences we found for the C-test.

A post hoc analysis makes it possible to find out whether all groups are different from each other. This turns out not to be the case. While all measures show there are significant differences between the Level 1 students and the native speakers and between the Level 3 students and the native speakers, the Level 1 and the Level 3 students do not differ from each other on the LRD. It should also be noted that the results for the Advanced Guiraud are only marginally significant for Level 1 and Level 3 (i.e. $p = .035$).

We also calculated Eta^2 to obtain an indication of the effect size of each measure. D and the Guiraud Index achieve the highest Eta^2, i.e. .66 and .67 respectively, with the LRD(basic/all) and the Advanced Guiraud receiving slightly less high Eta^2, namely .62 and .61. As the differences between the effect sizes are very small, they may not be so important. Finally, we should note that none of the measures obtains an Eta^2 that is as high as that of the C-test ($Eta^2 = .79$).

Correlations

Table 2 shows that all measures correlate strongly and significantly with the C-test, with *D* perhaps scoring marginally better than the other measures. Some exceptionally high correlations of the measures with each other should be noticed as well. It is remarkable that *D* correlates almost perfectly (*r* = .97, *p* <.001) with the Guiraud Index. In addition, the two measures that are based on the distinction between basic and advanced vocabulary, Advanced Guiraud and the LRD(basic/all), correlate almost equally well with each other (*r* = .90, *p* < .001).

Table 2   Pearson correlations between measures and C-test and among measures

	C-test	*D*	Guiraud Index	Advanced Guiraud
D	.76**	1		
Guiraud's Index	.75**	.97**	1	
Advanced Guiraud	.75**	.84**	.89**	1
LRD	.73**	.72**	.75**	.90*

** Correlations significant at *p* < 0.01 (2-tailed)

As we have seen above (see p. 145), the length of the stories told by the students differed strongly. The Level 3 students produced longer texts on average than the Level 1 students, and the native speakers produced the longest texts. Thus, text length is probably at least in part an indication of the students' language proficiency, and we expect there to be a positive correlation between text length and the different measures of vocabulary richness. This is indeed the case. Table 3 shows that the LRD (Basic/all) correlates slightly less strongly with the tokens than the three other measures. It is not clear at this point why the LRD(basic/all) differs from the other measures in this respect. This will need to be investigated in more depth at a later stage.

Table 3   Pearson correlations between measures and text length

	D	Guiraud Index	Advanced Guiraud	LRD(basic/all)	C-test
tokens	.61	.67	.678	.40	.40

All correlations significant at *p* < 0.01 (2-tailed)

Discussion and conclusion

The results presented above show that all measures of vocabulary richness investigated in this study are able to demonstrate that there are differences between the three groups, except for LRD, which does not reveal the differences between the Level 1 and the Level 3 students. In addition, all measures correlate strongly and significantly with the results of our general language proficiency test, which gives a clear indication that D, the Guiraud Index, the Advanced Guiraud and LRD(basic/all) are valid measures of lexical aspects of language proficiency. It is interesting to note here that Daller and Huijuan Xue (Chapter 8, this volume) arrive at the same conclusions, and note that the list-based measures correlate strongly with each other and the list-free measures (D and the Guiraud Index) correlate highly with each other.

The fact that all four measures perform very well lends support to Malvern and Richards' statement that there is no single, all-embracing measure of the quality of vocabulary deployment that can be seen as the solution to all problems.

The fact that the list-based measures (i.e. measures that distinguish between basic and advanced vocabulary) Advanced Guiraud and LRD(basic/all) performed slightly less well than the list-free measures D and the Guiraud Index calls for an explanation. In the first place, we note that there is a considerable amount of variation among the students in each group with respect to their use of advanced words. In other words, in each group there are students who use many advanced words and students who use few advanced words: in group 1 the number of advanced types used by the students ranges from 1–18 (SD 3.9) and in group 3 from 3–34 (SD 8.8). A t-test carried out on the differences between groups 1 and 3 shows that the variances in both groups are significantly different from each other in the case of Advanced Guiraud and LRD(basic/all), but not in the case of D or the traditional Guiraud Index. The students' different placement experiences (one year or one semester) can probably explain the different use they make of advanced words. While some have been able to expand the range of vocabulary used during their year or their semester abroad, others may not have used the opportunity to improve their language to the same extent. The wide range of ability in group 3 is reflected in the range of examination results the students obtain at the end of their studies.

Another possible explanation for these results is that, for this task and these groups, the type–token measures are more sensitive and that more of the variance is accounted for by diversity than rarity. As the elicitation materials were the same ones that were used in Daller et al. (2003), and the Advanced Guiraud did discriminate between the groups in that study, we do not think that the task itself was unsuitable for eliciting rare words.

A third reason for the results should probably be sought in our operationalisation of the notion of basic vocabulary. The advanced measures crucially depend on a valid distinction between basic and advanced words, but constructing a frequency-based list for the purposes of vocabulary assessment is far from easy. Relevant, well-constructed lists are hard to find, even for English (see also Nation, Chapter 1 in this volume). As the *Français Fondamental Premier Degré* is the only basic vocabulary list that is based to a large extent on oral French, we have assumed that it is probably better suited for our purposes than the lists that are based on literary corpora (see above, p. 140). It is clear, however, that a number of words in the FF1 list are not representative of current spoken French. Therefore it may well be the case that better results can be obtained for the Advanced Guiraud and the LRD(basic/advanced) if we try out more suitable operationalisations of the notion of basic vocabulary. An operationalisation based on teacher judgements, as used by Daller et al. (2003), is an interesting alternative that may well solve the problem. The strong significant correlations between the advanced measures and the C-test suggest that these are promising new ways of measuring lexical diversity and rarity, provided appropriate operationalisations of the notion of basic vocabulary are used.

In a follow-up project, we would also like to reflect further upon the correlations between the traditional Guiraud Index and *D*. In the current study we found that *D* and the Guiraud Index correlate almost perfectly, which appears to indicate that both measures are very similar, even though they are being calculated in very different ways. It is also clear that this result is not unique to the current data set (see Daller and Phelan, Chapter 13 in this volume). Finally, we are interested in exploring the effectiveness of *P-Lex* (Meara and Bell, 2001) on the current data set, and in exploring the dependency of the Advanced Guiraud and the LRD(basic/all) on text length, as this has not yet been investigated.

8 Lexical richness and the oral proficiency of Chinese EFL students

A comparison of different measures

Helmut Daller and Huijuan Xue

Introduction

The aim of this chapter is to develop Nation's final concern discussed in the opening chapter of this book: that of the importance of testing vocabulary in use. We have a variety of lexical measures available to us and the differences between them suggest that they may be useful in different ways and in different circumstances. It is not always clear which measure is most useful in any given set of circumstances. Indeed, as Fitzpatrick's Chapter 6 (in this volume) has made clear, we often lack basic information on the use of these tests from which to draw a conclusion. In this chapter, therefore, we intend to investigate which measurement of lexical richness appears the most suitable for measuring oral proficiency of Chinese EFL learners. This is a specific task and one where the vocabulary knowledge that a learner can bring to bear should play an important role in their success in carrying out the task. It might be expected that some measures would be more suitable than others. What, then, are the measures available which might prove suitable?

A person's language proficiency is closely related to the size and depth of their vocabulary, and this is true of both first and foreign languages. The *lexical richness* displayed in an oral or written text is a result of this underlying vocabulary knowledge. The term lexical richness covers several aspects of vocabulary use (see Read, 2000: 200ff.) such as lexical diversity, which is 'the variety of active vocabulary deployed by a speaker or writer' (Malvern and Richards, 2002: 87). Other aspects of lexical richness are lexical sophistication (the number of low frequency words) or lexical density (the ratio of content and function words used). Most researchers would agree that vocabulary knowledge and thus lexical richness play an important role in language proficiency. There are, however, many methodological problems in the actual measurement of lexical richness in written texts or speech.

One measurement proposed as early as 1944 is the Type–Token Ratio (TTR) (Johnson, 1944). According to Read's classification (2000: 200ff.) this would be regarded as a measure of lexical diversity. The TTR has been widely used in the past and is still being used today with equal text lengths (e.g. Jarvis, Grant, Bikowski and Ferris, 2003). However, the TTR has also been strongly criticised as unreliable (e.g. van Hout and Vermeer, 1988; Broeder, Extra and van Hout, 1993 and Vermeer, 2000) and it has a particular limitation because it is sensitive to text length.

A number of efforts have been made in the past to overcome this limitation. The most influential of these is Guiraud's Index (1954), which uses a square root for relating types and tokens: $G = \text{types}/\sqrt{\text{tokens}}$. This mathematical transformation is claimed to compensate for the systematic decrease of the TTR with longer texts, or in other words, it gives credit for maintaining the same TTR over a larger sample. The advantages of Guiraud over the TTR have been confirmed by many research studies (Broeder, Extra and van Hout, 1993; van Hout and Vermeer, 1988; and Vermeer, 2000). The superiority of Guiraud's Index over the TTR is, however, not undisputed. In a study of semi-spontaneous speech of school children, both Guiraud's Index and the TTR turned out to 'have poor reliability for small language samples' (Hess, Sefton and Landry, 1986, 133). Where the TTR systematically decreases with text length, Guiraud's Index seems to increase systematically in certain contexts and overcompensates for the falling TTR curve (see the study by Hess, Haug and Landry, 1989). Guiraud's Index only seems to be a valid measure in certain circumstances. More recently, Vermeer (2000) investigated the lexical richness of 4- to 7-year-old children learning Dutch as a foreign language. He found that in later stages of the language acquisition children learn more frequent function words and therefore neither of the measurements (TTR or Guiraud) is valid. One reason for this might be the fact that although the mathematical calculation on which Guiraud's Index is based may overcompensate for the decreasing TTR curve in some situations, it *undercompensates* for the same in other situations. A researcher can therefore never be sure beforehand whether Guiraud's Index is a valid measure in a given context.

Several other measures of lexical richness have been proposed in recent years. Malvern and Richards (1997, 2002) and Malvern, Richards, Chipere and Durán (2004) suggest a measure, *D*, which is designed to overcome the methodological problems mentioned above. Malvern and Richards's approach is based on a mathematical model which is based on the calculations of the falling TTR curve and is described in more detail in Chapter 4 of this volume. The effect of using D should be to allow the comparison of two speakers on the basis of the number of types and tokens they produce irrespective of the length of a text or utterance. Research on the construct validity of D often shows its clear advantages over other measures. Jarvis (2002) applies different measures of lexical richness, including Guiraud's Index and D, in a research study analysing 276 narratives written by foreign language learners and native speakers of English. He concludes (Jarvis, 2002: 71) that Guiraud's Index either over- or underadjusts and the problem of different text length remains. By contrast, D seems to be an accurate predictor of the actual TTR curve and is therefore, in principle at least, a better measure.

All measures discussed so far are based on types and tokens and mathematical transformations of the TTR (such as Guiraud's Index) or mathematical modelling of the TTR curve. It can be argued that all of them focus on lexical diversity. What all of them have in common is that every type has the same 'weight'. A weighting of different items is the central point of several other approaches, for example the MLR calculation described in van Hout and Vermeer's chapter (5) in this volume. Another is the Lexical Frequency Profile (LFP) developed by Laufer and Nation (see Laufer, 1994, 1995; Laufer and Nation, 1995). This approach was developed for the evaluation of EFL learners' essays. Laufer and Nation classify the words used by the students according to frequency bands. The more words used from higher frequency bands, the higher the profile of the student. Laufer recognises the sensitivity of this measure to text length, at least for shorter texts. She reports that compositions with 'approximately the same length' (Laufer, 1995: 267) were chosen to avoid difficulties with different text lengths. The profile seems to be stable between 200 and 400 words. According to Laufer (1995: 267) 'definite conclusions about sensitivity of the profile to text length have, however, not been reached yet'. Laufer (1995) also suggests a 'minimalist' version of the LFP with only two bands. This measure 'Beyond 2,000' distinguishes between words that are in a basic vocabulary (the most frequent 2,000 words) and those that are beyond this.

An approach that is also based on the notion of frequencies is *P-Lex* (Meara and Bell, 2001). Meara and Bell (2001: 6) illustrate the difference between TTR-based approaches and those that take frequencies into account with the following example: a speaker who describes a picture by saying 'the bishop observed the actress' reveals a higher proficiency than a speaker who describes the same picture by saying 'the man saw the woman'. Using measures that are only based on types and tokens, both speakers would yield the same score because the sophistication of the lexicon or the 'rareness' of the words used by the speaker is not taken into account. *P-Lex* is based on a probability distribution (Poisson distribution) that is taken as a model for the occurrence of rare or difficult words. The advantage of a Poisson distribution is that it depends only on one single parameter (lambda). This parameter can then, very much like *D*, be taken as a mark for the lexical richness of the text under investigation. It should be noted that the basis for these computations is different. The computation of *D* is possible without weighting the lexical item. *P-Lex* is based on a definition of rare words and therefore needs a word list. Both measures focus therefore on related but different aspects of lexical richness.

The last word-list-based approach under investigation is Advanced Guiraud (AG) (Daller, van Hout and Treffers-Daller, 2003). Like LFP/Beyond 2,000 it is based on a simple distinction between advanced and basic words. To mitigate the effect of text length, however, the same transformation was made as for Guiraud's Index. Advanced Guiraud is therefore computed by dividing the advanced types by the square root of tokens of a text. This approach also needs a basic word list or expert judgement on the difficulty of the words. It has been argued that word-list-free and word-list-based measures are quantitative but that the latter add a qualitative dimension to the analysis (Daller et al., 2003: 203). All word-list-based measures focus more on lexical sophistication, whereas the word-list-free approaches focus more on lexical diversity. Table 1 gives an overview of the two groups of measures.

Table 1   Measures under investigation

Word-list-free approaches	Word-list-based approaches
TTR Guiraud Index *D*	LFP/Beyond 2,000 *P-Lex* AG (Advanced Guiraud)

The subjects

The subjects of our studies are 26 Chinese students studying in the UK (UK Group) and 24 university students in China who have EFL teaching as part of their degree courses at a Chinese university (China Group). Table 2 gives an overview of the students of both groups.

Table 2   The background of the subjects

Group	Male	Female	Total	Age (mean)	Age (SD)
China	14	10	24	24.0	2.3
UK	14	12	26	23.3	2.6

Table 2 shows that both groups are quite similar with regard to age and sex. The main difference between the groups is their linguistic background.

Although teaching methodology is slowly changing, EFL in China still focuses on traditional grammar/translation methods. Oral skills do not play an important role. Chinese students who want to study abroad normally seek extra EFL tuition before leaving China. This is the case with the students in our study where the UK Group on average had almost 10 months of extra tuition before they came to the UK. In addition, on average, they had more than three months of EFL tuition after they started their studies in the UK, where a more communicative approach of language teaching is usual.

There is clear evidence that spending a year in a country where the target language is spoken natively can significantly improve the language proficiency of a language learner (for an overview see Coleman, 1995). Milton and Meara (1995: 31) even found that, 'the subjects in this study learned English as a foreign language nearly five times faster on average during their exchange than they did taking classes at home'. It can therefore be expected that the UK Group will have a higher level of proficiency in English in general, and that they are also more likely to have a higher oral proficiency than the China Group.

Hypotheses

1 The UK Group has a higher overall proficiency and will therefore have higher scores on a C-test than the China Group (see below on methodology). The UK Group will also have a higher oral proficiency in English than the China Group and will yield higher scores for lexical richness in a semi-spontaneous speech task (a picture description, see below).

2 All measures of lexical richness discussed above seem to work better in certain contexts than in others. There appears to be no measure that is valid in all circumstances. We therefore assume that the different measures applied will show the differences between the two groups in the present study to a different extent.

The scores for lexical richness will be higher for the UK Group but the magnitude of the difference between the two groups will be different for the measures applied in the analysis.

3 The length of residence in the UK has an influence on both oral and overall proficiency of the subjects. The longer they have been in the UK the higher their proficiency will be.

4 Word-list-based measures and word-list-free measures focus on different aspects of lexical richness. We expect that the former would correlate less strongly with the latter but that we will find high correlations within each group of measures. An exception might be the TTR, which generally shows a low reliability when used for different text lengths.

Methodology

Picture descriptions

All participants were asked to describe two short comic strips orally (father-and-son stories, see Plauen, 1996). These descriptions were tape-recorded and transcribed. They were then put into the Codes for Human Analysis of Transcripts (CHAT) format to apply the Computerised Language Analysis Program (CLAN) command *vocd* that produces the value for *D* (for further details see MacWhinney, 2003 and MacWhinney, 2000a,b). The transcribed picture descriptions were also analysed with the programs *P-Lex* and the LFP approach in its simplified version of 'LFP/Beyond 2,000'. Furthermore the TTR, Guiraud Index and Advanced Guiraud (AG) were computed with SPSS. It is necessary to have a basic word list for the computation of AG, *P-Lex* and LFP/Beyond 2,000. In all these cases the word list compiled by Nation (see Nation, 2003), based on West (1953), was used.

The C-test

The C-test is a gap-fill test where the second half of every second word is deleted. There is strong evidence that the C-test is a measure of general language proficiency (Klein-Braley, 1994 and 1997; Grotjahn, 1995). The C-test is a writing task but recent research shows that there are also high correlations between C-test results and scores in oral tasks. Arras, Eckes and Grotjahn (2002) report a correlation of .64 (Spearman) between a C-test and a 'simulated oral proficiency interview' (SOPI) in a study with 145 learners of German as a foreign language (for the SOPI technique see Shohamy, 1994,

Malone, 2000 and Kenyon and Tschirner, 2000). The C-test has also
been criticised and its validity has been questioned (see Alderson,
2002 and the debate between Jafarpur, 2002b and Hastings,
2002a,b). Hastings (2002b: 28) comes to the conclusion that 'There
seems to be a consensus that properly constructed and pre-tested
C-tests tend to have high reliability and concurrent validity'. The
C-test used in the present study had already been used in a different
study (Daller and Phelan, 2006) and yielded a value of more than .84
for Cronbach's alpha. It also showed significant correlations with the
well-established TOEIC test for EFL (TOEIC reading/C-test: $r = .483$,
$p = .007$; TOEIC listening/C-test: $r = .455$, $p = .011$, n for both $= 30$).
From our own findings on the specific C-test in use and from the
discussion on the C-test in general we conclude that the test used can
be seen as reliable and valid in the context of EFL.

Results

The proficiency of the students as measured with the C-test

In the present study the C-test turned out to be highly reliable
(Cronbach's alpha $= .842$, 6 items/sub-texts, 120 gaps, $n = 50$). The
scores for the groups are shown in Table 3.

Table 3   C-test scores for both groups

Group	n	Mean score	Standard deviation	Standard error
China	24	39.3	11.3	2.3
UK	26	61.3	11.1	2.2

As expected, the UK Group scored much higher than the China
Group. The difference is significant (t-test, two-tailed, $t = 6.963$,
df 48, $p < .001$). As mentioned above, the UK Group had received
more EFL tuition than the China Group. The question is whether the
difference between the groups in the C-test scores can be attributed
to the amount of EFL input or to the length of stay in the UK. If the
latter is the case a high correlation between the length of stay and the
level of proficiency (C-test scores) could be expected for the UK
Group. Figure 1 shows a scatter plot of the variables *C-test scores*
and *Length of stay in the UK* (measured in months).

There appears to be no correlation between the two variables. As
there are a few high values for 'months in the UK' and a lot of low
values, a logarithmic ($\log_e$) transformation for this variable might be
appropriate. This is shown in Figure 2.

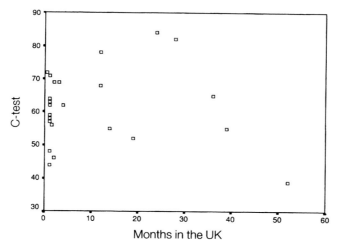

Figure 1   C-test scores and length of stay in the UK (n = 26)

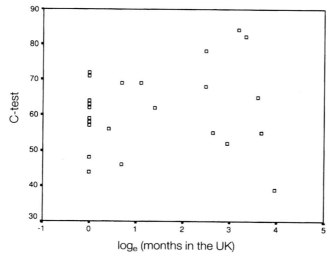

Figure 2   C-test scores and $\log_e$ (months in the UK), ($n = 26$)

Again there is no clear pattern. This is confirmed by parametric and non-parametric measures of association that yield no significant result at all (Pearson, two-tailed, $r = -.042$, $p = .839$). A possible explanation for this is that many overseas students from China have no intensive contact with English native speakers outside the class-room. The mere fact that they live in the country of the target language does not seem to improve their level of proficiency. The higher proficiency of the UK Group seems therefore not to be the result of the stay in the UK but of the EFL teaching received before and after the students' arrival in the UK. It could be the case that, after their arrival, the students initially made some progress in English, but after reaching a certain level they did not increase their proficiency any further. This is, however, difficult to measure.

The proficiency of the students as measured with the picture description task

In addition to the C-test the students were asked to give descriptions of two short comic strips. Tables 4 and 5 give an overview of the length of the picture descriptions (tokens) and the number of types. The computation of these figures can be made with the appropriate CLAN command after the texts have been transcribed into the CHAT format.

Table 4 Tokens in the picture descriptions

Group	*n*	Min	Max	Mean	Standard deviation
China	24	66	523	229.6	93.3
UK	26	61	602	290.8	137.6

Table 5 Types in the picture description

Group	*n*	Min	Max	Mean	Standard deviation
China	24	33	139	76.0	24.4
UK	26	36	184	104.8	36.0

The UK Group produced longer texts although the difference is not significant (t-test, two-tailed, $t = 1.824$, df 48, $p = .074$). The UK Group also produced more types. Here the difference is highly significant (t-test, two-tailed, $t = 3.288$, df 48, $p = .002$). This is a first indication that the lexical richness of the UK Group is higher than that of the China Group, which is in line with our expectations.

As a first summary we conclude that there is sufficient evidence that the English language proficiency of the UK Group is higher than that of the China Group. We will now consider which measure of lexical richness shows this difference most clearly and which measure is therefore the most appropriate in the specific context of the present study.

The proficiency of the students as measured with different measures of lexical richness

As outlined above, six measures of lexical richness were used in this study, three word-list-based measures (*P-Lex*/lambda, LFP and AG) and three word-list-free measures (*D*, TTR, and Guiraud's Index). All six measures were used to analyse the picture description of the two groups. Not surprisingly all measures show higher values for the UK Group than for the China Group, as shown in Table 6.

Table 6 Different measures of lexical richness
(China Group *n* = 24, UK Group *n* = 26)

Measure	Groups	Mean	Standard deviation
P-Lex/lambda	China	0.16	0.16
	UK	0.23	0.12
Advanced Guiraud	China	0.72	0.20
	UK	0.94	0.29
LFP/Beyond 2,000	China	10.96	4.21
	UK	16.38	7.68
D	China	28.59	5.57
	UK	36.22	7.59
Guiraud Index	China	5.03	0.83
	UK	6.18	0.79
TTR	China	0.35	0.07
	UK	0.39	0.08

All measures show differences between the groups in the expected direction. The results of a one-way ANOVA for all six measures are presented in Table 7. As an alternative, a series of t-tests could have been carried out. We computed a series of ANOVAs because SPSS also provides the values for Eta^2 with this procedure.

These results are interesting in several aspects. Firstly, all measures yield a significant p-value except the TTR (at least with a two-tailed test) and *P-Lex*. The two word-list-based measures Advanced Guiraud and LFP yield slightly higher (less significant) p-values than the two word-list-free measures, *D* and Guiraud's Index. In order to compare the effectiveness of the measures in discriminating between the groups we computed Eta^2, which describes the proportion of total variability attributable to a factor (effect size). These effect sizes are an indicator of how well the measures differentiate between the groups. Table 8 gives an overview of the effect size of the different measures.

Table 7   ANOVAs (one-way) for the six measures

Measure		Sum of squares	Df	Mean square	F	Sig.
P-Lex	Between Groups	.051	1	.051	2.591	.114
	Within Groups	.950	48	.020		
	Total	1.001	49			
Advanced Guiraud	Between Groups	3.048	1	.609	9.594	.003
	Within Groups	3.657	48	.064		
	Total	367.468	49			
LFP/ Beyond 2,000	Between Groups	367.468	1	367.468	9.347	.004
	Within Groups	1877.112	48	39.315		
	Total	2254.580	49			
D	Between Groups	710.076	1	710.076	15.707	.000
	Within Groups	2124.787	48	45.208		
	Total	2834.862	49			
Guiraud Index	Between Groups	16.495	1	16.495	24.912	.000
	Within Groups	31.782	48	.662		
	Total	48.277	49			
TTR	Between Groups	.021	1	.021	3.554	.065
	Within Groups	.280	48	.006		
	Total	.301	49			

Table 8   Effect size

Measure	Eta^2
P-Lex	.051
Advanced Guiraud	.167
LFP/Beyond 2,000	.163
D	.250
Guiraud	.342
TTR	.069

The p-values in Table 7 and the Eta^2 values given in Table 8 both indicate that Guiraud is the most appropriate measure in the given context, followed by *D* and then Advanced Guiraud and LFP/Beyond 2,000. *P-Lex* does not lead to significant differences between the groups. One reason why the three word-list-based measures lead to lower values for 'p' and Eta^2 than Guiraud's Index and D might be the fact that the word list used was not optimal in the given context. It is not a word list that was developed on the basis of everyday spoken language. A more appropriate word list would probably have led to better results for the word-list-based measures. Nevertheless, Advanced Guiraud and LFP/Beyond 2,000 lead to highly significant p-values. This means that the two measures are relatively robust even when used with an inappropriate word list. Earlier research (Daller et al., 2003) comes to the conclusion that Advanced Guiraud is superior to the traditional Guiraud. This judgement is based on the same picture descriptions as in the present study but with Turkish–German bilingual subjects. In the 2003 study German and Turkish word lists were used successfully. We conclude in general that researchers have to make sure that the word list itself is appropriate for the task.

One could argue that the larger values for Eta^2 obtained with Guiraud's Index in Table 8 might be the result of a systematic bias of this measure. Guiraud is meant to compensate for the falling TTR curve by increasing the value for the TTR systematically for longer tests. In the present study the mean TTR for the sample is .3693 and the text lengths vary between 61 and 602 tokens (Standard deviation 121.26). If we keep this TTR constant for different text lengths, the value for Guiraud's Index increases systematically, as is shown in Figure 3.

Figure 3 shows clearly that the Guiraud Index (and also Guiraud Advanced) is a function of the text length. This is exactly the notion

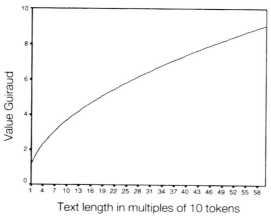

Text length in multiples of 10 tokens

Figure 3 Guiraud's Index for different text lengths with constant TTR (.3693)

behind Guiraud's Index. As it becomes difficult for longer texts to maintain the same TTR learners get credit if they can maintain the same TTR. Or, a systematically increasing Guiraud's Index value compensates for the systematically falling TTR. Ideally the compensation is as such that both effects even out. It could, however, be the case that Guiraud's Index overcompensates. In this case there would be a systematic bias for longer texts. The high Eta^2 values for Guiraud's Index could be the result of such a systematic bias. In order to investigate this we correlated the text length with the different measures of lexical richness. The results are given in Table 9.

Table 9   Text length and measures for lexical richness (Pearson, two-tailed, *n* for all = 50, except for *D* = 49)

	Tokens	TTR	Guiraud	AG	D	Advanced types	P-Lex lambda
Tokens	–	−.598	.636	.586	.390	.874	.120
Sig. (2-tailed)	–	.000	.000	.000	.006	.000	.405

For technical reasons it was not possible to compute *D* for one text.

In line with the expectations there is a negative correlation between text length (tokens) and the TTR. This reflects the fact that the TTR is systematically falling with increasing text length. There is a positive correlation between text length and the other measures. This correlation does not, however, necessarily mean that one of these measures 'overcompensates' for the falling TTR curve. The significant positive correlation between text length and the measures could be an indication that better students produce longer 'texts'and therefore get a higher value for these measures. In particular, the high correlation between Advanced Types and text length point in this direction. Students who produce longer 'texts' are also those who have a more sophisticated vocabulary at their disposal. Overall, there is no indication that a systematic bias leads to higher Eta^2 values for the Guiraud Index or one of the other measures. As discussed at the beginning of this chapter, the measures used focus on two different aspects of lexical richness. The word-list-based measures focus on lexical sophistication or rare words, the other three measures on lexical diversity. It therefore can be expected that measures with a focus on lexical sophistication will correlate significantly with each other and that a high correlation can be found between measures with a focus on lexical diversity (see hypothesis 4 on p. 155). In order to investigate this, we computed the correlation between the measures. The results are shown in Table 10.

Table 10   Correlations (Pearson, *n* = 50 for all cases except for correlations with *D*, for *D n* = 49)

	P-Lex	Advanced Guiraud	LFP/ Beyond 2,000	D	Guiraud Index	TTR
P-Lex	–	.33*	.26	.21	.19	.14
Advanced Guiraud	.33*	–	.89**	.47**	.66**	−.13
LFP/ Beyond 2,000	.26	.89**	–	.50**	.73**	−.37**
D	.21	.47**	.50**	–	.78**	.25
Guiraud Index	.19	.66**	.73**	.78**	–	.11
TTR	.14	−.13	−.37**	.25	.11	–

* significant at the .05 level, ** significant at the .01 level
For technical reasons it was not possible to compute *D* with the CLAN system for one subject.

The TTR does not seem to be suitable in the present context, where texts of different lengths are analysed. As a measure of lexical diversity it shows some very weak positive correlations with the other measures of lexical diversity but due to the effect of different text lengths these correlations are not significant. The measures of lexical sophistication show significant correlations between them except for *P-Lex*. This might be due to the fact that *P-Lex* is based on the occurrence of rare tokens. A rare word that is used more than once in a text is counted every time it is used. If we leave these two measures out then a clear picture emerges: the word-list-based measures Advanced Guiraud and LFP/Beyond 2,000 show a highly significant correlation with each other as do the word-list-free measures *D* and Guiraud's Index.

Conclusion

It is clear from the language acquisition history of our subjects and the C-test results that the two groups in our study have different proficiency levels in English. Most measures analysed show this difference and yield statistically significant results. This does not hold for the TTR, which does not seem to be a valid measure for spontaneous speech data and for the measurement associated with language proficiency in general when speech data of different lengths are compared. The remaining measures fall into two groups, word-list-based and word-list-free approaches, and they seem to tap into different aspects of lexical richness. This is indicated by the correlations between different measures. Guiraud's Index and D show the difference between the two groups of students most clearly and yield the highest values for Eta^2 and the highest significance levels. They seem to be the most appropriate measures in the given context. An explanation for this might be that they do not rely on word lists and are therefore applicable in different contexts. The results for Guiraud show that this measure, as simple as it is from a mathematical point of view, is still useful in certain contexts. Advanced Guiraud and LFP/Beyond 2,000 show the differences between the groups as well but seem to be less suitable in the given context. This might be the case because the word list they are based on is not appropriate for oral proficiency in an everyday context. We conclude that the word lists for these two measures have to be chosen carefully and have to be adapted to the specific task.

PART IV:
METAPHORS AND MEASURES
IN VOCABULARY KNOWLEDGE

9 Implementing graph theory approaches to the exploration of density and structure in L1 and L2 word association networks

Clarissa Wilks and Paul Meara

Introduction

The work described in this chapter grows out of a concern to explore the power and appropriacy of one of the most persistent and pervasive of the metaphors used in vocabulary research, that of the lexical network. Our attempts to investigate the network metaphor have led us to apply the principles of graph theory to word association data in order to compare the relative density and structure of L1 and L2 vocabularies. This chapter will briefly describe the background to this research and then report the findings of a new empirical study based on a graph theoretical approach. Our discussion and analysis of this work will focus in particular on one central issue raised by Nation in his overview of vocabulary models and measures in the opening chapter: the question of learner attitude in any form of vocabulary testing.

Any field of study that deals with things that we cannot directly observe is obliged to rely heavily on metaphors to describe and probe those phenomena. Research into the mental lexicon is no exception. Yet very often the 'metaphors we live by' in vocabulary research (to borrow Lakoff and Johnson's 1980 formulation) are so much part of the field's furniture that we no longer see them for what they are. We forget that they, and all the implications they bring with them, are only approximations to the phenomena we are seeking to capture and do not in fact translate any empirically verifiable reality. Our belief that the highly conventionalised analogies we use in lexical research deserve investigation is rooted in a constructivist view of metaphor. This position contends that metaphors not only help to explain ideas, but at the same time actively shape them. It is therefore very important to assess their potential impact on the way we conceive of and study the phenomena that interest us. As Boyd argues:

'It is part of the task of scientific theory construction involving metaphors (or any other sort of theoretical terminology) to offer the best possible explication of the terminology employed' (Boyd, 1993: 487).

As we have argued elsewhere (Wilks, 1999; Wilks and Meara, 2002) the notion of the lexical network, or 'word web', seems now so embedded in the vocabulary literature as to have developed a life of its own which at times obscures its own metaphorical status. We wanted, therefore, to step back from the intuitive attractions of this very plausible analogy to try to gauge the value of the insights it appeared to afford. Do they indeed bring us closer to an understanding of some aspects of the relative structure and development of L1 and L2 vocabularies? Or might they, on the contrary, be leading us into a number of unjustified assumptions?

Background to the current research

Our approach to these questions was to try to formalise some of the implications of the network metaphor by applying the principles of graph theory to word association data in order to compare some aspects of the mental lexicon in native and non-native speakers. graph theory is a branch of mathematics that deals with the presentation and analysis of 'relational data', that is, the way in which entities or agents – or in our case, words – are connected to one another. The graphs are simply sets of points that may be joined by lines, and graph theory's only concern is the nature of connections between those points; it is 'a body of mathematical axioms and formulae which describe the properties of the patterns formed by the lines' (Scott, 1991: 13).

Graph theory has increasingly emerged as a useful tool in modelling real-world problems that deal with relational data in fields ranging from genetics to sociology, and its appeal to those interested in word associations is not hard to understand. As early as 1968, Kiss, following up early structural work on word associations by Deese (1962a, 1962b, 1965) and Pollio (1963), called attention to 'the usefulness of graph theory as a tool in the structural analysis of relationships between words' (Kiss, 1968: 707). The formal, quantitative nature of graph theoretical work with word associations thus offered us a way of formalising and interrogating the implications of the network metaphor without getting bogged down in the descriptive detail that has beset much mainstream L2 word association research. It also allowed us to begin to explore some of the large-scale properties of L1 and L2 vocabularies rather than simply examining the qualitative detail of small sets of word associations. It thus promised a way of circumventing the difficulties inherent in trying to generalise the features of a system as large and complex as the mental lexicon on the basis of work conducted with very few lexical items (Meara, 1992b).

As a subject in its own right, graph theory is a highly complex and rapidly developing area as Schur, in the following chapter (this volume), demonstrates. Like other linguists and researchers in many other non-mathematical disciplines, we have not claimed to exploit the most arcane and mathematically complex aspects of graph theory. Instead we have simply adopted those features of graph theory most appropriate to illuminate our particular area of interest. (For an account of these basic principles see Wilks and Meara, 2002). We recognise, of course, that these simple graph theory models of the mental lexicon cannot attempt to represent the full complexity of the human vocabulary storage system. Their purpose is rather to offer a simple framework for investigating how particular aspects of the network metaphor may be formalised and explored.

Our project, therefore, has been to test some tacit assumptions about the density and structure of the mental lexicon that follow from the popular use of the web/network metaphor in much of the literature, as for example, in Aitchison's famous image of the 'giant, multidimensional cobweb' (Aitchison, 1987: 72). Graph theory offers us a formal way to investigate these issues. However, in practice, the implementation of graph theoretical approaches to the study of lexical networks has not proved to be a simple matter. We have applied graph theoretical principles to word association data in a range of empirical studies and large-scale computer simulations since the early nineties. This work has evolved in a number of directions, focusing on different simple properties of graphs, working with different graph theory models and developing a number of different elicitation tools to generate data (Meara, 1992b; Wilks, 1999; Wilks and Meara, 2002). Our findings have given us some answers to our questions, and in particular have prompted us to challenge some earlier methodologies and to argue for far greater caution in the use of the network metaphor which has tended to encourage unfounded assumptions about the extreme density of vocabulary networks.

At the same time, the interlocking development of methodological and theoretical concerns in this work have raised a number of new questions around the relationship between structure and density in even small core networks and about the behaviour of test-takers in these exercises. In the next section we will report our most recent empirical study, which we have designed in response to these emerging issues and which can be used to provide fresh insights into this approach.

Current study

Instrument

The word association data analysed in the current study were collected by means of an elicitation tool adapted from our earlier work. Our research had indicated the importance of reducing as far as possible the productive burden placed on informants in word association exercises. Early techniques that we had used (such as getting respondents to build chains of associations between random start and target words) had led to abnormally idiosyncratic word association behaviour, even among native speakers. We therefore developed a receptive methodology in which informants are simply asked to identify associations from a given set of randomly chosen words (Wilks, 1999; Wilks and Meara, 2002). The large-scale computer simulations that we conducted demonstrated that the number of associations identified (the 'hit rate') will rise as levels of linkage in the lexicon increase. As we have noted, however, density is not a straightforward concept and measures that only rely on calculating average numbers of links per word in a lexicon may be overlooking important differences in the way these links are clustered or arranged.

In our current study we therefore set out not only to test the sensitivity of the receptive word association technique further, but also to produce data that would be susceptible to a more detailed and sophisticated analysis of the performance of individual informants. Rather than participants being asked to identify a single association in a word set, this time they were required to indicate *all* the associations they perceived, as illustrated in Example 1.

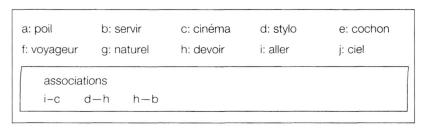

Example 1   Illustration of test format

The data were elicited by means of a 20-item word association questionnaire. Each item was composed of a set of words selected at random from the *Français Elémentaire* list (Gougenheim, 1956), which lists approximately the 1,000 most frequent words in French excluding grammatical items. The 200 words contained in the questionnaire were made up as follows: 109 nouns, 52 verbs, 25 adjectives, 3 adverbs, plus 11 other terms that fell into more than one of these categories (e.g. *rire, pouvoir, bleu* etc.).

Method

We collected data from 84 informants in all. Forty-eight of these informants were native English-speaking learners of French studying on the undergraduate degree programme at Kingston University. The learners fell into two proficiency groups. Half (Learner Group A) were first-year students who had completed the equivalent of 'A' level plus one semester of study in French. The other 24 learners (Learner Group B) were final-year students who had completed 'A' level plus seven semesters of study in French including one or two semesters spent in France. The remaining 36 informants were native speakers of French living in France.

The learners participating in the survey completed the questionnaires individually under supervision. They did not have access to a dictionary during the exercise. The students in each group spent approximately 20 minutes on the task. After each exercise, the two learner groups were invited to comment on their experience of the task. A number of first-year students reported finding the exercise difficult although they knew the majority of the words used in the questionnaire. The only unknown lexical items were *forgeron, caoutchouc* and *moisson.* Final-year students found the exercise 'challenging but interesting'. Native-speaker informants completed the questionnaire individually and returned them electronically or by post. All informants were instructed to work intuitively in completing the questionnaire and were reassured that there were no 'right' or 'wrong' answers. Note that the instrument used in this study was a simple pencil and paper exercise. Meara and Wolter (2004) are also currently experimenting with an online presentation of a similar elicitation tool in English (V_Links). We will return to a number of these issues in the 'Discussion' section on p. 173 when we consider the impact of methodology on test-taker behaviour.

Although not planned in our original research design, in the light of the issue of learner attitudes raised by Nation, we felt it would be illuminating to collect a small amount of further qualitative data.

Accordingly, we observed one new respondent (a learner of French corresponding to our Group A proficiency) as he completed the word association task, and then interviewed him in some detail about his approach to the exercise. This post hoc data is of course merely suggestive; we cannot for a moment claim to know how representative this single informant's behaviour is of our test-takers in general. Nevertheless, as we shall show in our Discussion, the additional data do offer some corroborating evidence, albeit very partial, for our interpretations and hint at some further avenues that we need to explore.

Results

We first analysed the completed questionnaires in terms of the number of word associations perceived (the number of 'hits') for each of the 20 items in the questionnaire and calculated the mean hit rate per item. These findings are summarised in Table 1.

Table 1   Perceived word associations ('hits') for the three groups

	Mean number of hits per word set	Standard deviation	n
Learner Group A	2.16	0.94	24
Learner Group B	2.86	1.17	24
French Native Speakers	3.96	1.98	36

As we can see, there is a progressive increase in the average number of word association hits as proficiency level increases. Statistical analysis (one-way ANOVA) shows that there is a significant group effect, that is, the level of proficiency of the groups does have a differential effect on the number of word associations perceived (F (2.81) = 10.409, p = < .05). Post hoc tests (Scheffé) reveal that while there is a highly significant difference between the native speakers and the two learner groups, the difference between the learner groups themselves is not significant on this test. However, a simple two-way comparison between learners in Group A and Group B (t-test paired two sample for means) does suggest that the mean hit rates for the less proficient learners are significantly lower than for their more advanced counterparts (t = 2.36, p = < .05). In addition, there proves to be a significant difference between the levels of variance in each of the two learner groups (F = 0.7, p = < .05), with the more proficient learners (Group B) showing greater variability in the test scores.

Discussion

In simple terms, then, we can say that, in common with our earlier findings (Wilks and Meara, 2002), L1 networks are shown to be denser than learner networks. The higher 'hit rates' observed in the native speaker data suggest that their lexical networks have higher levels of linkage than the learner vocabularies. In addition, the data suggest that the density of learners' vocabulary networks does increase as they become more proficient. However, it must be said that this finding is not as robust as we had anticipated and that there therefore remain some question marks over the sensitivity of our new instrument.

As we have indicated, apart from testing the ability of our revised elicitation tool to detect comparative differences in levels of linkage in L1 and L2 networks, our aim was to gain insights into the comparative distribution of links within learner and native-speaker vocabularies. We can of course do this at both group level and in terms of individual performance. However, once we begin to drill down into the detail of network structure that our instrument provides, it is clear that the relationship between group and individual data is by no means a straightforward one. It has been conventional in much L2 word association research to make extensive comparisons between groups of learners and native speakers. Very often the data produced by individual informants is pooled and group performance compared. Conclusions are then drawn about 'typical' L1 or L2 behaviours (for example, as regards the stereotypy or type of associations produced) which are assumed to be representative of individual learners or native speakers.

The possibilities offered by the data in our study make this type of group comparison seem tempting at first sight. The data produced by our current elicitation tool do appear to lend themselves to just this kind of analysis (and this is even more attractive where data are collected and manipulated online). It is possible for instance to draw up mini-networks for each of the three groups based on individual word sets and to compare these in terms of their density or the centrality of types of words within them. However, close inspection of the resulting graphs reveals the dangers inherent in this group approach. The group representations that we obtain are in fact extremely misleading since they mask extremely high levels of variability within each of the three groups.

The importance of focusing our detailed analysis on individual behaviour comes out very clearly if we consider the expected distribution of word association hits for our different groups. To do this we first calculate the probability of any given group scoring 0, 1, 2, 3 or 4 ... hits per questionnaire item. These group norms can then be matched against the performance of individual informants. Given that the chances of finding an association among a small set of randomly selected words, we originally thought that it might be possible to model the pattern of responses using simple Poisson distributions (Poisson distributions are typically used to model situations where there is a diminishing chance of multiple events occurring). Figure 1 shows the actual hit-rate data generated by the *three groups, and a best-fit Poisson curve that describes these data. It also shows that the theoretical curves are an astonishingly good fit to* the data. As we might expect, the curves move progressively to the right along the hits axis as proficiency increases. The curve for the lower-level learner group is skewed heavily towards the left, and falls away sharply to the right. The curve for native speakers peaks between 3 and 4 hits per item, and has an extended tail. The close fit between the data and the theoretical curves suggests that our thinking about the processes involved in recognising associations in random word sets is fundamentally correct.

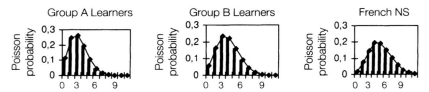

Figure 1   Expected distribution of word association hits for the three
        groups

So far, so good. However, when we compare the graphs of individual performance against the group curves, the extent to which individual performance deviates from group norms becomes apparent. Figure 2 shows some examples of individual hits distributions taken from the three different categories of informants. In each of the cases, the superimposed line indicates the expected curve derived from the group.

The nine cases shown in Figure 2 have been selected to illustrate the sorts of deviations from group norms that come to light when we scrutinise data provided by individual learners and native speakers. A review of all of the 84 informants in our study shows that not one of them matches exactly the curve drawn up for their group, and that even approximate matches are rare. This is true of all three groups. Even if we apply the very loose criterion of trying to identify those

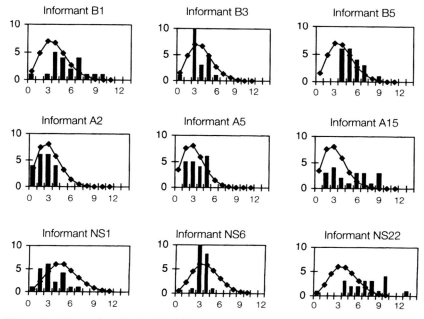

Figure 2 Example of individual hits distributions from the three groups

informants whose hits profiles follow the basic curve shape that group norms lead us to expect (as in the case of informant A2), we find relatively few instances. Amongst the native speaker informants, only some 50% of our sample display such profiles. For the other 50%, profiles are irregular and either contain unexpected peaks and troughs or are much flatter than expected. This split is also found in Learner Group A, while in Learner Group B as many as 16 out of the 24 profiles (67%) are 'irregular'.

It is clearly not within the scope of this chapter to undertake a full-scale analysis of all the individual informant data that are available from our study. We will focus instead on one possibility brought to the fore by the surprising degree of individual variation that we have found. That is, the notion that test-takers may in fact have been approaching our word association exercise in ways that we had not anticipated and that may threaten the validity of the data we have collected. We need, therefore, to address the question of the extent to which the precise methodology we have employed may foster, or indeed inhibit, certain types of associative behaviour. Of course, this is not a new question. Like Nation, in the opening chapter, we too have for some time been preoccupied by the possible impacts of methodology on learner attitude and test-taker behaviour. Indeed, as we have indicated, the receptive word association protocol within which our current instrument was developed was itself partly a response to issues of test-taker behaviour identified in earlier work.

However, it is not clear to us that L2 word association research has yet been explicit enough about what we think, or hope, our tests are measuring. It operates on the tacit assumption that word association measures (if only we can design them carefully enough) will enable us to 'tap into' the lexical networks of learners and native speakers in a way that is common to all informants. But how confident can we be of this assumption? The level of apparent randomness in distribution patterns that we have exemplified above invites us to question whether in fact all respondents are approaching or understanding the tests in the same way. We will now look at what the data on individual performance available from our tests can tell us about two key issues that arise when we begin to question these assumptions. Firstly, we will consider the problem of what counts as an association, both for test-takers and test-designer. Secondly, we will look at the question of strategies used by test-takers and will consider the possible impact of test presentation formats.

As we have reported, the written instructions for our questionnaire reassured respondents that there were no 'right' or 'wrong' answers. In the case of the two learner groups, this message was also reinforced orally as the tests were given out. Our intention in including this instruction was twofold. We wanted firstly to license our participants to work intuitively and to discourage an overly analytical approach. Secondly, we wished to forestall the problem that Nation has alluded to (Chapter 1, this volume) of learners being inhibited by a lack of confidence and consequently 'getting stuck' on the test. However, with hindsight, it may be that this explicit acceptance of any possible response in fact leads learners, and possibly also native speakers, to push the boundaries of what counts as a legitimate word association. The exercise may indeed become something of a game for some respondents who identify personal links between words that are only tenuously connected at any obvious cultural or linguistic level. The pairs *port–frapper* (port–hit) or *mars–couvercle* (March–lid), for example, both produced by native-speakers as a one-off response in the set, invite this kind of interpretation. We might also speculate that online versions of the test where the links appear on screen in network form will encourage this kind of behaviour if informants are tempted to 'just keep clicking' or simply to make patterns.

The interview and observation that we conducted subsequent to our main study lend some weight to the idea that respondents may be unsure of what 'counts' as an association. Whilst tackling the first few word sets, our test-taker commented, 'I can put whatever I like, can't I?' Despite this, he clearly did not opt for an entirely idio-syncratic or haphazard selection and his mean hit rate was slightly lower than the average for the lower-proficiency learners. When interviewed after the test, he volunteered that some of the links he had identified seemed 'a bit tenuous'. He had not consciously applied any criteria in selecting associations, although he was aware of having picked out a number of opposites. He had based his decisions only on the meaning of the words and not on their sound or shape. These comments suggest what we might characterise as a 'semi-intuitive' approach.

Researchers are thus faced with a twofold problem relating to test design on the one hand, and data analysis on the other. Firstly, to what extent, and how, should informants be guided in identifying associations? Secondly, how do we assess the legitimacy of the associations identified by test-takers? These problems are not easy to resolve in either theoretical or methodological terms. Theoretically speaking it would be hard to justify a research protocol that designed out all forms of idiosyncrasy. There is, after all, a fairly broad consensus in the literature that that purely 'personal' links do have a role to play in the organisation of the mental lexicon, and indeed there is some support for the idea that this role may be more significant in French than in English (Rosenzweig, 1961; Bogaards, 1994). Moreover, even if we can justify a design that will at least limit idiosyncratic associative behaviour to the levels suggested by large group norms (Postman and Keppel, 1970; Rosenzweig, 1961), this is not easy to implement.

A number of possible solutions have been mooted, but all have disadvantages. It would be possible, for example, to 'plant' certain associations in the word sets rather than selecting words completely at random. Scores would then be awarded on the basis of the predetermined links only. The problem with this method is justifying the selection of the agreed links. It is clearly too restrictive to limit types of associations to, for example, the major categories identified in the literature: co-ordination; collocation; superordination; and synonymy (Aitchison, 1987). To do so would fail to capture other equally well-attested but more elusive types of links, particularly certain syntagmatic associations that rely on cultural knowledge of all kinds, from pop music to works of literature. It is important to note that, notwithstanding the evidence for the so-called 'syn-tagmatic–paradigmatic shift' (Politzer, 1978; Söderman, 1993), this category of association is likely to be associated with more advanced learners or native speakers of a language.

Another solution to the problem of evaluating the legitimacy of word associations identified in these tests would be to ask native speaker judges to rate the strength of the associations. However, earlier experimental evidence (Wilks, 1999) suggests that test formats where judges have to rate large numbers of associations, tend to lead to a degree of inconsistency between judges, which limits their validity. Meara and Wolter (2004) have found similar inconsistencies in the use of rating scales in their current version of the English test (V_links) which requires informants to rate the strength of associations themselves.

A third possibility would be to use native-speaker test data as a benchmark for the validity of learner responses. This is the approach currently adopted by V_links, where only those associations which are also identified by at least two native speakers are deemed acceptable. Meara and Wolter acknowledge however, that this system is not entirely satisfactory because it fails to take account of L2 associations which arise out of specific local conditions (Meara and Wolter, 2004). There may also be a further theoretical difficulty with this very 'all or nothing' benchmarking approach in that it implicitly treats learners' lexical networks as defective versions of native-speaker networks and not as developing systems in their own right. If we weed out anything that doesn't conform to this minimal native-speaker benchmark then we confine ourselves to narrow observations of degrees of 'nativeness' and risk losing valuable insights into the dynamic patterning and development of learner vocabularies, their 'approximative system' (Nemser, 1971). A more sophisticated system of item analysis which is now being developed (Wolter, personal communication) may help to overcome this difficulty as it will be more sensitive to gradations of native-like or learner-like associative behaviour.

We will turn now to the question of whether informants may be adopting different test-taking strategies that influence performance. Analysis of our questionnaires suggests that a small but significant number of informants are adopting systematic approaches in completing the test. The most obvious of these is a systematic checking strategy. The answers of these informants indicate that they have worked their way alphabetically through the word sets looking first for any links with word 'a', then for links with word 'b' and so on. For example:

      ab aj bc bj ce ch   [item 12, NS1]

This is clearly a strategy that is in some sense invited by our test presentation format in a way that is not the case for online versions such as V_links. However, it is important to note that the strategy stands out precisely because most test-takers do not appear to approach the test 'from left to right'. Indeed our interviewee reported that he deliberately avoided this tactic as he felt that he was less likely to spot links in this way.

The systematic checking strategy is far more prevalent among native speakers, where some 22% (8 out of 36) have clearly used this technique in all, or nearly all, of the word sets. The partial users appear to have discovered the system after a few questionnaire items and then applied it for the rest of the test. Amongst the learner groups, only two of the higher-level learners use this systematic checking technique and only one lower-proficiency informant. Not surprisingly, test-takers applying this strategy tend to have high mean hits scores.

The prevalence of this strategy among native speakers invites us to speculate on a number of fronts. It could be that native speakers' more secure knowledge of the core vocabulary used in the questionnaire frees their attentional control and permits them the luxury of taking a systematic approach in a timed exercise. This interpretation receives some support from the qualitative feedback provided by informants. Many of the learners (including our post hoc interviewee) reported finding the exercise difficult or 'challenging'. They claimed to know most of the words but were conscious of knowing some of them 'better than others'. Our interviewee also commented that with more time he would have found more associations – and indeed did identify additional links on going back through the questionnaire when we interviewed him. More tentatively, as regards the checking strategy, we might suggest that there may be a cultural predisposition among our French informants to tackle tasks systematically given the value placed on such approaches in French pedagogic practice.

A second strategy that stands out from the data is that of the handful of informants (both learners and native speakers) who appear to decide at the outset on a fixed number of hits per word set. Thus we have respondents who identify, say, five or three associations in every questionnaire item. It is almost as though they 'get into a rhythm' in identifying associations. Given the very low probability of this distribution it is extremely unlikely that all of the links identified by these informants are 'intuitive' in any obvious sense.

The strategies outlined above are, of course, only those which are discernible from a scrutiny of the written data. It is entirely possible that more extensive qualitative feedback from individuals will in future enable us to identify other, less visible test-taker approaches. What is clear, however, is that we cannot be confident that we have any kind of direct access to lexical networks unmediated by conscious test-taking strategies, deliberate subversion or divergent understandings of what counts as a word association.

Of course the very idea of 'direct access' that we have just referred to shows the extent to which our models of the mental lexicon are still influenced by the very metaphor we are seeking to investigate. The 'access' question presupposes the existence of a more or less stable associative network. Of course the notion that such networks may be 'dynamic' is well rehearsed in the literature. McCarthy (1990: 42), for example, claims that: 'The webs of meanings and associations constantly shift and re-adjust; new connections are woven and old ones strengthened.' It is clear, nevertheless, that these adaptations are conceived of as changes to an existing structure. However, in the light of our evidence regarding the difficulty of implementing graph theoretical models, we are forced to try to step further outside the network metaphor. The problems of obtaining 'intuitive' responses, and the evidence of different test-taker strategies and understandings of the nature of associations surely oblige us to at least question whether links do in fact exist independently of the tasks or linguistic events that call them up. It may be that the lines on the graph are never in any sense permanently drawn. Instead, they may be created by the act of engaging in the tasks that are attempting to measure them.

We do not, at this point, advocate abandoning the metaphor of the lexical network. Despite its power to mislead in some respects, it still has much to offer in helping us to think about the way in which we learn, store and retrieve vocabulary – and offers particular advantages for a comparative investigation of L1 and L2 vocabularies. Nevertheless, the questions we have raised in the course of our research continue to argue for a cautious approach in the way we treat some of the implications of this particular bit of theoretical terminology.

Conclusion

In this chapter we have put the case for taking a formal approach to the highly conventionalised metaphor of the vocabulary network. We have shown that application of graph theoretical principles to word association data offers us a way of formalising and exploring the network metaphor. Graph theoretical approaches have led us to challenge some of the intuitive assumptions about density and structure in L1 and L2 vocabularies that flow from the implications of the 'word web' analogy.

The recent study that we have reported tests a new data elicitation tool intended to allow us to take our investigation of network structure and density a step further. Our results confirm that native-speaker networks have reliably higher levels of linkage than those of learners and offer some evidence that density increases as L2 proficiency develops. However, our data also show that even among native speakers, there is an unexpectedly high level of variability within the groups in our study. We argue therefore for a concentration on the analysis of data at the level of the individual informant.

Our discussion of test-taker attitudes and strategies shows that these factors remain a serious issue for the validity of measures of lexical density. We raise a number of methodological and theoretical issues. How direct can our access be to lexical networks given that many informants adopt, at best, only a semi-intuitive approach in identifying links? How best can we evaluate the legitimacy of the associations identified by learners (and indeed native speakers) without falling into the trap of treating learner networks only as deficient imitations of the native-speaker 'target'? More fundamentally, should we now review our own theoretical position as regards the nature of links in the mental lexicon?

We will finish with a couple of more general observations prompted by our experience of working on graph theoretical approaches to word associations over a number of years. The first is that this enterprise has led us to value the reflexive relationship between theory and methodology. There is undoubtedly a place in lexical research for an approach in which systematic analysis of data leads us to frame emerging theoretical positions in a manner in some ways analogous to the principles of Grounded Theory (Glaser and Strauss, 1967).

Secondly, we are persuaded of the benefits of taking a longer-term approach to the exploration of given problems in vocabulary research. Too many ideas in lexical research only see the light of day in a single study and are then shelved before they can be adequately pursued and developed (see Meara, 1993, for a more detailed critique of short-termism in lexical research). We hope, therefore, that our ongoing exploration of the network metaphor has to some extent adhered to Singleton's maxims for vocabulary research: 'be collaborative; be qualitative and quantitative; be durative' (Singleton, 1999: 276).

10 Insights into the structure of L1 and L2 vocabulary networks: intimations of small worlds

Ellen Schur

Introduction

This chapter examines a series of studies of individual L1, L2 and random vocabulary networks generated by a word association task and analysed according to graph theoretical criteria. It is a development and continuation of Wilks and Meara's preceding chapter in this volume and addresses questions as to the applicability of the metaphor we so commonly use of the lexicon as a web of words. It will consider this question in the light of the findings of three recent large-scale studies in which established corpora were analysed to determine whether semantic networks exhibit properties of a specific subclass of networks – small-world ones.

As noted in the previous chapter, the concept of semantic, vocabulary or lexical 'networks' appears quite often in second language acquisition literature as a metaphor which many researchers have used to explain the way words in the mental lexicon hang together (cf. McCarthy, 1990; Aitchison, 1994; Henriksen and Haastrup, 1998; Huckin and Coady, 1999). The metaphor of a web, or network, used by these researchers seems to be intuitively correct. Otherwise it would not be so prevalent, and we would not accept it so easily – to the point that we tend to forget that it is a metaphor, albeit an invaluable one insofar as it provides the impetus to explore the potential of an empirically based model of the structure and function of semantic networks.

This chapter, then, will approach semantic networks from the vantage point of graph theory, the study of the properties of networks. This approach is not a new one. Graph theoretical principles were implicitly or explicitly applied to the study of associative semantic networks in the 1950s and 1960s by researchers with backgrounds in the concepts and methodologies of experimental psychology (cf. Deese, 1962a; Marshall and Cofer, 1963; Pollio, 1963; Deese, 1965; Rapoport et al., 1966; Riegel, Ramsey and

Riegel, 1967; Riegel and Zivian, 1972; Kiss, 1968). More recently, Meara and his colleagues at the University of Wales, Swansea (cf. Meara, 1992b; Wilks and Meara, 2002; Wilks and Meara, Chapter 9, this volume) have built on this approach and continued to explore the applicability of graph theory to semantic networks. Following in this tradition, I have been exploring the potential of graph theoretical criteria to afford empirically based insights into the structure of lexical networks of individual native speakers, non-native learners and random computer-generated 'subjects'. These criteria may eventually offer a more holistic means of assessing the vocabulary knowledge of different language users than some of the traditional measures do, and provide us with a multi-faceted picture of this knowledge.

In this chapter, then, I will present some of the findings of a series of studies I carried out on native monolingual and bilingual English speakers and non-native learners from different cultural backgrounds using a restricted word association task. I used graph theoretical criteria to analyse the semantic networks of each subject group. In addition, a computer-generated random simulation of the task was also designed to provide a baseline against which the networks of the real-world subjects could be measured (Meara and Schur, 2002). The graph theoretical criteria not only shed light on the structural characteristics of the semantic networks, but also raise the question of whether these networks belong to a subclass of networks – small-world ones. I will discuss the key properties of this class of networks, and then present the findings of three recent large-scale studies carried out by mathematicians and physicists. These studies have identified small-world properties in networks formed by words in three established corpora. Finally, I will propose directions for future explorations of the semantic networks of individual language users suggested by these studies.

The concept of a small-world network comes from graph theory. It is a dynamic network which is neither completely regular nor completely random. A completely regular network would be one where each node is linked to its neighbours by an equal number of connections; a random network would be one where there would be varying numbers of connections and no discernible patterns in the connections. The small-world network is somewhere between these two extremes and can be used to describe a variety of things such as electricity grids, telephone networks and networks of personal and work-related contacts.

What these networks have in common is the *sparseness* of their connections and the *clustering* of these connections. They have a relatively small number of connections relative to their nodes, therefore, and these connections are not uniformly distributed but converge around some nodes and not others. Thus, they are said to have a high *clustering coefficient* – a small number of actual links in proportion to the hypothetical number of links they would have if the links were regular and equal in distribution. And they are also said to have a small *diameter*, that is, you only need a small number of nodes to get from one to another. This pattern of distribution is described according to a *power law curve*; a small number of nodes with large numbers of connections and a very large number of nodes with very few connections. When networks grow, new nodes tend to cluster around these existing nodes with high numbers of connections. It is a feature of these networks that there appears to be very little middle ground between these two extremes; there is no graduated scale or hierarchy with nodes which possess middling numbers of connections. The networks are said to be *scale-free*, with nodes falling either into a high-clustering or low-clustering group.

This model is very attractive from the point of view of trying to describe and measure a vocabulary network. The principles it describes will be familiar in language where we know that some words, like prepositions, are connected with large numbers of other words in phrasal verbs and collocations, while other words, generally infrequent, may have few such links. It is a mathematical model which could provide a principled explanation of how this aspect of the lexicon is acquired and organised into a cohesive system. It suggests that a limited number of words serve as well-connected hubs which provide the framework for an entire vocabulary network. If these words, or sets of words, can be identified it might enable us to build learner vocabularies according to an empirically testable model.

The word association studies

The subjects

There were four groups of subjects in the word association studies. Each group consisted of 32 subjects. Group 1 comprised adult bilingual native speakers of English whose L2 was Hebrew. Group 2 comprised Israeli 11th grade high-school students studying for their matriculation exam (*bagrut*) whose L1 was Hebrew. These were high-level students who had been studying English from grade 4 in classes where communicative teaching was emphasised. They had considerable exposure to English through movies and video clips, which, in Israel, are subtitled rather than dubbed. Group 3 comprised monolingual English speakers studying for a degree in Applied Linguistics at a British university. Group 4 comprised Chinese students in the first week of a pre-academic preparatory course at the same British university. These students learned English vocabulary primarily by rote, mostly in paired lists of the English word and its Chinese translation equivalent. Their exposure to English through the media was limited because in China both movies and video clips are dubbed. A set of data from a random computer simulation of the task was also generated (Meara and Schur, 2002).

The instrument

The subjects were given a randomly ordered list of 50 verbs selected from Nation's (1986) first 1,000-word frequency band. High frequency words were used to ensure that the non-native learners would be familiar with the vocabulary used in the task. The same 50 verbs were presented in two formats. They appeared in a 'Verb Box' in alphabetical order (Figure 1) and then on a facing page in a randomly ordered list (Figure 2). Each word on the list was followed by a blank space.

to argue	to drive	to help	to obey	to show
to assist	to earn	to imagine	to pay	to spend
to build	to expect	to invent	to point	to study
to buy	to explain	to learn	to prepare	to tell
to clean	to fight	to listen	to prove	to test
to cost	to find	to look	to ride	to try
to cut	to fly	to lose	to sail	to wash
to describe	to grow	to love	to scream	to win
to discover	to hate	to make	to see	to work
to dream	to hear	to measure	to shout	to yell

Figure 1 The verb box

The task was restricted to verbs for two reasons. Firstly, research has shown that for both L1 children (cf. Gentner, 1981; 1985) and L2 adult learners (cf. Ellis and Beaton, 1995; Källkvist, 1998), verbs are more difficult to learn than nouns and other parts of speech. This suggested that, even though the verbs were high-frequency ones, the non-native learners might not have the same degree of knowledge of these words as the native speakers. Thus, a task restricted to verbs might tap quite different native-speaker and non-native learner responses to the same set of stimulus words. Secondly, other research has shown that stimulus words of different parts of speech elicit

1.	to help:	26.	to describe:
2.	to study:	27.	to fly:
3.	to scream:	28.	to drive:
4.	to tell:	29.	to point:
5.	to expect:	30.	to yell:
6.	to wash:	31.	to sail:
7.	to love:	32.	to build:
8.	to cost:	33.	to fight:
9.	to shout:	34.	to prove:
10.	to imagine:	35.	to prepare:
11.	to show:	36.	to work:
12.	to dream:	37.	to explain:
13.	to invent:	38.	to hate:
14.	to ride:	39.	to see:
15.	to lose:	40.	to learn:
16.	to listen:	41.	to argue:
17.	to grow:	42.	to pay:
18.	to make:	43.	to assist:
19.	to cut:	44.	to obey:
20.	to measure:	45.	to discover:
21.	to find:	46.	to try:
22.	to spend:	47.	to test:
23.	to clean:	48.	to win:
24.	to look:	49.	to buy:
25.	to earn:	50.	to hear:

Figure 2   The randomly ordered word list

different numbers of responses (cf. Brown and Berko, 1960; Deese, 1962b). It was expected, then, that stimulus words taken from different word classes would add an unwanted confounding factor.

The subjects were given a three-page questionnaire, with the title *Pair the Words that Go Together* printed on the top of each page. The first page consisted of a short questionnaire to determine their language background, and several practice examples which they worked through before embarking on the main task. The second page contained a Verb Box (Figure 1), and the third page a randomly ordered Word List (Figure 2). The instructions were:

On this page you will see 50 verbs that are arranged in
alphabetical order in a Verb Box. On the next page you will
see the same 50 verbs, but these have been arranged in
random order in a Verb List. Read each verb in the list. Then
decide which one of the verbs in the Verb Box best completes
the pair for each verb in that list. Write this verb next to the
appropriate verb in the list. You can use a verb from the Verb
Box as many times as you need to.

Both the bilingual and the monolingual native speakers completed
the task in 10 to 15 minutes, whereas it took the non-native learners
in both groups from 20 to 50 minutes to complete it.

Results

The results were then coded and mapped out to create a semantic
network for each subject in each group. Each set of individual
networks was analysed according to the following graph theoretical
criteria: number of components, pairs, bi-directional arrows and
degrees per node.

Let us look carefully at one such network in order to clarify some
of these terms and concepts. Figure 3 shows the network of a
monolingual subject. Words are represented by nodes shaped as
ellipses. The number in each ellipsis refers to a word as it appeared in
the randomly ordered list (see Figure 2). For example, in the first two
verb pairs at the top left of Figure 3, number 5 = *to expect*, number
35 = *to prepare*, number 6 = *to wash*, number 23 = *to clean*. The nodes
in the diagrams are connected by arrows which represent the associations among them. The arrows may be one- or two-directional. For
example, nodes 6 and 23 are connected by a bi-directional arrow.
This means that verb 6, *to wash*, has elicited verb 23, *to clean*, and
verb 23, *to clean* has also elicited verb 6, *to wash*. The arrow
connecting nodes 5 and 35 goes only in one direction. This means
that verb 35, *to prepare*, has elicited verb 5, *to expect*, but verb 5 has
not elicited verb 35. A bi-directional arrow implies a greater strength
of association between words than a one-directional arrow.

Another key concept is that of node degree: the number(s) of
connections to and from each node in the network. For example,
node 37 at the top right of Figure 3 has 4 degrees, node 1 has 2
degrees, node 43 has 1 degree, etc. Graph theory also allows us to
discuss the connectedness of a network. Like all of the networks in
the study, this network is not connected. It contains 11 separate
segments or components: 2 components have 8 nodes, 2 have 6, and

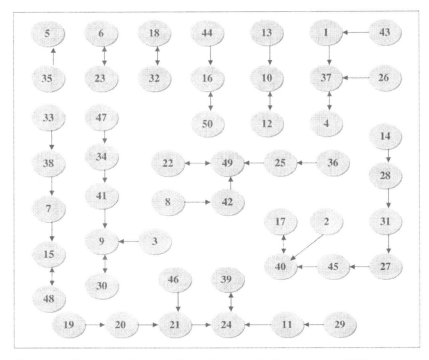

Figure 3   Network of a monolingual native English speaker (E32)

2 have 5; an additional 2 components have 3 nodes, and there are 3 components with 2 nodes each. A final key term is that of path length. This refers to the mean number of steps it takes to get from any one node to another in the network. For example, we can go from node 17 to node 2 in two steps, and from node 17 to node 14 in six steps. However, since this network is non-connected we cannot go from node 17 to node 42, or to any of the nodes in the other components. Since all of the networks in this study were non-connected, their average path lengths could not be ascertained. The implications of this will be noted later on. At this point, let us take a brief look at the mean numbers of components, pairs, bi-directional arrows and degrees per node found in each network set.

Components

As noted above, none of the networks were connected ones. Table 1 shows the mean number of components per network set. The Hebrew learners produced the smallest number of network components per network (conversely their network components comprised more nodes), followed in increasing order by the monolinguals, the bilinguals and the Chinese learners. The random 'subjects' produced considerably fewer components per network than any of the real-world subjects. These differences and those that will be discussed below, are illustrated in Figures 4, 5 and 6, representative examples of a Hebrew learner network, a Chinese learner network and a random network, respectively.

Table 1 Mean number of components per network set ($n = 32$)

	Mono-linguals	Bilinguals	Hebrew	Chinese	Random
Mean	9.56	10.6	8.9	10.63	2.4
Standard deviation	3.28	4.0	4.19	5.6	0.98

The standard deviations indicate that the largest variation in the number of network components could be found among the Chinese learners. This variation reflected a greater range in the number of components per network, from 2 to 23, on the part of the Chinese learners, as opposed to 2 to 17 for the other real-world network sets and 2–5 for the random one. The mean numbers of components per network set tend to mask this variation. In fact, a comparison of the network sets according to the distribution of the network components in each (Table 2) reveals that, although the mean number of components in the bilingual and Chinese network sets seem almost identical, their distribution is quite different: we can observe identical distribution patterns for the native-speaker networks and quite different ones for the non-native learner networks. (See Schur, 2003, for detailed descriptions and statistical analyses of the distribution of components, the number of nodes in each component and the range of components per network set.)

Table 2 Distribution of network components ($n = 32$)

	Mono-linguals	Bilinguals	Hebrew	Chinese	Random
Number of networks with 7 or fewer components	7	7	14	12	32
Number of networks with 8 or more components	25	25	18	20	0

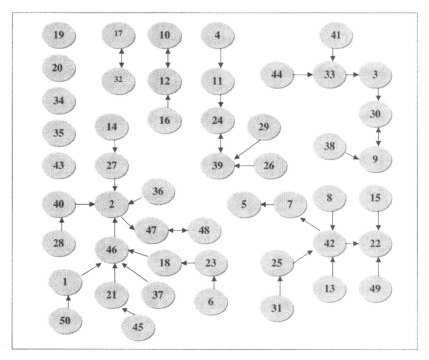

Figure 4   A network of a Hebrew L1 non-native learner of English (H3)

Paired components

There was a considerable difference in the number of paired components found in the networks of the Chinese learners and those found in the network sets of the three other real-world subject groups, as we can see in Table 3. The other real-world network sets contained fewer paired components than the Chinese learner set. The standard deviations indicate that the number of paired components were the least variable for the monolingual networks and the most variable for the Chinese learner networks. It can also be observed that the random 'subject' network set is again markedly different from all

Table 3   Mean number of paired components per network set ($n = 32$)

	Mono-linguals	Bilinguals	Hebrew	Chinese	Random
Mean	3.13	3.59	2.97	4.84	0.19
Standard deviation	2.12	2.61	2.49	4.44	0.47

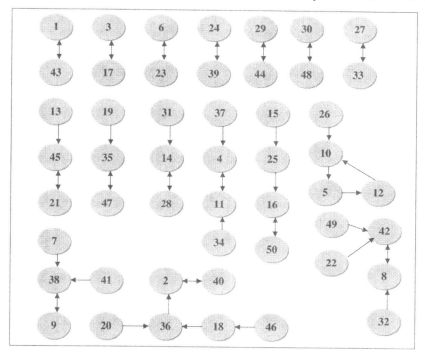

Figure 5   Network of a Chinese L1 non-native learner of English (C43)

four of the real-world network sets: there were hardly any pairs or individual variation.

Bi-directional arrows

Table 4 shows that the Hebrew-speaking high-school learners produced the fewest bi-directional arrows per real-world network, whereas the Chinese learners produced the most. The mean number of bi-directional arrows produced by the bilingual adults was quite similar to that of the Chinese learners, and that of the bi-directional

Table 4   Mean number of bi-directional arrows per network set ($n = 32$)

	Mono-linguals	Bilinguals	Hebrew	Chinese	Random
Mean	8.28	9.2	6.8	9.25	0.66
Standard deviation	3.63	4.4	4.5	5.85	0.83

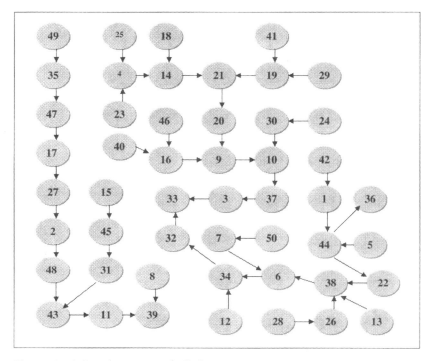

Figure 6   A Random network (R6)

arrows produced by the monolinguals was somewhere in-between. The standard deviations indicate that for the real-world network sets, the variation for the monolinguals was less than that found in the other three sets and greatest for the Chinese learners. The random set showed almost no variation at all.

Node degree distribution

The final criterion used to analyse the networks was the node degree distribution in each network set. The degree of each node for each subject in the network set was counted, and the distribution pattern of the nodes for each set was then plotted out. The resulting graphs for the five sets can be seen in Figure 7. Whereas each of the three previous criteria yielded differences among the network sets, this criterion indicated that all five were quite similar. They were all characterised by large numbers of 1- and 2-degree nodes followed by sharp decreases in the number of nodes with 3, 4 and 5 or more degrees.

We can also see from Figure 7 that all the network sets contained fairly similar numbers of 3-degree nodes, and that there were small differences in the numbers of 4-degree nodes. The means of the 4-degree nodes for the monolingual and the random network sets were almost identical (3 and 2.9 nodes per degree, respectively), and quite similar for the bilingual and the Chinese network sets (2.1 and 1.84, respectively). The mean number of 4-degree nodes for the Hebrew speaker network set fell in-between (2.5). We can also see that the network sets were similar in the numbers of nodes with 5 or more degrees, although the monolingual sets contained the largest number of these nodes (a mean of 0.94), and the random set the smallest (a mean of 0.69). Within the 5-or-more-degree category subtle differences were found. Unlike the random network set for which the highest node degree was 6, the real-world network sets had between 1 and 4 nodes with 7, 8 or 9 degrees. (See Schur, 2003, for a detailed description and analysis of the node distribution per network set.)

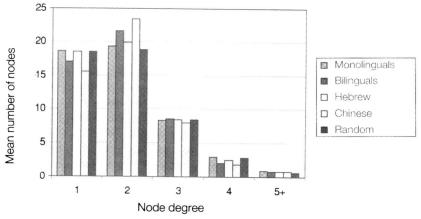

Figure 7　Node degree distribution

Discussion

Space considerations preclude a full discussion of various implications of this data. I will focus, therefore, on the differing strengths of associations among the subject groups, the inter-relatedness of the four analytical criteria and the issue of the centrality of certain nodes in the real-world networks. I will then discuss the importance of the similar node degree distribution pattern obtained for all the network sets. This pattern suggests a potentially rewarding area for further research: the exploration of the small-world properties of the semantic networks of individual language users.

First of all, we can conclude that there were differences in the ways each subject group perceived associative connections among words. The disproportionately large number of pairs and bi-directional arrows in the Chinese network set, and the concomitantly larger number of separate network components, suggests that the Chinese learners' perceptions of associative connections were the strongest, perhaps overly so. The small number of pairs and bi-directional arrows in the Hebrew learner network, and the concomitantly smaller number of separate network components, indicates that these learners' perceptions of associative connections were much weaker.

In addition, comparisons between the two native-speaker network sets, which showed somewhat smaller numbers of pairs and bi-directional arrows for the student monolinguals than for the adult bilinguals, indicated that the bilinguals' perceptions of the associations among words were stronger than those of the monolinguals. The question that this raises is whether the bilinguals' stronger associative connections were the result of their age and experience with their native language or can be put down to the influence of their second language.

Furthermore, comparisons between the monolingual and bilingual native-speaker network sets and the Hebrew and Chinese learner ones showed that the latter two were clearly non-native-like, albeit in different ways. The preponderance of one-off pairs and bi-directional arrows that marked the Chinese learner networks might reflect a very limited type of vocabulary knowledge: one word is associated only with one other word. On the other hand, the relatively smaller number of pairs and bi-directional arrows that characterised the Hebrew learner networks might indicate that their awareness of which words can be associated with another was far too broad.

A possible explanation for the marked differences between the learner networks of the Chinese students and those of the Hebrew-speaking students can be found in informal feedback from both the teachers of both groups and the students themselves. As noted above, the Chinese students seemed to have learned vocabulary primarily by rote, mostly in paired lists – the word in English and its Chinese translation equivalent – and they were accustomed to tests that focused on one-to-one translation equivalents. Both teachers and students acknowledged that, although many of the Chinese learners had a very large single-meaning vocabulary as a result of their decontextualised method of learning and test preparation, they had tremendous difficulties in understanding and producing English in context. Their tendency to focus on a single meaning of a particular word meant that many times they were totally lost when confronted with different combinations of words whose definition they thought they knew, i.e., when they had to deal with vocabulary in context. This was reflected in the difficulties they experienced in both reading and aural comprehension and in speaking and writing. This was especially so at the very beginning of their course, which was when the association task was administered.

In contrast, the approach to vocabulary learning experienced by the Israeli high-school students was quite different. Although the learners were encouraged to keep lists of words and their translation equivalents to facilitate the learning process, the focus of their vocabulary acquisition was on vocabulary as a communicative tool. The learners were assigned projects in which the fluent and correct use of the written and spoken word in context was the objective. Their progress was evaluated not on the basis of periodic discrete item tests, but through cumulative portfolios. The more holistic communicative approach to language learning to which they were exposed meant that they were more comfortable with the possibility that one word could be combined with others in a variety of ways, with the slight shifts in meaning that this might entail.

It would seem, then, that most of the Chinese learners were not at ease with the kind of task used in this study, one that required an openness to the possibility that words may combine in different ways. When the nature of the task was explained to them and they worked through the practice examples, the fact that all of the verbs could be used more than once to complete the pairs was emphasised. But as they worked their way through the task on their own, they seemed to return to the more familiar vocabulary learning strategies with which they were most comfortable. They tended to perceive the best answer as *one* verb that best completed *only* one other verb, creating one-off reciprocal word pairs. Thus, for the most part, their individual networks were organised in many discrete pairs. In contrast, the number of pairs produced by the Hebrew-speaking learners was closer to the number of pairs produced by the two native-speaker subject groups. This would seem to indicate that, although this learner group found the task difficult, their approach was a more native-like one. They seemed to be more sensitive to the different possible connections that any one verb may have.

However, the most consistent and significant finding of these comparisons needs to be kept in mind: even the associative choices of the non-native learners were far from random. Like the native

[handwritten marginal notes: "perhaps learning background needs to be investigated as part of the individual profiles?"; "Surely this is a test taking strategy – not a comm strategy."]

speakers, they too were making meaning-governed choices as they worked their way through the association task. More work would need to be done with other groups of language users if norms of associative strength are to be established. The in-depth discussion in Wilks and Meara's Chapter 9 in this volume explores the complexity of and challenges inherent in researching these issues.

A second point that needs to be stressed is the inter-relatedness of the four analytical criteria. Node degree distribution seems to be the most inclusive. The findings reported in my results on pp. 187–93 show that, although the five network sets had a similar overall distribution pattern, there were subtle differences among the various network sets. These differences reflect the findings of the other three measures. For example, the markedly greater number of 2-degree nodes in the Chinese learner network set is a direct reflection of the large number of pairs and the concomitant large number of separate network components produced by these students. The relatively large gap between the number of 1- and 2-degree nodes in this network set also echoes the huge number of pairs linked by bi-directional arrows. The smaller gap in the numbers of 1- and 2-degree nodes of the bilingual network set mirrors the smaller, but still relatively large, number of pairs linked by almost the same number of bi-directional arrows that were found in the Chinese learner networks.

A final point concerns the issue of the centrality of certain nodes. The small graduated decrease in nodes with more than 5 degrees as we move from the monolingual to the Chinese network set suggests that the monolinguals tended to perceive more verbs as central than the bilinguals, Chinese or Hebrew speakers. However, two verbs (*to show*, number 11, and *to discover*, number 45) in the monolingual networks consistently have nodes of 5 or more degrees. This, along with their low level of variation, implies that the monolinguals were more homogeneous in their perceptions of which words were the most central ones, a finding consistent with the results of earlier studies showing greater stereotypy of response on the part of native speakers (cf. Rosenzweig, 1961; Rosenzweig, 1964; Lambert and Moore, 1966; Riegel et al., 1967; Postman and Keppel, 1970; Riegel and Zivian, 1972; Szalay and Deese, 1978).

Moreover, the fact that all the real-world networks had some nodes with more than 7 degrees, whereas the random networks had none, points to further differences between the random networks and the real-world ones. The large-degree nodes found in the real-world networks can be seen as a product of a conscious awareness that certain nodes are more central than others, which, by definition, is lacking in the random set of networks.

These differences, then, some of which are quite subtle, indicate that we cannot make across-the-board generalisations about the properties of the semantic networks of learners from very different language and cultural backgrounds, or even about the networks of monolinguals and bilinguals. They also suggest that the restricted word association technique is a sensitive one. In addition, the findings clearly reflect the inter-related nature of the four-graph theoretical criteria. Particularly intriguing are the similar overall node distribution pattern and the presence of a small number of central nodes in the real-world networks. Both suggest, albeit tentatively, that these networks might belong to a subclass of networks described by graph theory – small-world ones.

Three key properties of these networks can be found in two seminal works which initiated a recent explosion of graph-theory-related research, Watts and Strogatz (1998) and Watts (1999). These properties are: sparseness, (relatively) large clustering coefficients and small path lengths. Thus, exemplars of these networks would necessarily have: (1) very few connections relative to the large number of nodes found in these graphs; (2) large clusters around some central nodes, and (3) a minimal number of steps separating any one node from another. Other graph theory researchers and theoreticians, Barabási and Albert (1999) and, more recently, Strogatz (2001), have investigated an additional property of small-world networks. They have shown that in addition to the three properties mentioned above, small-world networks are also scale-free. This means that, although most of the nodes in these networks have very few connections, they also have some central nodes that are connected to large numbers of other nodes. When the numbers of connections of all the nodes in these networks are plotted out, a power law distribution graph can be seen: many nodes with small numbers of connections and a progressively steady decrease, which never reaches zero, in the number of nodes with increasing larger numbers of connections. (For basic and easily accessible explanations of these properties, cf. Hayes, 2000a,b; Barabási, 2002; Buchanan, 2002; Watts, 2003.)

The node distribution pattern in the five sets of networks sets in my studies, with their 'standard wiring' of many 1- and 2-degree nodes, and decreasingly smaller numbers of 3- to 9-degree nodes and clustering patterns around several central nodes, suggest such a graph. Obviously, the small number of data points in the node distribution graph, the very few nodes which exhibited clustering patterns and the non-connected nature of the networks, which meant that their average path length could not be determined, preclude any definitive statements as to whether these networks are small-world ones. However, three recent papers have identified these properties in the semantic networks of large corpora. In the next section, I will review these findings and discuss some directions for future research that they suggest.

Three large-scale studies

The main findings of these studies are summarised in Table 5. In the first study, Motter, de Moura, Lai and Dasgupta (2002) analysed an online thesaurus comprising 30,000 words. The authors constructed their network by connecting each word listed in the entry of another word. The resulting network was sparse: each word had an average of 60 links to the other words in the network, a very small fraction of the total number of words in the thesaurus. The network had an average path length of 3.2. The authors remark that the network's large clustering coefficient (0.53) was due to the presence of short-cuts, several words belonging to more than one conceptual domain. These words, or nodes, were characterised by many connections and formed the basis of the scale-free property of the network. Motter et al. attribute the presence of these nodes to the dynamic nature of small-world networks: nodes which already have several connections will attract even more connections. They argue that, since semantic networks are small-world networks which have evolved over time, their growth was characterised by the preferential attachment of new words to words which already had other links (cf. Dorogovtsev and Mendes, 2001).

In the second study, Sigman and Cecchi (2002) investigated the small-world properties of semantic networks derived from the 66,025 different meanings of the nouns in the Wordnet1.6 lexicon.

Table 5 Findings of three studies of the small-world properties of large corpora

Study	Corpora	Size	Word types	Path length	Clustering coefficient	Scale-free
Motter et al. (2002)	On-line thesaurus	30,000	Content words	3.2	0.53	✓
Sigman and Cecchi (2002)	Wordnet 1.6	66,025	Nouns in logical relationships	11.9→ 7.4	0.0002 → 0.06	✓
Ferrer i Cancho and Solé (2001)	BNC	750,000	Functors and content words	2.63 or 2.67	0.687 or 0.437	✓

This lexicon is organised according to logical relationships among words. The authors considered four of these logical relationships: antonymy, hypernymy (sic), meronymy and polysemy. They created two graphs by mapping out the links formed by words in the hypernymy and meronymy categories. These two graphs also illustrated the power law distribution discussed above. However, the authors note that the power law distribution in and of itself was not sufficient to indicate that the networks were small-world ones. A small average path length and large clustering coefficients were also necessary. When the polysemous words were introduced into the two networks, they reorganised themselves into small-world ones: their average path length was reduced from 11.9 to 7.4, and their average clustering coefficient increased from 0.0002 to 0.06. The resulting reduction in path length and the larger clustering coefficient converted the networks in each of the two categories into small-world ones.

In the third study, Ferrer i Cancho and Solé (2001) constructed networks derived from three-quarters of the one million words in the British National Corpus. They built their networks on the basis of common words in co-occurring consecutive pairs. The authors note the highly clustered nature of the resulting network, the scale-free node degree distribution graph they obtained and its small path length (2.63 or 2.67, depending on the basis of their calculations). They attribute the highly clustered nature of the graph and the scale-free distribution of node degree to the large numbers of connections found in a subset of function words, i.e. particles such as *and*, *the*, *of*, and *in*. They claim that although these words have 'very low or zero semantic content' they do 'speed-up navigation' around the network (Ferrer i Cancho and Solé, 2001: 2264–5).

The analyses of three large word compilations, an online thesaurus, the Wordnet lexicon and the British National Corpus, clearly indicate that semantic networks are small-world ones. These studies, carried out by mathematicians and physicists, raise several issues that need to be teased out by applied linguists. The first issue concerns the role of the functors in the high clustering coefficients and the short path lengths obtained. Motter et al. (2002) and Sigman and Cecchi (2002) indicate that content words are sufficient to determine the small-world nature of semantic networks. However, the Ferrer i Cancho and Solé (2001) study indicates that the functors may also play a significant role in the formation of these networks. In order to distinguish between the roles of the content words and that of the functors, an interesting follow-up to the latter study would be to reanalyse the data omitting the functors. Such a study might show that two interrelated sets of two different lexical networks need to be considered: syntactic networks formed by co-occurring adjacent words in a running text which includes functors, and semantic networks comprising words linked only by the concepts they represent.

The different types of words comprising the networks in the three studies raises a second issue: which content words generate sufficient links to form a small-world network with the shortest average path length? Both the network in Motter et al. (2002) and those in Sigman and Cecchi (2002) were formed by the semantic links among content words. However, the former study comprised associatively linked words (as determined by cross-references in a thesaurus), whereas the latter included both rigorously logical relationships among words (hypernymy and meronymy) and the more associative relationships generated by polysemous words. There were clear differences between the three types of networks found in these studies. The average path length of the Motter et al. (2002) network was much smaller (3.2) than the Sigman and Cecchi networks constructed from both logically related and polysemous words (7.4). The networks constructed from words which were linked only logically by their logical relationship were self-generating, but they were not small-world networks. This implies that the most direct semantic links among words can be found exclusively in their associative connections, and it is these connections that make them small-world networks.

The Sigman and Checchi (2002) study is worth considering in more detail. This used the words in the Wordnet1.6 lexicon as the basis for study. These words were categorised according to their *relationships with other words. They mapped out the links formed by the words in two of the categories, hypernymy and meronymy.* The graphs they created showed that the power law – a few words with large numbers of connections and many words with very few connections – applied to the words in each of these categories. But the two other features that characterise small-world networks, large clustering coefficients and small path lengths did not obtain. When the authors introduced the words in a third category, the polysemous words, the resulting networks exhibited these two necessary properties of small-world networks as well. The fact that it was the polysemous words that 'did the trick' is striking. These are words that have connections to different domains, e.g. *light* can take us to a series of relationships that deal with weight or a series of relationships that deal with brightness/darkness. Thus it seems that the multi-faceted associative connections of these words to different domains, as opposed to the logically determined connections of others within a single domain, made the networks small-world ones.

A third issue is the concept of the dynamic nature of small-world networks and the principle of preferential attachment which explains how these networks grow. As we have seen, Motter et al. (2002) claim that this principle explains the evolutionary growth of a language: words which already have some connections are the ones that tend to attract more connections. Dorogovtsev and Mendes (2001) present a theoretical mathematical model that shows the growth of an evolving language system. This model posits that a set of initial words forms a kernel lexicon whose size does not vary as a language develops, and that these words are the ones that attract increasing numbers of other connections over the course of its evolution. An interesting challenge for linguists would be to find empirical evidence of how this actually happens in a specific language: what words does the kernel lexicon consist of? Can evidence for the patterns of growth predicted by this model be found? The concept of preferential attachment might provide a valid explanation not only of how languages evolve, but also of how the semantic networks of native speakers and second language learners develop.

In light of the Motter et al. (2002) and Sigman and Cecchi (2002) studies which indicate that *associative* connections among words are the ones necessary for the formation of small-world networks, it is worth reconsidering the word association task used in my studies. All of the recent studies examining the graph theoretical properties of real-world phenomena (cf. Hayes, 2000b; Watts, 1999) are large-scale ones, including the three studies presented above. Thus it would seem that the 50 vocabulary items in the task used in my studies might have been too few to allow the small-world properties of individual semantic networks to emerge. The main consideration in using 50 items was that a larger vocabulary sample size would have made it impossible for most of the non-native learners to carry out the task. However, the experimental design did prove to be a sensitive one, in that it illuminated the different structural properties of the real-world network sets and the computer-generated random ones. For this reason, it would seem wise to retain the basic paradigm but with modifications. These modifications might include a much larger vocabulary sample size that would enable us to ascertain whether the small-world properties noted above can be identified in the semantic networks generated by individual native speakers and non-native learners.

Before radically expanding the sample size, however, we need to consider expanding the single response format to a two- or three-response format (the associations tend to become tenuous beyond three responses), thus retaining a doable 50-item task. This task could be piloted on native speakers to establish whether this revised format will result in connected networks which could then be analysed to determine whether they are in fact small-world ones. If the sample still proves too small even in a multiple-response format, the number of stimulus words could be slowly increased to determine the point at which they do form complete networks and ones that are clearly identifiable as small-world ones. Once we have determined these thresholds, the task could be repeated with different groups of non-native learners and the differences and/or similarities in the findings compared. An alternative approach might be to use single native-speaker and non-native learner subject studies repeated over a long period of time. The advantage of this method would be that the cumulative results could tap very large lexicons.

In any event, we would definitely need to reconsider the choice of words: the verbs in my studies were taken from the first 1,000-word frequency band to ensure that the non-native learners would be familiar with them. We would still want to use words from this frequency band, but not restrict it to verbs. Other content words, especially polysemous ones that belong to different grammatical categories, e.g., *light, book, house*, would need to be included. These words might generate responses which belong to the different conceptual domains noted by Motter et al. (2002), and thus facilitate the formation of complete networks (cf. Marshall and Cofer, 1963).

An additional research project could also be carried out along the lines of the Motter et al. (2002) study. The cross-references of the thesaurus entries for the content words in the first 1,000-word frequency band could be linked up. The questions to be addressed in such a study would be: (1) Are these words sufficient to form a small-world network? (2) If they are sufficient, at what threshold does this occur? (3) Is there any evidence to support Dorogovtsev and Mendes' (2001) claim of the existence of a kernel lexicon?

Conclusion

The word association studies presented in this chapter show that graph theoretical concepts can provide a solid empirical basis to explore the all too prevalent metaphor of semantic networks. My studies used graph theoretical criteria to determine the structural differences in the associative networks of individual native speakers and non-native learners and between real-world network sets and computer-generated random ones. These criteria may eventually offer a more holistic means of assessing the vocabulary knowledge of different language users than some of the traditional measures do, and provide us with a multi-faceted picture of this knowledge. More work needs to be done to establish norms for these structural differences.

Some of the results of my studies intimated that these networks might be small-world ones, and recent large-scale studies have unequivocally identified the small-world properties of semantic networks in established corpora. Their findings suggest directions for further research to determine whether individual semantic networks are indeed small-world ones. If they are, we would have an empirically based explanatory model which could give us a better understanding of the structure and function of the mental lexicons of different language users.

PART V:
VOCABULARY MEASURES IN USE

11 Assessing vocabulary for the purpose of reading diagnosis

Hilde Hacquebord and Berend Stellingwerf

Introduction

This chapter, and the others in this part, take up the challenge raised by Nation in the opening chapter, to investigate vocabulary in use in order to gain a balanced picture of overall vocabulary knowledge. It focuses upon vocabulary assessment as part of the general language screening that is carried out by many secondary schools in multi-lingual settings. It is argued that the assessment of vocabulary, as a part of reading diagnosis, may shed light on diverse reading problems that both L1 and L2 students encounter at school. It may help answer the question which is often raised by these problems: Are we dealing with a reading problem or a language problem?

In the past decades, the school population in the Netherlands, as in many other European countries, has become more and more linguistically diverse as a consequence of immigration. Currently, some 15% of students in their first year of secondary education are non-native, and some inner city schools welcome more than 80% immigrant students. For most of them, Dutch is the second language, although there is much variety in the use of home and school languages. As a result of the growing diversity of the school population, there is a need for a general assessment of academic language proficiency of students in their first year of secondary school. Many schools carry out such an assessment of the academic language proficiency of their students in order to identify, on their entry to secondary school, students at risk of failing (among them bilingual and dyslexic students). There is a strong focus on reading proficiency, and on the diagnosis of reading problems specific to the school subjects taught in school. The use of vocabulary tests must be understood in that context. The assessment of vocabulary is not for the selection of students but for the purpose of diagnosis.

In this chapter we will present the design of a vocabulary test as part of a broader diagnostic instrument. A prerequisite is that, in this context, vocabulary testing is carried out functionally and adaptively.

It must be related to vocabulary in use, related to a specific context, for example, the secondary school subject areas. Computerised testing is a promising way to achieve adaptability so that students will be assessed according to their actual reading level, and with respect to the reading materials that they encounter in their classes. Vocabulary should be assessed in a flexible way so that it is not only accurate and range-specific, but is also meaningful in the light of reading diagnosis.

Vocabulary and reading

Vocabulary knowledge is strongly related to text comprehension, as word recognition is an important aspect of the reading comprehension process. Although it is not considered a reading skill in itself, word recognition and lexical access skills (potentially two separate abilities for L2 readers) are strongly connected with the result of reading, which is the understanding of meaning (Grabe, 2002). Recent models of reading proficiency (Grabe, 1999; Kintsch, 1998) are based on the theoretical and empirical insight that text comprehension is not simply a process of understanding a collection of individual words and sentences. It is an active process of meaning construction, in which so-called 'top-down processing' interacts with the 'bottom-up processing' of textual elements, including words.

While constructing the meaning of a text, a fluent reader alternates between both processes, reading 'top-down' if possible, and 'bottom-up' if necessary (Stanovich, 1980). However, a top-down reading style requires highly automatised and rapid word recognition and lower-level, micro-processing. For readers with limited word knowledge, or for readers with decoding difficulties, lower-level processing is difficult and they may become stuck even at the beginning of a text. This is especially true when texts become either linguistically or cognitively difficult. The higher-level, macro-processing of the text as a whole may be frustrating to them. Thus, limited word knowledge may cause reading problems. For dyslexic readers, however, it is not vocabulary knowledge *per se*, but a deficit of automatised word recognition which may cause similar reading problems. On the other hand, we know that many of these readers (including dyslexics and those reading in a second language) compensate for their difficulty by using greater higher-level processing strategies (Stanovich, 1980). Their reading comprehension does not appear deficient because they compensate for an inadequate micro-processing by relatively strong macro-processing and the use of top-down reading strategies. It has become apparent that there are several underlying patterns that characterise different types of readers (Hacquebord, 1999) and these are listed in Table 1.

Table 1   Types of readers and scoring patterns on reading and vocabulary

Reading style	Vocabulary	Reading strategies	Reading comprehension
Fluent	+	+	+
Bottom-up	+	−	+/−
Top-down	−	+	+/−
Frozen	−	−	−

Fluent readers alternate between bottom-up and top-down processes, according to their reading needs. In the school context, these reading needs mostly imply full and intensive comprehension of school-subject textbooks for learning purposes. Bottom-up readers can be characterised as students who do not alternate flexibly between the two processes, but mainly hold on to bottom-up processing. These students do not grasp the meaning of the text as a whole. Although they can rely on good word knowledge, and are not hampered in their lower-level processing, they do not process the higher-order levels of text comprehension adequately: they do not grasp the main idea or the 'thread' and the function of a text. If we know that it is not a vocabulary problem, but merely a reading problem, we can offer these students a reading course with an emphasis on top-down reading strategies. Top-down readers are students with the opposite reading profile: they read for meaning and for comprehension of the text as a whole, even if they have difficulties on the word and sentence level. In that case, they compensate by using top-down strategies, such as guessing word meanings from the context, constructing meaning on the basis of their background knowledge, and making use of text cues. For this group of students, it is important to know whether they have a lack of vocabulary knowledge, even if they have an average reading score, because they might encounter greater problems when they have to read more difficult texts in higher classes. If a student in their first year of secondary school compensates for a vocabulary deficit by using macro reading strategies, vocabulary assessment in relation to their reading score is very useful. The student might, for example, be directed to a vocabulary building course specific to the subject areas of their study.

A third group of readers are 'frozen' readers who have many problems and fail to make progress. Their reading scores are low on the whole spectrum. We found that 10–12% of the students on each educational level belong to this group of 'frozen' readers. These 'frozen' readers can be found not only in vocational secondary schools, but in general secondary schools as well, if we give them reading tasks at their own level. 'Frozen' readers might not only have reading problems, but a vocabulary deficit as well. If so, they have two problems, and both reinforce each other. These students are at immediate risk of failing, because they have no motivation to read, and therefore avoid reading tasks. They need a reading course *and* a vocabulary course in a stimulating and motivating learning environment.

Aims and functions of vocabulary assessment in multilingual schools

One of the major issues in the field of second language reading is the question: If reading in L2 is weak, as measured by standardised reading tests, is it a language or a reading problem (Alderson, 1984)? The answer to this question depends on the general language proficiency level of the reader on the one hand, and on the text difficulty on the other. There seems to be a 'linguistic threshold', below which reading problems are due mainly to a language problem, especially a lack of vocabulary knowledge (Alderson, 1984). This appears to be true for L1 readers as well, if they are young or have poor language skills. However, this threshold is relative to the difficulty of the reading text as well as to the language proficiency of the reader (Mushait, 2003).

Therefore, it is important to bear in mind that the actual scoring patterns or the reading style of an individual may be dependent on the reading level. So, vocabulary, reading strategies and reading comprehension should be assessed on the right difficulty level, that is to say, they need to be related to the level of difficulty of the reading task in the context of the school. Further, the assessment of vocabulary should be related to the actual reading level of the individual students. This implies a need for a kind of dynamic assessment (Poehner and Lantolf, 2003), that can be realised by computer adaptive testing (Chalhoub-Deville, 2002).

This raises the question of a design for a computerised vocabulary test that is adaptive to the actual reading level of the individual student, and to the textual difficulty of the school books. In addition to the reading test, we also need to be able to assess the vocabulary in use, that is, the vocabulary of the actual reading tasks. In our case, we need representative samples of the vocabulary that is used in the school context of secondary education in the Netherlands, differentiated according to educational level. There are two separate levels of schooling in the Netherlands: vocational and general education. However, in both levels, the same 14 school subjects are taught in the first three years, with textbooks that are edited for the two educational levels separately. Therefore, a vocabulary source list for the first year of secondary school must represent all school subjects in both levels. Further, the list needs to be extended with vocabulary relevant to the school subjects taught at primary school. The source list we compiled (Hacquebord and Struiving, 1998) is based on a screening of representative textbooks for all school subjects, in addition to the list for primary school subjects compiled by Schrooten and Vermeer (1994).

Table 2 A developmental model for reading/vocabulary difficulty related to level of education

Vocabulary	Level 0 (basic)	Level 1 (easy)	Level 2 (intermediate)	Level 3 (advanced)
Reading level 1 (grade 1, vocational)	✗	(✗)		
Reading level 2 (grade 1, general)	✗	✗	(✗)	
Reading level 3 (grade 2, vocational)	✗	✗	✗	(✗)
Reading level 4 (grade 2, general)	✗	✗	✗	✗

What we have here is a model for vocabulary development related to reading level. It is anchored on a level-based description of the vocabulary used in the different educational levels and grades. This was done on the basis of the sampling of the vocabulary from representative school books for all subjects, which we divided into Levels 0, 1, 2 and 3. This was done on the basis of (a) frequency, (b) source and (c) judgement of teachers (Hacquebord and Struiving, 1998).

The assumption is that students develop their vocabulary on the basis of reading texts that increase in difficulty during the school years (Nation, 1993). As linguistic difficulty of texts can be ascertained on the basis of the percentage of basic vocabulary they contain (Laufer, 1998), advanced text difficulty can also be predicted by the increased percentage of vocabulary of lower frequencies. In our research we have tested this theoretical and hypothetical model empirically.

The construct of a developmental vocabulary scale

The model presented in Table 2 can be applied to the design of our vocabulary test, which we want to be adaptive to the reading level of the learner. The underlying model in Table 2 offers the advantage of level-adaptive vocabulary testing such that a subject enters the test on the vocabulary level that is determined by their own actual reading level. Thus, if a student is on reading level 2, the vocabulary test starts on vocabulary level 2, and so on. Adaptive testing in this way is not only efficient and time saving, but also pedagogically justified because it tests learners in their zone of proximal development (Poehner and Lantolf, 2003). For this reason, we want to construct a developmental scale for the vocabulary test, as we did previously with the reading test (Hacquebord and Andringa, 2000). The scores of the reading test are given in terms of DLE (*Didactisch Leeftijds Equivalent:* Educational Age Equivalent), that is, educational age. The DLE score represents the student's score on a standardised test for reading or vocabulary, in comparison with other students in various grades and educational levels with respect to the reading or vocabulary level that is required in that grade and educational level. Some subjects' scores may correlate with scores of younger subjects, others with subjects who are older. For example, a student is 12 years and five months old, and has an educational age (as measured by one test) of 11 years. Alternatively, a 12-year-old's educational age may be 13 years and six months (Kagan and Gall, 1998). The DLE model has been introduced widely in primary schools in the Netherlands and we adopted it for the secondary schools, on the basis of extrapolation and empirical research that we present below. The concept of DLE implies that there is a 'normal' growth of 10 points in each school year (i.e. 10 months of education in one school year). Starting at the age of 6, school year 1, after six years of education, the 'normal' child has an educational 'age' of 60 by the end of primary school (grade 8). So, on starting secondary school, if the students are measured in the first month, we can assume an average educational age of 61. However, of course there is a lot of individual variation, as students are streamed into the two different educational levels even at the age of 12. There is also a lot of variation within the streams. We stipulated the next model (Table 3).

The vocabulary test that we developed is scaled into this DLE

Table 3 Educational age (DLE) and reading/vocabulary levels related to the levels of education

	DLEs	Reading level	Vocabulary level	Text difficulty
Primary school, grade 8	51–60	1	1	1
Grade 1, vocational	51–60	1	1	1
Grade 1, general	61–70	2	2	2
Grade 2, vocational	61–70	2	2	2
Grade 2, general	71–80	3	3	3
Grade 3, vocational	71–80	3	3	3
Grade 3, general	81–90			

model, which is uni-dimensional by nature. It is based on the growing difficulty of vocabulary specific to the different school subjects, which implies that more low-frequency vocabulary is used. The underlying idea of building a test around word frequency is that more knowledge of less frequent words reflects a larger vocabulary size. Wesche and Parikbakht (1996) mention a problem with this method of testing: the lack of evidence for a clear link between the frequency of a word in a given corpus and the likelihood of its being known by an individual. This question has been tackled in Chapter 2 of this volume and although there is no one-to-one relationship between word frequency and word knowledge, especially in the later stages of L2 acquisition, it does appear possible to distinguish levels of difficulty based on the frequency of vocabulary. The advantages of a developmental model have been mentioned already; we will now see if it holds empirically.

Empirical design of the test

Research questions

The first question is part of the construction process of the vocabulary test, which should be based on clearly distinctive difficulty levels, related to the use of texts in the actual school subjects. This question is aimed at modelling the test into the theoretically presumed model:

1 Do the vocabulary and reading scores of students of different educational levels fit into the model presented in Table 2?

The second question has to do with the rationale behind the whole project we are involved in, to test the value of a vocabulary test in addition to a reading test with respect to reading diagnosis:

> 2 Is there evidence for the reader typology presented in Table 1, as related to the scores on reading and vocabulary?

Subjects and sample

As many as 2,718 students in their first year of secondary school, from 19 schools spread across the Netherlands, made up our sample. The sample can be considered as representative for the Dutch school population with respect to school type, geographical spread, urbanisation and denomination (the percentages of public vs private, and Roman Catholic, Protestant and other religion-based schools), as well as with respect to the percentage of second language students (12.8%), the percentage of diagnosed dyslexics (3.2%) and educational level (low: 39%, middle: 21%, high: 40%). All subjects have been tested on reading comprehension and reading strategies using the standardised *Elektronische Tekstbegriptoets voor de Brugklas*, and on vocabulary by the test we are reporting on here.

The reading test

The reading test that was administered is the *Elektronische Tekstbegriptoets voor de Brugklas* (see Hacquebord and Andringa, 2000). It was constructed on the basis of a discourse analysis of propositions as proposed by van Dijk and Kintsch (1983), who take the text as a starting point for information processing by a reader. The computerised test yields DLE scores, and it is adaptive to reading performance. Thus, each student is tested on their own level, and the reading texts are more or less representative of their actual educational level. The reading test has been standardised and is reliable in all subsets of texts (Cronbach's alphas between 0.81 and 0.86) (Hacquebord, 1999).

The reading strategy test

The reading strategies are measured by a subtest of the reading test, the so-called macro reading test, which consists of a subset of 'macro items' concerning the 'macro level' of the texts. These macro items measure the overall text structure, including the main theme and function of the text. Students who are able to comprehend the macro items will use or apply top-down reading strategies. As a subtest the strategy test is less reliable than the reading test as a whole (Cronbach's alpha = 0.60), and significantly correlated to this test (r = 0.44).

The vocabulary test under construction

The vocabulary test, *Diawoord*, consists of 50 multiple-choice items in which the vocabulary is presented in the context of short sentences. The learner has to choose the correct alternative (out of three or four alternatives) to the underlined word. Care was taken to phrase these synonyms or description in easy language. The items appear one by one on a computer screen and an example of the screen display is given in Figure 1.

---

2 De leeringen <u>dienen</u> allen aanwezig te zijn.

Kies uit een van de onderstaande antwoorden:

    A. moeten

    B. mogen

    C. willen

Translated item:

2 The pupils <u>are required to</u> be there.

Select one from the answers below:

    a. have to

    b. may

    c. want to

Figure 1 Screen display of *Diawoord* test

The vocabulary was taken from a source list based on a screening of a representative selection of school textbooks for the first year of secondary school (Hacquebord and Struiving, 1998 (extended in 2003)). Four different levels of vocabulary difficulty were distinguished on which the adaptive nature of the test is based. Depending on the test-taker's performance on the first 25 items, the test will offer a lower or higher level of vocabulary items for further testing.

The scaling in DLEs was carried out by applying the general model (see Table 3) on the actual found frequencies of three subsets between two sub-samples (lower- and higher-level subjects). The result is an acceptable spread of scores slightly skewed to the right, which implies that the test should be extended with more difficult items. The construction of the difficulty levels (see research question 1 on p. 213) was accomplished in the following way: after the deletion of psychometrically weak items the remaining items were divided over the three difficulty levels, according to the percentages we found for the different groups of subjects. The results are shown in Table 4.

Table 4   Mean vocabulary percentage scores for reading and vocabulary levels

	Vocabulary level 1	Vocabulary level 2	Vocabulary level 3
Reading level 1	**86**	56	37
Reading level 2	93	**72**	53
Reading level 3	96	83	**67**

The found spread of mean percentage scores is acceptable, and fits well enough the postulated model in Table 2. The percentages in bold can be considered as the 'zone of proximal development', and point to the vocabulary levels to which the test should be adaptive. The skew that we found in the DLE spread is visible again in Table 4: the vocabulary level for Reading level 1 seems a little easy, whereas the vocabulary level for Reading level 3 seems to be difficult. Analysis of variance showed a significant difference between vocabulary levels and reading levels: between reading levels (main effect): F (2, 2074) = 3406, $p < .05$; between vocabulary levels (repeated measures) 1 and 2: F (2, 93) = 4799, $p < .05$, between vocabulary levels 2 and 3: F (2, 65) = 881, $p < .05$.

Results with respect to research question 2

Is there evidence for the reader typology presented in Table 1, as related to the scores on reading and vocabulary? In order to address this question we calculated the percentage of students in each cell for specific vocabulary and reading comprehension profiles on the one hand, and on the other the percentage of students with specific vocabulary and reading strategy profiles (Tables 5 and 6).

In Table 5 we see the percentage of students in all hypothesised groups. The results show that a small majority of students have a fluent reading style. About 23% of the students have problems with both vocabulary and reading comprehension. The groups of bottom-

Table 5   Distribution of students by reading style calculated using vocabulary and reading comprehension scores

Reading style	Vocabulary	Reading comprehension	Students (%)
Fluent	+	+	57.4
Bottom-up	+	−	10.0
Top-down	−	+	9.4
Frozen	−	−	23.3

Table 6   Distribution of students by reading style calculated using vocabulary and reading strategy scores

Reading style	Vocabulary	Reading strategy	Students (%)
Fluent	+	+	52.2
Bottom-up	+	−	18.3
Top-down	−	+	15.0
Frozen	−	−	14.5

up and top-down readers each consist of, respectively, 10% and 9.4% of the students, which indicates the relevance of these categories of readers with specific scoring profiles in reading and vocabulary.

In Table 6 the same pattern of percentages of the reading groups emerges with respect to vocabulary and reading strategy, using the macro reading sub-test scores. Again, the majority of students (52.2%) have a fluent reading style, while 14.5% of the students have problems with both vocabulary and reading strategy. The groups of bottom-up (18.3%) and top-down readers (15%) are clearly manifest in this analysis, which once more indicates the relevance of these categories of readers with specific scoring profiles.

Additionally, the correlations between reading strategy and reading comprehension scores were calculated, as is shown in Table 7. The overall vocabulary scores correlate with the overall reading scores: $r = 0.716$, indicating an overall correspondence between reading scores and vocabulary.

As shown in Table 7, the correlations between reading comprehension and reading strategy are moderate for the fluent and the frozen readers. For the bottom-up and the top-down readers statistically significant correlations are absent. The same pattern can be found for the correlations between vocabulary and reading strategy, although the correlations are weaker. In both cases, the absence of a significant correlation with the vocabulary scores is meaningful in the light of

Table 7   Correlations between reading comprehension and vocabulary
scores, and between reading strategy and vocabulary scores,
divided by reading-style group

Reading style	Reading comprehension	Reading strategy
Fluent	.525**	.264**
Bottom-up	.012	.032
Top-down	.129	.105
Frozen	.472**	.232**

** $p < .01$

our hypothesised typology. Top-down readers have limited vocabulary, but reasonable reading comprehension as a result of effective
reading strategies; the latter two compensate for the former. In
contrast to the style of the top-down reader, the bottom-up reader
has difficulties with reading strategies for comprehension of the text,
despite having a good vocabulary. Thus, for both reader types an
absence of correlation between vocabulary and reading comprehension and reading strategy, was to be expected.

Summary and discussion

The results indicate that the postulated reader typologies are valid.
We found significantly different groups of readers. This implies that a
vocabulary test is a potentially useful addition to a reading comprehension test for the purposes of a diagnosis of reading strategies.
First we calculated frequency tables for the different subgroups
(Fluent, Bottom-up, Top-down and Frozen). The results displayed in
Tables 5 and 6 indicate that the assumption of subgroups holds
empirically. Moreover, the bottom-up top-down readers are characterised by atypical correlations between vocabulary and reading
comprehension on the one hand and vocabulary and reading strategy
on the other.

Our vocabulary levels model appears to be valid; we found
significantly different levels of difficulty of words. These last findings
show that adaptive testing is possible. Students can be offered a
subset of the test depending on the level of school entrance (school
type). Adaptive testing of vocabulary could be realised by adding
items from increasingly difficult levels after the first subset of test
items have been successfully completed, and students who perform
poorly can be re-tested on items that are less difficult. This method
of adaptive testing is useful for the diagnostic screening of large

heterogeneous groups of students, it is fair to the individual student, and it is indicative of a student's proximal developmental stage. However, a major concern in constructing the test is the reported ceiling effect. In order to overcome this problem more different items will be added and some other items will be removed.

12 The best of both worlds?

Combined methodological approaches to the assessment of vocabulary in oral proficiency interviews

Nuria Lorenzo-Dus

Introduction

In this chapter I discuss how different research methodologies can inform the design and validation of vocabulary assessment in oral proficiency interviews. The rationale is twofold. Firstly, despite the profuse literature on vocabulary testing, the assessment of spoken vocabulary is under-researched and a number of key questions thus remain unanswered, such as: What role do the various dimensions of vocabulary knowledge play in speaking tests contexts? What is the relationship between candidate production of different types of vocabulary (for example, (in)frequent words and colloquialisms) and examiner ratings for vocabulary? Secondly, in oral proficiency interviews vocabulary is assessed as part of a larger construct, namely the ability of candidates to interact with an examiner. Consequently, the validity of this assessment is affected by factors that go beyond candidates' lexical output *per se*. As this chapter will show, these factors can be best ascertained and understood by applying different research methodologies to their study.

Oral proficiency interviews vary considerably. One manifestation of this is whether the roles of interlocutor and rater are performed by the same person or by two different people. For simplification, this chapter uses the term examiner throughout, except when it is important for the discussion to make a distinction between the two roles.

Although the chapter's emphasis is mainly methodological, I analyse illustrative extracts and report findings from empirical work on the assessment of spoken vocabulary. This work draws extensively on a corpus of oral proficiency interviews of Spanish as a second language (L2) collected over a four-year period (2000–2004).

Assessing vocabulary in oral proficiency interviews: to count or not to count?

A quick review of the leading journal *Language Testing* over the past 30 years or so suffices to show that quantitative methodologies have been the predominant framework of analysis in the field of L2 assessment. A similar emphasis is found within the sub-discipline of *oral proficiency assessment*, where an extensive body of quantitative-based research has accumulated over time. This has ranged from studies on the construct validity of L2 speaking tests (e.g. Bachman and Palmer, 1981, 1982; Reed, 1992) to comparisons among different testing methods (e.g. Douglas and Selinker, 1992; Stansfield and Kenyon, 1992). One study worth particular mention here is McNamara and Lumley (1997), as it addresses an important but under-researched aspect of validity in oral proficiency assessment: the relationship between examiner performance and candidate ratings. These authors used multifaceted Rasch measurement to examine the impact on test scores of rater perceptions of audibility of tapes and of interlocutors' ability both to carry out competently their role in the role-play task and to establish rapport with candidates. With regard to the latter two, McNamara and Lumley found that raters compensated for what they regarded as 'a relative incompetence of interlocutors' (1997: 150) and that they (the raters) favoured candidates whose interlocutors were perceived to achieve poor rapport during the examinations.

Regarding the assessment of vocabulary in oral proficiency interviews, the limited number of published studies on this topic have mainly applied quantitative methodologies. In two related studies, for example, Richards and Malvern (2000) and Malvern and Richards (2002) investigated the relationship between examiner and candidate's performance using a measure of lexical diversity. Their analyses revealed that examiners accommodated their vocabulary primarily to the perceived lexical ability of the class that they were examining (either a low-level or a high-level class) and only less often to the perceived lexical ability of individual candidates.

Nonetheless, qualitative methodological approaches to the assessment of oral proficiency have been undertaken and found to be useful. Grotjahn (1986), for instance, argued that statistical analysis was not conducive to gaining a *full* understanding of the construct validity of L2 speaking tests. Douglas and Selinker (1992), for their part, made a case for the use of rhetorical and grammatical interlanguage analysis, a qualitative methodology, to disambiguate subjective gross ratings on oral language tests. Lazaraton (1992, 1995,

1996, 2000) has successfully applied conversation analysis to the validation of L2 speaking tests. Two relatively recent publications (Lazaraton, 2002; Young and He, 1998) concentrate exclusively on the role of qualitative methods in the field of L2 speaking testing. Lazaraton (2002: 2) describes the introduction of qualitative research methodologies as 'the most important development in language testing over the last ten or so years.' And in the preface to Young and He's (1998) edited collection, Celce-Murcia (1998: ix) reminds readers that 'until very recently studies of LPIs (language proficiency interviews) ignored the *central validity issue of oral proficiency assessment* namely, the ways in which the LPI is accomplished *through discourse*' (my emphasis).

The nature of variation in examiner performance is one of the areas of enquiry to which qualitative methods have been applied. Pioneering work on examiner accommodation strategies by Ross (1992) and Berwick and Ross (1996) paved the way for the systematic investigation of the interdependence of examiner and candidate performance. Brown (2003) provides a particularly good example of how this work has evolved into detailed microanalysis of the talk-in-interaction of examiners and candidates in speaking tests. Brown examined two interviews involving the same candidate with two different interlocutors. The interlocutors had been judged to differ considerably in their 'difficulty', that is, the raters had graded them as more or less difficult to interact with. Brown's turn-by-turn analysis of the interviews, coupled with data obtained from retrospective rater verbal protocols, revealed that the raters were in general more positive about the candidate's performance when she was interviewed by the interlocutor with a 'teacherly' style than when she was interviewed by the interlocutor with a 'casual' style. The teacherly style was characterised by abundant support-yielding strategies of accommodation, while the casual style resembled more closely the norms of (English) first language (L1) conversational strategies and thus included, among other features, more minimal responses, in-explicit questions and unnatural topic shifts.

Notwithstanding these studies, research on the assessment of spoken vocabulary remains both limited and predominantly quanti-tatively based. The way forward, though, is not to continue to use *either* quantitative *or* qualitative measures in the assessment of vocabulary and spoken language performance. Rather, a truly inte-grated approach seems likely to be insightful. The remainder of this chapter discusses why this is the case, providing illustrative examples of the kind of work that such a methodological approach may help to achieve.

Assessing vocabulary in oral proficiency interviews: to count *and* not to count

Keeping separate the work on oral proficiency assessment conducted via quantitative and qualitative methodologies runs the risk of reinforcing the widespread and seldom challenged assumption that it is possible to establish a strict separation between the two methodologies. This, however, is not the case. For one, the quantitative versus qualitative distinction is an artificial one at heart. It is based on the assumption that quantification is essentially objective, whereas qualitative work is mainly driven by a researcher's subjectivity. Yet quantitative research includes qualitative judgements, such as which variables will be selected for investigation and how to interpret the results. And, while there is no consensus on actual universal or permanent criteria for judging qualitative research, it would be wrong to dismiss the existing body of this research on language testing as the result of researchers' personal views. It is work, after all, that follows well-established and validated methods in other disciplines, such as those of interactional sociolinguistics on intercultural communication, and of conversation analysis on workplace communication. Differences between quantitative and qualitative methodologies are matters of degree rather than of nature.

Another reason why it is not advisable to continue to treat quantitative and qualitative methodologies as completely separate is in itself a validity-ridden one. Nation positively appraises, in Chapter 1 of this volume, research that uses multiple measures to investigate issues such as vocabulary growth (Waring and Takaki, 2003), depth of vocabulary (Webb, 2002) and vocabulary learning effects in retelling tasks (Joe, 1998). If the area of investigation is the *validity* of language testing, it is even more imperative that evidence be drawn from more than one measure and/or method. As Davidson (2000: 616) puts it:

> The practice of language testing should be monitored and modified such that determining the world from statistical evidence is balanced by knowledge and perspectives from other world views. From time to time a new statistical procedure will emerge that passes the test of epistemological flexibility. Even still, at the end of the day, it is probably best never to rely on a single tool or even a single toolbox alone.

Research that draws upon the strengths of quantitative and qualitative methodologies can contribute significantly to the design, description and validation of L2 speaking tests. An illustration of this might be Koike's (1998) comparative study of the American Council on the Teaching of Foreign Languages (ACTFL) oral proficiency interview (OPI) for Spanish and of the corresponding simulated oral proficiency interview (SOPI). In the OPI, candidates perform the tasks and functions of the examination via a series of interactive exchanges with the examiner. In the SOPI candidates generate mono-logic discourse for the same tasks and functions. In light of this, and despite prior quantitative-based evidence of the concurrent validity of both tests (Stansfield and Kenyon, 1992), Koike sets out to investigate the features of the discourse produced in the SOPI and the OPI conditions by the same candidates. Data obtained from the actual tests were coded according to a set of management strategies used by candidates, such as self-corrections, fillers, code switching, propositions and speech acts. These data were subsequently analysed via descriptive statistics and t-tests. In line with previous quantitative research, the results of Koike's analysis failed to show significant variation between the OPI and the SOPI. However, when a selection of the corpus was also examined using the methods of discourse analysis, this qualitative analysis did show *some* important areas of variation between the two tests. For example, the SOPI candidates produced 'better organized talk' than the OPI candidates did, although the SOPI candidates' talk was also 'more formal and some-what more awkward' than that of the OPI candidates (1998: 92). Based on these results, Koike (1998: 93) concluded that the mono-logic and interactive discourse generated by the SOPI and the OPI tests, respectively, were both different in some ways and useful in assessing candidates' communicative competence.

Lorenzo-Dus and Meara (2004) provide another example of combined methodologies being applied to research into the assess-ment of spoken *vocabulary*. Specifically, they conducted statistical analysis of the lexical performance of candidates and examiners during a role-play task set as part of an intermediate-level Spanish L2 speaking examination. Although no ratings for vocabulary were made available for analysis purposes, the study nevertheless indicated clearly the added value of a two-pronged methodological approach. For instance, quantitative analysis revealed that examiners contri-buted over 50% of the word types generated in the role-plays. This meant that, upon providing their assessment of the candidates' lexical output, these examiners were drawing upon a rather limited amount of data. It also suggested that candidates were not contri-buting as many word types as might be expected. Subsequent qualitative analysis, involving detailed examination of the talk gener-ated by candidates and examiners in the role-plays, revealed further interesting patterns and raised key questions about task design and test variables. Firstly, a role analysis revealed that the actual distribution of interactional parts in this particular examination task was not conducive to candidates generating a larger amount of vocabulary than their examiners. Thus, limited vocabulary production was not necessarily a reflection of candidate ability alone but also of structural constraints imposed by task design. Secondly, a discourse analysis revealed that contextualisation of the task during the opening stage of the role-plays differed across examiners and that this was an important variable in candidate performance. Candidates generally displayed better their interactional competence, including their lexical competence, where openings were fully contextualised by reminding participants of their part and aims in the task. Where opening turns included little or no contextualisation, there often resulted awkward exchanges, long pauses and lower levels of vocabulary being subsequently displayed by the candidates.

Assessing spoken vocabulary: what evidence can different methodologies provide?

Under the previous heading, I have indicated advantages of applying combined methodologies to the validation of the assessment of oral proficiency, including vocabulary. In what follows, I draw extensively on Lorenzo-Dus and Meara (2005) to illustrate these with reference to two specific concerns in the assessment of spoken vocabulary: (1) the relationship between candidate vocabulary output and examiner ratings for vocabulary; and (2) the relationship between examiner accommodation and both candidate vocabulary output and examiner ratings for vocabulary.

The relationship between candidate vocabulary output and examiner ratings for vocabulary

The assessment of vocabulary in oral proficiency interviews rests on the assumption that, regardless of the structure and context of the interview, there should be a relationship between the lexical output of the candidates and the ratings for vocabulary that examiners award to them. This relationship can be effectively investigated by using quantitative measures once, that is, the less easy question of how to measure lexical output has been answered. In Lorenzo-Dus and Meara (2005) both word types and lexical diversity were used to measure the lexical output of 30 candidates who took a pre-university Spanish L2 speaking test. Full details about the examinations have not been included here as it is the methodological underpinnings of the study, rather than its findings, that this chapter is concerned with. For full details of the findings of the study see Lorenzo-Dus and Meara (2005). The data were subjected to an analysis of variance, which showed an effect for vocabulary ratings for the word type measure (F [3, 25] = 10.55 p < .001) but not for the lexical diversity measure (F [3, 25] = 1.99 p = .14). It was therefore concluded that the examiner in this study found it more difficult to rate lexical diversity than other constructs of vocabulary in use. Specifically, the results showed that this examiner was sensitive to the overall size of the vocabulary displayed in the examinations, that is, to the number of different words (word types) generated by the candidates.

The number of word types generated by candidates was, nonetheless, not the only factor that affected the examiner's ratings. Statistical analysis of the candidates' lexical output also revealed that the two high scoring groups in the corpus (candidates who scored ≥ 7 out of 10, n = 18) were considerably less homogenous than the two low scoring groups (those with a rating for vocabulary < 7, n = 12). In fact, 33.3% of the candidates in the high-scoring groups generated a higher number of word types than might be expected given their ratings for vocabulary. In the low-scoring groups, only 8.3% of the candidates generated a higher number of word types than may be expected from their ratings for vocabulary. In a recent study of vocabulary in IELTS speaking tests administered in New Zealand, Read and Nation (2004) also report a higher level of intra-variation in high-scoring groups than in low-scoring groups. Something other than word types must therefore have had an important effect upon vocabulary ratings at the high-level end of the rating continuum, but what was it?

Given that previous research in comparable settings (cf. Malvern and Richards, 2000; 2002) suggests examiner sensitivity to low-frequency vocabulary in rating candidates' performance, the candidates' lexical output was analysed for frequency too. On account of the well-known problems of analysing specific corpora according to general frequency lists (Nation, Chapter 1, this volume), however, vocabulary items were defined as infrequent, or rather as *rare*, when they displayed a maximum frequency of three occurrences in the reference corpus regardless of their frequency status in general frequency lists for Spanish (Alameda and Cuetos, 1996). Specially designed computer software was used to identify and classify these items (Meara, 2003). The analysis showed that rare words were both low-frequency words in the Spanish language, such as *consejero* ('advisor', frequency = 1), *and* high-frequency words in Spanish (words within the first 1,000-word frequency band) such as *conocimientos* ('knowledge', frequency = 402) and *precisamente* ('precisely', frequency = 348). The analysis also showed that the majority of these rare words occurred in the talk generated by the high-scoring candidates. Furthermore, the high-scoring candidates with fewer word types than might be expected given their rating for vocabulary were those with the highest number of rare words per examination (approximately double that of the rest of the candidates). Rareness of vocabulary proved to have a significant effect, alongside size of vocabulary, for ratings in this corpus.

Further insights into the candidates' lexical output were gained through a discourse analysis of the entire corpus. From this analysis, it became clear that one factor had particular bearing upon the relationship between vocabulary size and rareness, on the one hand, and ratings for vocabulary, on the other: the perceived naturalness of candidates' vocabulary. The concept of naturalness is, of course, complex in the context of oral proficiency interviews, in particular, low- and intermediate-level ones where candidates often render a performance of skills and knowledge that they have memorised and practised beforehand. In fact, teachers routinely prepare candidates for oral proficiency interviews by practising possible answers to a number of pre-set topics that are made publicly available by the various examination bodies. In this case, pre-set topics fell into three broad thematic categories: the candidates' hobbies, plans for the future and current studies. The examiner's specific wording of questions relating to these pre-set topics varied only slightly from candidate to candidate, for instance: *¿Qué estudias este año en el colegio?* ('What are you studying in school this year?') and *¿Qué asignaturas estudias este año?* ('What subjects are you studying this year?') To allow for production of memorised talk, I use the term 'naturalness' to designate stretches of interaction during these speaking tests where a number of indicators strongly suggested that the candidates were no longer following a pre-memorised script. One such strong indicator was the position of the candidate turn, and of rare vocabulary therein, within the examination. Candidate contributions occurring three or four turns after 'expected questions' were no longer thematically connected in any direct way to the pre-set topics. Using the current studies topic, for example, an initial answer may have included the candidate explaining that he/she studied a foreign language such as Welsh or Catalan. After three candidate–examiner turns, the topic of the conversation may have moved on to the right of minority-language speakers to be schooled through the medium of these languages. Another, concomitant, indicator of naturalness in the corpus was a higher number of self-corrections, hesitations and errors (mainly noun–verb or noun–adjective agreement) in these later candidate turns than in follow-up turns to expected questions.

By looking qualitatively at the position of rare vocabulary in the overall turn structure of the interviews, a pattern could be identified whereby the candidates in the high-scoring bands produced more rare words within stretches of spontaneous talk than their low-scoring band counterparts. In more than half of the cases, *all* the rare words actually occurred in naturally occurring stretches of talk. As for the low-scoring candidates, not only did they generate less rare vocabulary overall, but the rare words in their speech tended to occur in follow-up turns to expected questions. Thus, while the quantitative analysis of the candidates' lexical output revealed that the number of different words that they used and the 'rareness' of these words affected examiner ratings, the qualitative analysis provided insights into the processes whereby these factors may have become salient for the examiner.

The relationship between examiner accommodation, ratings for vocabulary and candidate lexical output

I started this chapter by stating that one main reason why the assessment of vocabulary in oral proficiency interviews merits considerably closer attention than it has received hitherto, is that it is part of candidates' ability to interact with an examiner. This ability, or 'interactional competence' (Kramsch, 1986) is co-constructed by candidate *and* examiner in the here-and-now of the oral proficiency interview. Candidates' interactional competence, including their lexical competence, is to varying degrees shaped by that of examiners. Conversely, examiners often fine-tune their talk, including their vocabulary, to that of the candidates. Improving our understanding of the product and the process of assessing vocabulary in oral proficiency interviews thus requires consideration of the performance of both candidates and examiners. *How* do they react to one another's contributions? And what are the actual effects of this on ratings?

An obvious line of enquiry here is that of examiner accommodation, where past research has already established both variation according to candidate level (e.g. Ross, 1992; Cafarella, 1994; Young, 1995; Berwick and Ross, 1996; Lazaraton, 1996) and, in general terms, the impact of such accommodation on assessment outcomes (e.g. McNamara and Lumley, 1997; O'Loughlin, 2000 and Brown, 2003). In addition to the quantitative and qualitative analysis of candidates' vocabulary reported above, in Lorenzo-Dus and Meara (2005) the examiner's lexical output and use of accommodation strategies were also statistically analysed. Of these two factors, only accommodation strategies had an overall significant effects for ratings (F [3, 25] = 10.578 $p < .001$).

The picture that emerged, therefore, from the quantitative analyses of examiner *and* candidate performance was one of interdependence. The more accommodation strategies used by the examiner, the lower the ratings for vocabulary. Conversely, the fewer accommodation strategies used, the higher the ratings for vocabulary. This suggests that examiner accommodation was not as subconscious as it may have been perceived to be in the past. As far as the examiner in this study was concerned, variation in terms of accommodation strategies was factored into ratings for vocabulary.

It order to ascertain the actual ways in which examiner accommodation took place in these interviews – a key factor in determining the impact on candidates' lexical output and, hence, ratings – a discourse analysis of the corpus was undertaken. This entailed close examination of the interactional function that each of the examiner accommodation strategies fulfilled, their antecedent triggers and the interactional context in which they were delivered. Let us consider, for instance, the examiner's use of Confirmation Questions (CQs), which I have selected here for two reasons. Firstly, CQs were one of the few accommodation strategies which, when independently analysed, failed to show a significant effect for ratings (F [3, 25] = 1.365 $p = .276$). The two other strategies with a direct impact upon vocabulary were Supply or Complete Vocabulary and Simplify Statement or Question. Both showed a significant effect for ratings. Secondly, CQs were one of the three strategies that showed a demonstrable impact upon candidates' vocabulary, as can be seen in Extract 1. A key to transcription conventions is given in Appendix 4.

CQs like the one in Extract 1 tended to result in candidate follow-up turns that included one or more of the vocabulary items used in the CQ. On this occasion, the candidate produced two nouns (*uvas* and *reyes*) as examples of what the examiner interpreted in the CQ (arrowed in the extract) as two Spanish traditions associated with the Christmas festive season. One refers to the New Year's Eve tradition of eating twelve grapes at midnight to bring good luck during the twelve months of the New Year. The other is a reference to the Three Wise Men, rather than Santa Claus, bringing gifts for Spanish children on January 6. The candidate had not been able to produce the word *tradiciones* before the examiner's CQ. Thereafter, she was able to do so.

Extract 1

E	*te gusta la Navidad en España?*	do you like Christmas in Spain?
C	*sí claro (.) la Navidad es bien (.)*	yes of course (.) Christmas is nice
	er España (.) los reyes (.) las uvas er	(.) er Spain (.) the wise men (.)
	(.) sí (.) cosas diferentes en España	the grapes er (.) yes (.) different
		things in Spain
E→	*muy bien (.) la Navidad en España*	good (.) there are many traditions
	tiene muchas tradiciones (.) verdad?	in Spain at Christmas (.) aren't
		there?
C	*ah sí (.) tradiciones (.) me gustan*	ah yes (.) traditions (.) I like them
	en España	in Spain

Examining CQs across the corpus, it became apparent that they performed two different interactional functions. They were used either as pre-closing/closing turns within particular topics in the examinations or as checks on comprehension. Crucially for this discussion, the analysis revealed that most of the CQs in the examiner's interaction with the high-scoring candidates (75% of the total) fulfilled the closing or pre-closing turn function. These CQs therefore aided the examiner's own discourse, rather than that of the candidate. Extract 2 provides an example of the pre-closing topic function of CQs.

Extract 2

01	E	*y cuando tienes tiempo li[bre*	and in your free ti[me
02	C	*[sí*	[yes
03	E	*qué te gusta hacer?*	what do you like doing?
04	C	*er los sábados ir al centro (.)*	er on Saturdays (I like to) go to
05		*a las tiendas er ropa cuando*	the town centre (.) shopping er
06		*tengo dinero*	clothes when I have money
07	E	*gastas mucho dinero en ropa?*	do you spend a lot on clothes?
08	C	*no (.) porque compro en*	no (.) because I shop during the
		rebajas =	sales =
09	E	*= aha*	= aha
10	C	*porque me gusta las rebajas (risa)*	because I like the sales (laughs)
11	E	*no te gustan las marcas? (risa;*	you don't like the brand names?
12		*entonación muestra sorpresa)*	(laughs; intonation indicates
			surprise)
13	C	*no (risa)*	no (laughs)
14	E→	*eres una chica muy sensata*	you're a very sensible girl then
15		*entonces[no?*	[aren't you?
16	C	*[sí (risa) sensata*	[yes (laughs) sensible
17	E	*muy bien (risa) muy sensata (.)*	very good (laughs) very sensible
18		*vamos ahora a pasar a otro tema*	(.) let's now move on to another
			topic

In Extract 2, the examiner did not use the CQ in lines 14–15 to confirm that the candidate was a sensible teenager. Instead, the examiner used it to create a transition turn (a pre-closing sequence) between the previous topic (pastimes) and the next one in the examination. The whole exchange was conducted in a relaxed way, as demonstrated by the participant's paralanguage (lines 10–12, 13, 16 and 17) and obvious ease in expressing their views. It is therefore very unlikely that CQs as (pre)closing turns such as the one in this extract affected negatively the assessment of this candidate's vocabulary output.

The situation was, however, different with CQs used as checks on comprehension. This was the predominant function of CQs in the examinations with low-scoring candidates (68% of the total number of CQs). Consider Extract 3:

Extract 3

01	E	*te gusta salir al cine con tus*	do you like to go to the cinema
02		*amigos?*	with your friends?
03	C	*sí (.) me gusto mucho (risa)*	yes (.) I like myself [it] a lot
			(laughs)
04	E	*sí? por qué ?*	really? why is that?
05	C	(3.0)	(3.0)
06	E	*te gusta más ver películas en el*	do you prefer watching films in
07		*cine?*	the cinema?
08	C	*erm no =*	erm no =
09	E	*= no? por qué te gusta ir al cine*	= you don't? why do you like
10		*entonces? puedes ver la tele*	going to the cinema then? you
			can watch TV
11	C	*°porque erm (.) gust- erm (4.0)*	°because erm (.) lik- erm (4.0) I
12		*gusto me er amigos divierte-?°*	like myself (.) er friends [you]
			have fun-?°
13	E→	*aha (.) muy bien (.) te gusta*	aha (.) good (.) you like to have
14		*divertirte con tus amigos verdad?*	fun with your friends right?
15	C	*sí (.) divertirte con amigos*	yes (.) [you] have fun with
			friends

In Extract 3, the examiner's CQ in lines 13–14 served to put together the pieces of information that the candidate had provided in the previous turn (lines 11–12). The CQ was used here to obtain confirmation that the examiner had understood the candidate's argument that he liked to go to the cinema a lot (line 03) but that he did not prefer going to the cinema to watching films on television (lines 06–10). The candidate was clearly struggling to answer the examiner's questions, as evident in the long pauses (lines 05, 11), hesitations (lines 08, 11–12), markedly quiet delivery (lines 11–12), and grammatical errors and reformulations when conjugating the verb *gustar* (lines 11–12). It was the combination of these features that most likely led the examiner to afford the candidate lexical support in the form of a CQ (lines 13–14).

Put together, the various results discussed above point towards examiner consistency in the practice of assessing vocabulary, with use of accommodation strategies revealing statistically significant effects for vocabulary ratings across the corpus. This may be seen by some as a threat to the validity of such assessment since examiners' factoring of their own performance is largely subjective. I am more inclined to see it as reflecting what is, for all intents and purposes, a natural feature of interaction and to call for further research on the precise ways in which various types of accommodation impact upon ratings. This further research, as the discussion above shows, needs to encompass both quantitative and qualitative methods. The statistical analysis of accommodation strategies in the study by Lorenzo-Dus and Meara (2005) was essential to establishing whether or not their use had an impact on ratings for vocabulary. It was also instrumental in identifying which individual accommodation strategies were used consistently across scoring bands, as well as their relative frequency of use. The qualitative analysis, for its part, provided valuable insights into the rationale behind the use of specific accommodation strategies. Taking the case of CQs as an example, the discourse analysis revealed that, while these CQs were used with a similar frequency across scoring bands (hence the lack of effect for ratings), there were clear and important differences regarding the functions that they were performing and the consequent potential impact on examiner ratings for vocabulary.

Conclusion

Two are not always better than one. Research into the assessment of vocabulary and oral proficiency has progressed considerably over the past years using *either* quantitative *or* qualitative methodologies. One is also often simpler than two, a fact that has particular bearing on contemporary research given its nature and the structures within which it is, at times, developed. Use of a single methodological approach is a natural product of specialisation and is encouraged by a research environment that, in its 'publish or perish' overtones, militates against taking the extended time that is almost inevitably required to combine methodologies. Moreover, as Koike's (1998) study illustrated, where qualitative results seemingly contradict those of previous quantitative analyses, combining methodologies can complicate as well as elucidate.

Yet however understandable, and often justifiable, it may be to use a single methodological approach to the assessment of vocabulary in oral proficiency examinations, the question remains whether this is sufficient. This chapter suggests that it is not always so. Qualitative methodologies, specifically discourse analytic ones, can offer detailed investigation of the process of such assessment. Quantitative methods can effectively measure the product according to a range of variables and factors. Combining them can truly enrich the investigation of what the assessment of spoken vocabulary actually entails. Lorenzo-Dus and Meara (2004), for instance, used quantitative analysis to reveal that examiners contributed over 50% of the word types generated in the role-plays but needed qualitative analysis to clarify why this was the case. Had this not been done, then the logical assumption drawn from the quantitative analysis of relatively low student capability could not have been mitigated by findings regarding task design.

The potential benefits of drawing upon quantitative and qualitative methodologies thus seem compelling, even when balanced against the technical and structural disincentives to do so. However, there is one final caveat. In past studies that have sought to combine methodologies, qualitative work has tended to follow quantitative work. This is problematic in that the results of the latter are inevitably evaluated in relation to the results of the former. For research into the assessment of spoken vocabulary in oral proficiency examinations to truly benefit from the best of both worlds, we need to consciously design research that enables us to move beyond merely combining methodologies to developing integrated methodologies. The quantitative and qualitative toolboxes need to be incorporated from the very beginning, and until the very end, of the study of spoken (vocabulary) assessment.

13 What is in a teacher's mind?
Teacher ratings of EFL essays and different aspects of lexical richness

Helmut Daller and David Phelan

Introduction and overview

The findings of the present chapter are a contribution to the discussion on the role of lexical richness within the construct of foreign language proficiency. The present study investigates to what extent teacher judgement of EFL essays can be predicted by measuring the lexical richness of these texts. Thirty-one essays from students on English for Academic Purposes (EAP) short courses were analysed with various measures of lexical richness (*D*, Advanced Types, *P-Lex*, Guiraud's Index, Advanced Guiraud and Type–Token Ratio (TTR)). Four experienced EFL teachers rated the essays according to a set of band descriptors that was familiar to the teachers, and is also used in EAP exams. The raters were asked to judge the overall proficiency and a number of other linguistic aspects of the texts. Although the teachers did have different individual preferences in the detailed analysis of the essays, there was a highly significant correlation between them, especially on the overall score (rho > .9), which is an indication of reliable rating. Other studies on teacher ratings of oral texts (Richards and Malvern, 2000; Malvern and Richards, 2002; Malvern, Richards, Chipere, and Durán, 2004: 103) suggest that teacher rating is influenced by the use of advanced vocabulary or rare words. The present study confirms this for written texts as well. In line with our expectations this chapter shows that the measures based on the occurrence of infrequent words are most useful in predicting teacher judgement. This is a further indication that the aspect of lexical sophistication (the use of rare words) is an important consideration for teachers in their marking. One explanation could be that this is the most 'economical' marking strategy. However, this has implications for the discussion of what foreign language proficiency actually is, at least in the eyes of the teachers. The results of the present study suggest that in an educational setting the advanced parts of the lexicon play a crucial role in the construct of foreign language proficiency.

Teacher judgements

This chapter investigates how teacher judgements are based on the lexical richness of EFL essays. It addresses directly the concern raised by Nation in the opening chapter that vocabulary measures must be related to language use if they are to be considered valid, and it picks up the relationship between lexical richness and overall writing ability which Nation specifically addresses. The measures used in this study tap into different aspects of lexical richness, and a major research question is whether lexical diversity or lexical sophistication has more influence on the judgement of the teachers. Lexical diversity is typically seen as an aspect of lexical richness that relates the number of types to the number of tokens. The most basic measure of it is the Type–Token Ratio. Lexical sophistication, however, has its focus on the rareness of words in a text. Several studies on oral interviews (Richards and Malvern, 2000; Malvern and Richards, 2002; Malvern et al., 2004: 103) suggest that it is possibly the use of rare words that leads teachers to positive judgements rather than lexical diversity. Teachers 'are likely to respond to other aspects of lexical richness, such as the use of low-frequency words, or, at least, words which are less common in the foreign language classroom' (Malvern and Richards, 2002: 95).

Teachers obviously need to have economical marking strategies to cope with the daily burden of marking. A focus on lexical sophistication rather than diversity could be the result of such strategies. A further example of a time-saving strategy that leads to judgements in a very short period of time is illustrated by Meara and Babí (2001). In an experimental study, they found that experienced teachers only need a short text segment (about 30 words) to decide whether a text is written by a native speaker or not. It is, however, unclear how the teachers come to this decision. In their study on oral interviews Malvern and Richards (2002) asked their raters to judge the oral proficiency of their candidates according to six different aspects (vocabulary range, fluency, complexity of the structure, content, accuracy and pronunciation). The overall scores on these aspects show very high intercorrelations which can be interpreted as results of halo effects. High intercorrelations between different aspects of rating suggest that the raters – at least in this situation – make a holistic judgement and do not or cannot differentiate between the different linguistic aspects of the performance (for further discussion on holistic teacher rating see Williamson and Huot, 1993, Page, Poggio and Keith, 1997).

Aspects of lexical richness and their measurement

The previous paragraph discusses the possible relevance of lexical diversity and lexical sophistication for teacher judgements. Table 1 lists the measures that are used in the present study. They are the same measures as used in Chapters 7 and 8 of this volume. All word-list-based approaches take the frequency or rareness of a word into account and are therefore mainly measures of lexical sophistication; word-list-free measures are measures of lexical diversity. Table 1 gives an overview of these measures.

Table 1 Measures of lexical richness used

Word-list-free approaches	Word-list-based approaches
TTR	LFP/Beyond 2,000
Guiraud's Index	*P-Lex*
D	AG (Advanced Guiraud)

It is worth bearing in mind that the TTR is a function of the sample size, and falls systematically with larger texts. This makes it difficult to use the TTR when comparing texts of different lengths. Guiraud's Index, Advanced Guiraud, *P-Lex* and *D* try to overcome this problem in different ways. Guiraud's Index uses a simple mathematical transformation to compensate for the falling TTR curve, *P-Lex* uses the parameter of a Poisson distribution (lambda) for the occurrence of rare words as a single measure, and finally *D* employs a single parameter for a function that models the falling TTR curve. The aim of this study is not to compare the general validity of these measures but to investigate empirically their usefulness in predicting teacher ratings.

Hypotheses

1 Teachers will have different preferences when rating students' essays but will come to a highly reliable overall, holistic score.
2 Word-list-based measures will correlate highly with teacher ratings whereas measures of lexical diversity will show only low correlations.

Methodology

Data collection and analysis

The subjects in the present study are 31 students (14 female, 17 male) who took part in English for Academic Purposes (EAP) short courses in the UK. The data collection took place in September 2003. The students came from a variety of countries, with the majority from China and Mexico; the average age was 20. The short courses were part of their preparation for degree study in the UK. The students were asked to write an essay about their home country.

The essays were then transcribed into CHAT (Codes for the Human Analysis of Transcripts, see MacWhinney, 2000a,b) which enabled us to compute D and the other word-list-free measures. For the word-list-based approaches we used Nation's word list (see Nation, 2003), which is based on West (1953). Every word that is not included in the first two bands of this list and that is not a proper noun was counted as an advanced type.

The teacher ratings of the essays

We asked four experienced EFL teachers to rate the essays on the following aspects:

a Overall rating
b Vocabulary range
c Arguments and ideas
d Cohesion and coherence
e Grammar complexity
f Errors in lexis and grammar

All aspects had to be rated on a 9-point scale. For the overall ratings the teachers were provided with a band descriptor which was similar to the overall band descriptor of the International English Language Testing System (IELTS). For the other aspects we used a 9-point scale with a short description of the end point ('an error-free text will give a score of 9').

Results

The essays

An overview of text length (tokens) and the number of types is given in Table 2.

Table 2   Text lengths and number of types of the essays

	n	Minimum	Maximum	Mean	Standard deviation
Types	31	95	273	143.81	41.07
Tokens	31	169	563	280.77	93.25

It is obvious that the texts vary considerably in text length and number of types used. This might cause problems for some of the measures that are a function of text length, such as the TTR.

The teachers' ratings

As a first step we will investigate the teachers' ratings before we compare them with the results of the different measures of lexical richness. There are considerable differences between the raters. The spread of marks for the *overall rating* and the rating of *vocabulary range* is shown in Figure 1.

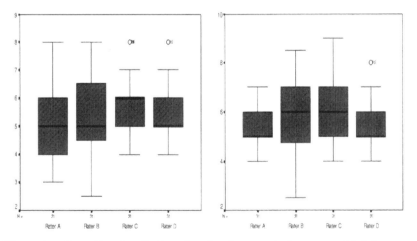

Figure 1   *Overall rating* (left) and rating for *vocabulary range* (right)

The ratings of the four teachers vary considerably; for example, rater B uses the whole range of marks, whereas rater D has a much narrower spread of marks. Rater A applies a wide range of marks for the *overall rating* but only a limited range for the *vocabulary range*. Rater C displays precisely the opposite tendency. This raises the question of whether the rating itself is reliable. Table 3 shows that the raters differ in their marks on the *overall rating*, *vocabulary range*,

Table 3   Agreement between raters

	Ratings (maximum 9)					
	Overall rating	Vocabulary range	Arguments and ideas	Coherence and cohesion	Grammatical complexity	Errors in lexis and grammar
Rater A	5.16	5.29	6.07	6.13	5.10	4.81
Rater B	5.34	5.76	6.84	6.60	5.29	4.87
Rater C	5.71	6.03	6.81	6.61	5.23	5.23
Rater D	5.23	5.65	5.65	5.61	5.32	5.00

arguments and ideas and *coherence and cohesion*. There is no significant difference for *grammar complexity* and *errors in lexis and grammar*. Table 3 shows the mean ranking (mark) of the raters. Overall, this shows that the teachers differ widely in the marks they give for the different aspects. This is, however, not the case for *grammar complexity* and *errors in lexis and grammar*. These two linguistic aspects are probably easiest to rate for experienced teachers.

The statistics of Table 3 are represented graphically in Figure 2. This graph shows how the different raters marked the six aspects

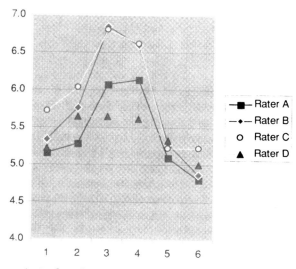

(Labels for the x-axis: 1 = Overall rating, 2 = Vocabulary range, 3 = Arguments and ideas, 4 = Coherence and cohesion, 5 = Grammatical complexity, 6 = Errors in lexis and grammar)

Figure 2   Different mean ranks of the four raters

of the essays mentioned above. It can also be interpreted as a representation of markers' preferences. The profile of the raters is reflected by the fact that they give relatively high marks in a certain area and low marks in another. Figure 2 shows these rater profiles. Rater D, for example, is very critical in areas such as *coherence and cohesion* and *arguments and ideas*. Raters B and C by contrast are more lenient when judging these aspects of the texts. This raises the question of whether the combined judgement of the raters can be regarded as a reliable measurement. It is vital that the judgements of the teachers are reliable if we want to draw conclusions about the relationship between the judgements and the lexical richness of the texts. We therefore computed Cronbach's alpha as a measure of inter-rater reliability (for a discussion on the use of Cronbach's alpha as a measure for rater reliability see Rietveld and van Hout, 1993: 187ff.). Table 4 shows the value for Cronbach's alpha based on the judgements of the four teachers.

Table 4   The reliability of the raters

Aspect of rating	Cronbach's alpha
Overall rating according to band descriptors	.911
Vocabulary range	.818
Arguments and ideas	.694
Coherence and cohesion	.631
Grammatical complexity	.846
Errors in lexis and grammar	.851

It appears that Cronbach's alpha is generally acceptable with the exception of *arguments and ideas* and *coherence and cohesion*. Although all correlations are highly significant (see Table 5) there is less agreement in these two areas. These two aspects of the texts seem to be difficult to judge. Apart from that, the correlations between the raters are modest to high. Table 5 shows the correlations between the raters when judging different linguistic aspects of the tests.

These correlations show that there is a large overlap between the ratings of the different linguistic aspects of the essays. This overlap is, however, lower than reported in a study on the rating of oral proficiency (Malvern et al., 2004), where all correlations were above .9 and are interpreted as the result of halo effects. It is likely that these halo effects play a role in the present study as well, albeit to a lesser extent. It could be argued that these high correlations are an indication that teachers always judge on an overall impression and do not, or cannot, distinguish between the other aspects. There may

Table 5 Correlations between the judgements

	Overall rating	Vocabulary range	Arguments and ideas	Coherence and cohesion	Grammatical complexity
Overall rating	–				
Vocabulary range	.947	–			
Arguments and ideas	.837	.846	–		
Coherence and cohesion	.863	.857	.899	–	
Grammatical complexity	.935	.882	.791	.895	–
Errors in lexis and grammar	.967	.920	.739	.795	.895

($n = 31$ for all, Spearman's rho, p for all cases < .001, two-tailed)

well be an important halo effect from the *overall rating*, which was done first. The exceptions are *arguments and ideas* and *coherence and cohesion*. These two aspects might be more difficult to quantify. It may be concluded that the high correlation between the *overall rating* and the other aspects, plus the high value for Cronbach's alpha for the *overall rating* (Table 4) are strong indications that the overall (holistic) rating yields the most reliable results. The high correlation between the *overall rating* and *vocabulary range* means that the vocabulary range or lexical richness of the essays might be one of the best predictors of teacher judgement. The high correlation between these two ratings means that they are interchangeable.

As a first summary, we can conclude that the teacher ratings can be seen as a reliable measure for overall proficiency. However, the high correlations between the ratings of the different aspects make it difficult to differentiate between these aspects. In the remainder of this chapter we will therefore focus only on the *overall rating*. The main question now is how this holistic rating is related to the scores obtained by different measures of lexical richness, or in other words: which aspect of lexical richness is valued most or can be judged more easily by the teachers?

Firstly, we computed the correlation between the scores obtained from the different measures of lexical richness. These correlations are displayed in Table 6. For all measures, except for *P-Lex* where for technical reasons only 20 essays could be analysed, $n = 31$.

It is striking that the TTR shows no significant correlation with

242   *Helmut Daller and David Phelan*

Table 6   Correlations between the measures

	TTR	Guiraud's Index	D	Advanced types	P-Lex
TTR	–				
Guiraud's Index	.309	–			
D	.483**	.726**	–		
Advanced types	−.067	.832**	.507**	–	
P-Lex	.094	.591**	.392	.674**	–
AG	.198	.806**	.565**	.939**	.738**

(Pearson, two-tailed, n for all = 31, except *P-Lex*, n = 20) * = $p < .05$, ** $p < .01$

most of the other measures. We conclude that the TTR is not a reliable measure for texts of different lengths, which is in line with our expectations. Various other studies have come to the same conclusion (e.g. Daller et al., 2003; Malvern et al., 2004: 95ff.). Secondly, there is a very high correlation between AG (Advanced Guiraud) and Advanced types which means that they measure the same aspect of the lexicon (lexical sophistication). There are also very high correlations between the traditional Guiraud Index and all other measures (except TTR). This is an indication that Guiraud's Index is a useful measure, at least in the given context.

The main question is how these different measures of lexical richness correlate with the teacher judgements of the essays. Table 7 shows correlations between the *overall rating* and the scores obtained by the different measures of lexical richness.

Table 7   Correlations between the judgements and the measures (Spearman, two-tailed)

	D	Advanced types	P-Lex	AG	Guiraud's Index	TTR
Overall rating	.235	.549**	.494*	.471**	.577**	−.030

n = 31 for all measures, except *P-Lex* (n = 20), * = $p < .05$, ** = $p < .01$

All word-list-based measures correlate highly with the teacher ratings. This supports our hypothesis that lexical sophistication is indeed an important aspect for teacher ratings. As a measure of lexical diversity D does not correlate significantly with the teacher judgements. This is in line with previous findings (Richards and Malvern, 2000; Malvern and Richards, 2002; Malvern et al., 2004: 103). We therefore conclude that lexical diversity probably influences teacher ratings to a lesser extent than lexical sophistication. However, high correlations between Guiraud's Index and the teacher ratings does not support this as Guiraud's Index is also a measure of diversity. In the present context it is safe to conclude that the TTR does not give any predictions of teacher judgements, which is not surprising since texts of different lengths are involved.

The measurement of lexical richness and text length

Comparing texts with different lengths is a methodological problem in research on lexical richness. The traditional TTR is especially sensitive since this measure falls systematically the longer a text becomes (for a discussion and references to earlier research, see Daller et al., 2003, Malvern et al., 2004). Many measures have been developed in order to overcome this methodological problem (see Chapter 7). They try to compensate for the systematic fall of the TTR *within* the same text (which should not be the case since the proficiency of the speaker/writer does not change while they produce the text). However, differences in length *between* texts are an aspect of the quality of the texts. Many studies show that more-proficient learners produce longer texts than less proficient learners when carrying out the same task (for an overview see: Jarvis, Grant, Bikowski and Ferris, 2003). Not surprisingly the teacher ratings in our study change in accordance with text length. The positive correlation between the *overall rating* of the teachers and text length is significant (rho = .502, *p* = .004, two-tailed). One can therefore also expect a positive correlation between measures of proficiency and text length. A negative correlation would be an argument against the measure. Table 8 shows the correlation between the scores obtained by different measures and text length (tokens).

The negative correlation between the TTR and text length is a

Table 8   Text length and scores of lexical richness obtained by different measures

	D	Advanced types	P-Lex	Guiraud's	AG	TTR
Tokens	.307	.818	.453	.673	.579	− .479
Significance level	.094	.000	.045	.000	.001	.006

(Pearson correlation, two-tailed, *n* = 31 for all measures, except *n* = 20 for *P-Lex*)

clear indication that this measure is not valid in the given context. All other measures show a positive correlation with text length, although for D this would only be significant with a one-tailed test of significance. It is not possible to draw further conclusions from the magnitude of the correlations apart from the fact that positive correlations were expected.

Conclusions

The teachers in the present study show both high inter-rater correlations and high correlations between the ratings of different linguistic aspects of the essays. From the latter we conclude that large halo effects allow only an overall rating. This supports our first hypothesis, which assumes that teachers will have different individual preferences when rating students' essays but will come to a highly reliable overall, holistic score.

This reliable overall rating turns out to be closely connected to the occurrence of low-frequency, rare words. The use of these words is highly rated by the judges. Measures that are based on lexical sophistication (Advanced types, *P-Lex*, Advanced Guiraud) yield highly significant correlations with the teacher ratings. However, D, a measure that was developed to measure lexical diversity, yields only moderate and not significant correlations with the teacher ratings. These findings support our second hypothesis, that word-list-based measures would correlate highly with teacher ratings as they are based on lexical sophistication rather than lexical diversity, and that measures of diversity correlate with the teacher ratings only to a lesser extent. However, the significant correlation between the traditional Guiraud Index and the teacher ratings was unexpected and needs further investigation. Overall, we conclude that our findings are a clear indication that teachers focus on rare, infrequent words, perhaps as result of an economical marking strategy. The focus on rare words allows a reliable judgement in a short period of time, whereas the focus on other aspects of lexical richness would take more time and effort, and would probably be too difficult. This is in line with other findings on the rating of oral proficiency. Measurements of advanced lexis are therefore useful tools for predicting teacher ratings. These teacher judgements, however, reflect only one view of language proficiency, which is related to a classroom setting. One could argue that foreign language proficiency in this setting is a construct based on the teachers' view. Further studies are necessary to give more insight into proficiency and lexical richness in a setting outside the classroom.

References

Adamopoulou, R. (2000) The equivalence of a computer-delivered and a paper-delivered Yes/No vocabulary test. Unpublished MA thesis, University of Wales, Swansea.

Ágnes, A. and Kormos, J. (2004) Creativity and narrative task performance: an exploratory study. *Language Learning* 54, 277–310.

Aitchison, J. (1987) *Words in the Mind: An Introduction to the Mental Lexicon.* Oxford: Blackwell.

Aitchison, J. (1994) *Words in the Mind: An Introduction to the Mental Lexicon.* Oxford: Blackwell.

Alameda, J.R. and Cuetos, F. (1996) *Diccionario de frecuencias de las unidades lingüísticas del castellano. Vol. 1 y 2.* Oviedo: Servicio de Publicaciones de la Universidad de Oviedo.

Alderson, J.C. (1984) Reading in a foreign language: a reading problem or a language problem? In Alderson, J.C. and Urquhart, A.H. (eds.) *Reading in a Foreign Language.* London: Longman.

Alderson, J.C. (2002) Testing proficiency and achievement: principles and practice. In Coleman, J.A., Grotjahn, R. and Raatz, U. (eds.) *University Language Testing and the C-Test.* Bochum: AKS-Verlag, 15–30.

Al-Hazemi, H. (1993) Low-level EFL vocabulary tests for Arabic speakers. Unpublished PhD thesis, University of Wales, Swansea.

Alekseev, P.M. (1984) *Statistische Lexikographie.* Brockmeyer: Bochum.

Anglin, J.M. (1993). *Vocabulary Development: A Morphological Analysis.* Monographs of the Society for Research in Child Development Serial No. 238, vol. 58, No. 10. Chicago, IL: Society for Research in Child Development.

Arnaud, P.J.L. (1984) The lexical richness of L2 written productions and the validity of vocabulary tests. In Culhane, T. Klein-Braley, C. and Stevenson, D.K. (eds.) *Practice and Problems in Language Testing.* Colchester: University of Essex, 14–28.

Arras, U., Eckes, T. and Grotjahn, R. (2002) C-Tests im Rahmen des 'Tests Deutsch als Fremdsprache' (TestDaF): Erste Forschungsergebnisse. In Grotjahn, R. (ed.) *Der C-Test. Theoretische Grundlangen und praktische Anwendungen*, vol. 4. Bochum: AKS-Verlag, 175–210.

Baayen, R.H. (1989) A corpus-based approach to morphological productivity. Statistical analysis and psycholinguistic interpretation. Unpublished PhD thesis, University of Amsterdam.

Baayen, R. H. (2001) *Word Frequency Distributions*. Dordrecht, Boston, London: Kluwer.

Bachman, L.F. (1990) *Fundamental Considerations in Language Testing*. Oxford: Oxford University Press.

Bachman, L.F. and Palmer, A.S. (1981) The construct validity of the FSI oral interview. *Language Learning* 31 (1), 67–86.

Bachman, L.F. and Palmer, A.S. (1982) The construct validation of some components of communicative proficiency. *TESOL Quarterly* 16 (4), 409–65.

Bachman, L.F. and Palmer A.S. (1996) *Language Testing in Practice*. Oxford: Oxford University Press.

Barabási, A. (2002) *Linked: The New Science of Networks*. Cambridge, MA: Perseus.

Barabási, A. and Albert, R. (1999) Emergence of scaling in random networks. *Science 286*, 509–12.

Bates, E., Bretherton, I. and Snyder, L. (1988) *From First Words to Grammar: Individual Differences and Dissociable Mechanisms*. Cambridge: Cambridge University Press.

Baudot, J. (1992) *Fréquence d'utilisation des mots en Français écrit contemporain*. Presses de Montréal.

Bauer, L. and Nation, I.S.P. (1993) Word Families. *International Journal of Lexicography* 6 (4), 253–79.

Beeckmans, R., Eyckmans, J., Janssens, V., Dufranne, M. and Van de Velde, H. (2001) Examining the Yes/No vocabulary test: some methodological issues in theory and practice. *Language Testing* 18, 235–74.

Berman, R.A. and Verhoeven, L. (2002) Cross-linguistic perspectives on the development of text-production abilities: speech and writing. *Written Language and Literacy 5*, 1–43.

Bertram, R., Baayen, R. and Schreuder, R. (2000) Effects of family size for complex words. *Journal of Memory and Language 42*, 390–405.

Bertram, R., Laine, M. and Virkkala, M. (2000) The role of derivational morphology in vocabulary acquisition: get by with a little help from my morpheme friends. *Scandinavian Journal of Psychology* 41 (4), 287–96.

Berwick, R. and Ross, S. (1996) Cross-cultural pragmatics in oral proficiency interview strategies. *Studies in Second Language Acquisition* 10 (1), 149–64.

Biber, D. (1988) *Variation across Speech and Writing*. Cambridge: Cambridge University Press.

Bland, J.M. and Altman, D.G. (1986) Statistical methods for assessing agreement between two methods of clinical assessment. *The Lancet* February 8, 307–10.

Boers, F.M., Demecheleer and Eyckmans, J. (2004) Etymological elaboration as a strategy for learning figurative idioms. In Bogaards, P. and Laufer, B. (eds.) *Vocabulary in a Second Language: Selection, Acquisition and Testing*. Amsterdam and Philadelphia, PA: John Benjamins, pp. 53–78.

Bogaards, P. (1994) *Le vocabulaire dans l'apprentissage des langues*. Paris: Didier.

Bogaards, P. (2000) Testing L2 vocabulary knowledge at a high level: the case of the Euralex French Tests. *Applied Linguistics* 21, 490–516.

Boyd, R. (1993) Metaphor and theory change. In Ortony, A. (ed.) *Metaphor and Thought*. Cambridge: Cambridge University Press.

British National Corpus. http://www.natcorp.ox.ac.uk.

Broeder, P., Extra, G. and van Hout, R. (1987) Measuring lexical richness and variety in second language use. *Polyglot* 8, 1–16.

Broeder, P., Extra, G. and van Hout, R. (1993) Richness and variety in the developing lexicon. In Perdue, C. (ed.) *Adult Language Acquisition. Volume II: The Results*. Cambridge: Cambridge University Press, 145–63.

Brown, A. (2003) Interviewer variation and the co-construction of speaking proficiency. *Language Testing* 20 (1), 1–25.

Brown, C. (1993) Factors affecting the acquisition of vocabulary: frequency and saliency of words. In Huckin, Th., Haynes, M. and Coady, J. (eds) *Second Language Reading and Vocabulary Learning*. Norwood, NJ: Ablex, 263–86.

Brown, R. (1973) *A First Language: The Early Stages*. London: Allen and Unwin.

Brown, R. and Berko, J. (1960) Word association and the acquisition of grammar. *Child Development* 31, 1–14.

Buchanan, M. (2002) *Nexus: Small Worlds and the Groundbreaking Science of Networks*. New York: W.W. Norton.

Bucks, R.S., Singh, S., Cuerden, J.M. and Wilcock, G.K. (2000) Analysis of spontaneous, conversational speech in dementia of Alzheimer type: Evaluation of an objective technique for analysing lexical performance. *Aphasiology* 14, 71–91.

Cafarella, C. (1994) Assessor accommodation in the V.C.E. Italian oral test. *Australian Review of Applied Linguistics* 20 (1), 21–41.

Celce-Murcia, M. (1998) Preface. In Young, R. and He, A.W. (eds.) *Talking and Testing: Discourse Approaches to the Assessment of Oral Proficiency*. Amsterdam and Philadelphia, PA: John Benjamins, ix–x.

Chalhoub-Deville, M. (2002) Technology in standardized language assessments. In Kaplan, R.B. (ed.) *The Oxford Handbook of Applied Linguistics*. Oxford: Oxford University Press, 471–84.

Chaudron, C. (2003) Data collection in SLA research. In Doughty, C.J. and Long, M.H. (eds.) *The Handbook of Second Language Acquisition*. Oxford: Blackwell, 762–828.

Cole, K.C., Truman E.C. and Vanderstoep, C. (1999) The influence of language/cognitive profile on discourse intervention outcome. *Language, Speech, and Hearing Services in Schools*, 30, 61–7.

Coleman, J.A. (1995) The current state of knowledge concerning student residence abroad. In Parker, G. and Rouxeville, A. (eds.) *The Year Abroad: Preparing, Monitoring, Evaluation*. London: Association of French Language Studies, 17–42.

Coxhead, A. (2000) A new *Academic Word List*. TESOL *Quarterly* 34 (2), 213–38.

Daller, H. (1999) *Migration und Mehrsprachigkeit* (Migration and Multilingualism). Frankfurt: Lang.

Daller, H. and Phelan, D. (2006) The C-test and TOEIC[R] as measurements of students' progress in intensive short courses in EFL. In Grotjahn, R. (ed.) *Der C-Test: Theorie, Empirie, Anwendungen. (The C-test: Theory, Empirical Research, Applications)*. Frankfurt am Main: Lang, 101–19.

Daller, H., Treffers-Daller, J., Ünaldı-Ceylan, A. and Yıldız, C. (2002) The development of a Turkish C-Test. In Coleman, J.A., Grotjahn, R. and Raatz, U. (eds.) *University Language Testing and the C-Test*. Bochum: AKS-Verlag, 187–99.

Daller, H., van Hout, R. and Treffers-Daller, J. (2003) Lexical richness in spontaneous speech of bilinguals. *Applied Linguistics* 24 (2), 197–222.

Davidson, F. (2000) The language tester's statistical toolbox. *System* 28 (4), 605–17.

Deese, J. (1962a) On the structure of associative meaning. *Psychological Review* 69, 161–75.

Deese, J. (1962b) Form class and the determinants of association. *Journal of Verbal Learning and Verbal Behavior* 1, 79–84.

Deese, J. (1965) *The Structure of Associations in Language and Thought*. Baltimore, MD: Johns Hopkins.

Dieltjens, L., Vanparijs, J., Baten, L., Claes, M.-T., Alkema, P. and Lodewick, J. (1995) *Woorden in Context Deel 2*. Brussels: De Boeck.

Dieltjens, L., Vanparijs, J., Baten, L., Claes, M.-T., Alkema, P. and Lodewick, J. (1997) *Woorden in Context Deel 1*. Brussels: De Boeck.

Dörnyei, Z. and Kormos, J. (2000) The role of individual and social variables in oral task performance. *Language Teaching Research* 4, 275–300.

Dorogovtsev, S.N. and Mendes, J.F.F. (2001) Language as an evolving word web. Proceedings of the Royal Society of London B, 268, 2603–6.

Douglas, D. and Selinker, L. (1992) Analyzing oral proficiency test performance in general and specific purpose contexts. *System* 20 (3), 317–28.

Durán, P., Malvern, D., Richards, B.J. and Chipere, N. (2004) Developmental trends in lexical diversity. *Applied Linguistics* 25, 220–42.

Ellis, N.C. and Beaton, A. (1995) Psycholinguistic determinants of foreign language vocabulary learning. In Harley, B. (ed.) *Lexical Issues in Language Learning*. Amsterdam and Philadelphia, PA: John Benjamins, 107–65.

Engwall, G. (1984) *Vocabulaire du roman français (1962–1968), Dictionnaire des Fréquences*. Stockholm: Almqvist and Wiksell.

Eyckmans, J. (2000) De Ja/Nee woordenschattoets: klaar voor gebruik in de klas? *Toegepaste Taalwetenschap in Artikelen* 2, 117–28.

Eyckmans, J. (2001) De vertekening van het antwoordgedrag in de Ja/Nee woordenschattoets. *Toegepaste Taalwetenschap in Artikelen* 2, 79–90.

Eyckmans, J. (2004): *Measuring Receptive Vocabulary Size: Reliability and Validity of the Yes/No Vocabulary Test*. Utrecht: LOT.

Fenson, L., Dale, P.S., Reznick, J.S., Bates, E., Thal, D.J. and Pethick, S.J. (1994) *Variability in Early Communicative Development*. Monographs of the Society for Research in Child Development 59 (5), Serial No. 242. Chicago, IL: Society for Research in Child Development.

Ferguson, G.A. (1981) *Statistical Analysis in Psychology and Education* (5th edn.) London: McGraw-Hill.

Ferrer i Cancho, R. and Solé, R. (2001) The small world of human language. Proceedings of the Royal Society of London B, 268, 2261–5.

Fitzpatrick, T. and Meara, P.M. (2004) Exploring the validity of a test of productive vocabulary. *Vigo International Journal of Applied Linguistics* 1, 55–74.

Francis, W. and Kucera, H. (1982) *Frequency Analysis of English Usage.* Boston, MA: Houghton Mifflin.

Fulcher, G. (2003a) Interface design in computer-based language testing. *Language Testing* 20, 384–408.

Fulcher, G. (2003b) *Testing Second Language Speaking.* London: Longman Pearson.

Gentner, D. (1981) Psycholinguistic determinants of foreign language vocabulary learning. In Harley, B. (ed.) *Lexical Issues in Language Learning.* Amsterdam and Philadelphia, PA: John Benjamins, 107–65.

Gentner, D. (1985) Why nouns are learned before verbs: linguistic relativity versus natural partitioning. In Kuczaj, S. (ed.) *Language Development: Language, Thought and Culture,* Hillsdale, NJ: Lawrence Erlbaum Associates, 301–34.

Gervais, C. (1997) Computers and language testing: a harmonious relationship? *Francophonie,*16, 3–7.

Glaser, B. and Strauss, A. (1967) *The Discovery of Grounded Theory: Strategies For Qualitative Research.* Chicago, IL: Aldine.

Goldfield, B. (2002) When comprehension meets production. In Skarabela, B., Fish, S. and Do, H.-J. (eds.) *Proceedings of the 26th annual Boston University Conference on Language Development.* Sommerville, MA: Cascadilla Press, 232–42.

Gougenheim, G. (1956) *L'élaboration du français élémentaire.* Paris, Didier.

Gougenheim, G., Michéa, R., Rivenc, P. and Sauvageot, A. (1964) *L'élaboration du Français fondamental, 1er degré* (2nd edn.) Paris: Didier.

Goulden, R., Nation, P. and Read, J. (1990) How large can a receptive vocabulary be? *Applied Linguistics* 11, 341–63.

Grabe, W. (1999) Developments in reading research and their implications for computer-adaptive reading assessment. In Chalhoub DeVille, M. (ed.) *Issues in Computer-Adaptive Testing of Reading Proficiency.* Cambridge: Cambridge University Press, 11–47.

Grabe, W. (2002) Reading in a second language. In Kaplan, R.B. (ed.) *The Oxford Handbook of Applied Linguistics.* Oxford: Oxford University Press, 40–60.

Grotjahn, R. (1986) Test validation and cognitive psychology: some methodological considerations. *Language Testing* 3, 159–85.

Grotjahn, R. (1995) Der C-Test: state of the art. *Zeitschrift für Fremdsprachenforschung* 6 (2), 37–60.

Grotjahn, R. (ed.) (2002) *Der C-Test. Theoretische Grundlagen und praktische Anwendungen* (vol. 4). Bochum: Brockmeyer.

Grotjahn, R. and Allner, B. (1996) Der C-Test in der Sprachlichen Aufnahmeprüfung an Studienkollegs für ausländische Studierende an Universitäten in Nordrhein-Westfalen. In Grotjahn, R. (ed.) *Der C-Test. Theoretische Grundlagen und praktische Anwendungen* (vol. 3). Bochum: AKS-Verlag, 279–335.

Guiraud, P. (1954) *Les caractères statistiques du vocabulaire*. Paris: Presses Universitaires de France.

Hacquebord, H.I. (1999) A Dutch comprehension test for identifying reading problems in L1 and L2 students. *Journal of Reading Research* 22 (3), 299–304.

Hacquebord, H.I. and Andringa, S. (2000) *Elektronische Tekstbegriptoets voor de basisvorming. Verantwoording en normering (technical report)*. Groningen: Etoc (Rijksuniversiteit Groningen).

Hacquebord, H.I. and Struiving, J.P. (1998) *Streefwoordenlijst voor de eerste fase van het voortgezet onderwijs (met verantwoording)*. Utrecht: APS.

Hall, J.W., Paus, C.H. and Smith, J.A. (1993) Metacognitive and other knowledge about the mental lexicon: do we know how many words we know? *Applied Linguistics* 14 (2), 189–206.

Harris, M., Yeeles, C., Chasin, J. and Oakley, Y. (1995) Symmetries and asymmetries in early lexical comprehension and production. *Journal of Child Language* 22, 1–18.

Hastings, A. (2002a) In defense of C-testing. In Grotjahn, R. (ed.) *Der C-Test. Theoretische Grundlagen und praktische Anwendungen* (vol. 4). Bochum: AKS-Verlag, 11–26.

Hastings, A. (2002b) A response to Jafarpur. In Grotjahn, R. (ed.) *Der C-Test. Theoretische Grundlagen und praktische Anwendungen* (vol. 4). Bochum: AKS-Verlag, 28–9.

Hayes, B. (2000a) Computing science, graph theory in practice: Part I. *American Scientist* 88, 1, 19–13.

Hayes, B. (2000b) Computing science, graph theory in practice: Part II. *American Scientist* 88, 2, 104–9.

Hazenberg, S. and Hulstijn, J.H. (1996) Defining a minimal receptive second-language vocabulary for non-native university students: an empirical investigation. *Applied Linguistics* 17 (2), 145–63.

Henriksen, B. (1999) Three dimensions of vocabulary development. *Studies in Second Language Acquisition* 21, 303–17.

Henriksen, B. and Haastrup, K. (1998) Describing learners' lexical competence across tasks and over time: a focus on research design. In Haastrup, K. and Viberg, Å. (eds.) *Perspectives on Lexical Acquisition in a Second Language*. Lund: Lund University Press, 61–95.

Hess, C.W., Haug, H.T. and Landry, R.G. (1989) The reliability of type–token ratios for the oral language of school age children. *Journal of Speech and Hearing Research* 32, 536–40.

Hess, C.W., Sefton, K.M. and Landry, R.G. (1986) Sample size and type–token ratios for the oral language of school age children. *Journal of Speech and Hearing Research* 29, 129–34.

Hickey, T. (1991) Mean length of utterance and the acquisition of Irish. *Journal of Child Language*, 18, 553–69.

Hindmarsh, R. (1980) *Cambridge English Lexicon*. Cambridge: Cambridge University Press.

Holmes, D.I. and Singh, S. (1996) A stylometric analysis of conversational speech of aphasic patients. *Literary and Linguistic Computing* 11, 133–40.

Huckin, T. and Coady, J. (1999) Incidental vocabulary acquisition in a second language: a review. *Studies in Second Language Acquisition* 21 (2), 181–93.

Hughes, A. (1989) *Testing for Language Teachers*. Cambridge: Cambridge University Press.

Huibregtse, I. and Admiraal, W. (1999): De score op een ja/nee-woordenschattoets. In Kuczaj, S.A. (ed.) *Language Development. Vol. 2: Language, Thought and Culture*. Hillsdale, NJ: Lawrence Erlbaum Associates, 301–44.

Hunston, S. and Francis, G. (2000) *Pattern Grammar: A Corpus-Driven Approach to the Lexical Grammar of English*. Amsterdam and Philadelphia, PA: John Benjamins.

Huttenlocher, J., Haight, W., Bryk, A., Seltzer, M. and Lyons, Th. (1991) Early vocabulary growth: relation to language input and gender. *Developmental Psychology* 27 (2), 236–48.

Institut National de la Langue Française (INALF) (1971) *Dictionnaire des fréquences du trésor de la langue française* Paris: Didier.

Jacobs, H.L., Zingraf, S.A., Wormuth, D.R., Hartfiel, V.F. and Hughey, J.B. (1981)*Testing ESL Composition: A Practical Approach*. Rowley, MA and London: Newbury House.

Jafarpur, A. (1995) Is C-testing superior to cloze? *Language Testing* 12 (2), 194–216.

Jafarpur, A. (2002a) A comparative study of a C-test and a cloze test. In Grotjahn R. (ed.) *Der C-Test. Theoretische Grundlagen und praktische Anwendungen* (vol. 4). Bochum: AKS-Verlag, 31–51.

Jafarpur, A. (2002b) A response to Hastings. In Grotjahn, R. (ed.) *Der C-Test. Theoretische Grundlagen und praktische Anwendungen* (vol. 4). Bochum: AKS-Verlag, 26–7.

Janssens, V. (1999) Over 'slapen' en 'snurken' en de hulp van de context hierbij. *ANBF-nieuwsbrief* 4, 29–45.

Jarvis, S. (2002) Short texts, best-fitting curves and new measures of lexical diversity. *Language Testing* 19 (1), 57–84.

Jarvis, S., Grant, L., Bikowski, D. and Ferris D. (2003) Exploring multiple profiles of highly rated learner compositions. *Journal of Second Language Writing*, 12, 377–404.

Jiménez Catalán, R. and Moreno Espinosa, S. (2004) Assessing L2 young learners' vocabulary: which test should researchers choose? Paper presented at BAAL/CUP *Workshop in Vocabulary Knowledge and Use*, Bristol: University of the West of England, 8–9 January.

Joe, A. (1998) What effects do text-based tasks promoting generation have on incidental vocabulary acquisition? *Applied Linguistics* 19 (3), 357–77.

Johnson, W. (1944) Studies in language behavior: I. A program of research. *Psychological Monographs* 56, 1–15.

Juilland, A., Brodin, D. and Davidovitch, C. (1970) *Frequency Dictionary of French Words*. The Hague and Paris: Mouton.

Kagan, J. and Gall, S.B. (eds.) (1998) *Gale Encyclopedia of Childhood and Adolescence*. London and Detroit, MI: Gale. See also: http://www.gale.com.

Källkvist, M. (1998) Lexical infelicity in English: the case of nouns and verbs. In Haastrup, K. and Viberg, A. (eds.). *Perspectives on Lexical Acquisition in a Second Language*. Lund: Lund University Press, 149–74.

Kamimoto, T. (2005) The effect of guessing on vocabulary test scores. Paper presented to EuroSLA, September 14–17, Dubrovnik, Croatia.

Kenyon, D.M. and Tschirner, E. (2000) The rating of direct and semi-direct oral proficiency interviews: comparing performance at lower proficiency levels. *Modern Language Journal* 84 (1), 85–101.

Kibby, M.W. (1977) Note on relationship of word difficulty and word frequency. *Psychological Reports* 41, 12–14.

Kintsch, W. (1998) *Comprehension: A Framework for Cognition*. Cambridge: Cambridge University Press.

Kiss, G.R. (1968) Words, associations and networks. *Journal of Verbal Learning and Verbal Behavior* 7, 707–13.

Kiss, G.R., Armstrong, C. and Milroy, R. (1973) *An Associative Thesaurus of English*. Wakefield: P Microfilms.

Klein-Braley, C. (1994) Language testing with the C-Test. A linguistic and statistical investigation into the strategies used by C-Test takers and the prediction of C-Test difficulty. Unpublished Habilitationsschrift, University of Duisburg.

Klein-Braley, C. (1997) C-Tests in the context of reduced redundancy testing: an appraisal. *Language Testing* 14 (1), 47–84.

Klein-Braley, C. and Raatz, U. (1984) A survey of research on the C-Test. *Language Testing* 1, 134–46.

Koike, D.A. (1998) What happens when there's no one to talk to? Spanish foreign language discourse in simulated oral proficiency interviews. In Young, R. and He, A.W. (eds.) *Talking and Testing. Discourse Approaches to the Assessment of Oral Proficiency*. Amsterdam and Philadelphia, PA: John Benjamins, 69–98.

Kramsch, C. (1986) From language proficiency to interactional competence. *Modern Language Journal* 70, 366–72.

Lado, R. (1961) *Language Testing*. London: Longman.

Lakoff, G. and Johnson, M. (1980) *Metaphors We Live By*. Chicago, IL: Chicago University Press.

Lambert, W.E. and Moore, N. (1966) Word association responses: comparisons of American and French monolinguals with Canadian monolinguals and bilinguals. *Journal of Personality and Social Psychology* 3(3), 313–20.

Laufer, B. (1991) The development of L2 lexis in the expression of the advanced language learner. *Modern Language Journal*, 75 (4), 440–8.

Laufer, B. (1992) How much lexis is necessary for reading comprehension? In Arnaud, P.J. and Béjoint, H. (eds.) *Vocabulary and Applied Linguistics*. London: MacMillan, 126–32.

Laufer, B. (1994) The lexical profile of second language writing: does it change over time? *RELC Journal* 25(2), 21–33.

Laufer, B. (1995) Beyond 2,000. A measure of productive lexicon in a second language. In Eubank, L., Selinker, L. and Sharwood Smith, M. (eds.) *The Current State of Interlanguage. (Studies in Honor of William E. Rutherford)*. Amsterdam and Philadelphia, PA: John Benjamins, 265–72.

Laufer, B. (1998) The development of passive and active vocabulary in a second language: same or different? *Applied Linguistics* 19, 255–71.

Laufer, B. and Nation, P. (1995) Vocabulary size and use: lexical richness in L2 written production. *Applied Linguistics* 16, 307–22.

Laufer, B. and Nation, P. (1999) A vocabulary-size test of controlled productive ability. *Language Testing* 16, 33–51.

Lazaraton, A. (1992) The structural organization of a language interview: a conversation analytic perspective. *System* 20 (4), 373–86.

Lazaraton, A. (1995) Qualitative research in TESOL: a progress report. *TESOL Quarterly* 29, 455–72.

Lazaraton, A. (1996) Interlocutor support in oral proficiency interviews: the case of CASE. *Language Testing* 13, 151–72.

Lazaraton, A. (2000) Current trends in research methodology and statistics in applied linguistics. *TESOL Quarterly* 34, 175–81.

Lazaraton, A. (2002) *A Qualitative Approach to the Validation of Oral Language Tests*. Cambridge: University of Cambridge Local Examinations Syndicate and Cambridge: University Press.

Leech, G. and Fallon, R. (1992) Computer corpora – what do they tell us about culture? *ICAME Journal* 16, 29–50.

Leech, G., Rayson, P. and Wilson, A. (2001) *Word Frequencies in Written and Spoken English*. Harlow: Longman.

Lorenzo-Dus, N. and Meara, P. (2004) Role-plays and the assessment of oral proficiency in Spanish. In Márquez Reiter, R. and Placencia, M.E. (eds.) *Current Trends in the Pragmatics of Spanish*. Amsterdam and Philadelphia, PA: John Benjamins, 65–85.

Lorenzo-Dus, N. and Meara, P. (2005) Examiner support strategies and testtaker vocabulary. *IRAL* 43, 239–58.

Mackey (1965) *Language Teaching Analysis*. London: Longman.

MacWhinney, B. (2000a) *The CHILDES Project: Tools for Analyzing Talk, Vol. 1: Transcription Format and Programs* (3rd edn.). Mahwah, NJ: Lawrence Erlbaum Associates.

MacWhinney, B. (2000b) *The CHILDES Project: Tools for Analyzing Talk: Vol. 2: The Database* (3rd edn.). Mahwah, NJ: Lawrence Erlbaum Associates.

MacWhinney, B. (2003) http://childes.psy.cmu.edu.

Malone, M. (2000) Simulated oral proficiency interviews: recent developments. *Eric Digest*. EDO-FL-00–14.

Malvern, D.D. and Richards, B.J. (1997) A new measure of lexical diversity. In Ryan, A. and Wray, A. (eds.) *Evolving Models of Language. Papers from the Annual Meeting of the BAAL held at the University of Wales, Swansea, September 1996*. Clevedon: Multilingual Matters, 58–71.

Malvern, D.D. and Richards, B.J. (2000) Validation of a new measure of lexical diversity. In Beers, M., Van de Bogaerde, B., Bol, G., de Jong, J. and Rooijmans, C. (eds.) *From Sound to Sentence: Studies on First Language Acquisition*. Groningen: Centre for Language and Cognition, 81–96.

Malvern, D.D. and Richards, B.J. (2002) Investigating accommodation in language proficiency interviews using a new measure of lexical diversity. *Language Testing* 19, 85–104.

Malvern, D.D. and Richards, B.J. (2004) A unified approach to the measurement of vocabulary diversity, morphological development and lexical style. Keynote address to the BAAL/CUP Colloquium *Vocabulary Knowledge and Use: Measurements and Applications*. Bristol: University of the West of England, 8–9 January.

Malvern, D.D., Richards, B.J., Chipere, N. and Durán, P. (2004) *Lexical Diversity and Language Development: Quantification and Assessment*. Basingstoke: Palgrave Macmillan.

Marsden, E., Myles, F., Rule, S. and Mitchell, R. (2003) Using CHILDES tools for researching second language acquisition. In Sarangi, S. and Van Leeuwen, T. (eds.) *Applied Linguistics and Communities of Practice*. London: Continuum, 98–113.

Marshall, G.R. and Cofer, C.N. (1963) Associative indices as measures of word relatedness: a summary and comparison of ten methods. *Journal of Verbal Learning and Verbal Behavior* 1, 408–21.

McCarthy, M. (1990) *Vocabulary*. Oxford: Oxford University Press.

McKee, G., Malvern, D.D. and Richards, B.J. (2000) Measuring vocabulary diversity using dedicated software. *Literary and Linguistic Computing* 15, 323–38.

McKeown, M.G. (1993) Creating effective definitions for young word learners. *Reading Research Quarterly* 28 (1), 17–31.

McNamara, T. and Lumley, T. (1997) The effect of interlocutor and assessment mode variables in overseas assessments of speaking skills in occupational settings. *Language Testing* 14, 140–56.

Meara, P. (1990) Some notes on the Eurocentres vocabulary tests. In Tommola, J. (ed.) *Foreign Language Comprehension and Production*. Turku, Finland: AFinLa, 103–13.

Meara, P. (1992a) *EFL Vocabulary Tests*. Swansea: University College, Centre for Applied Language Studies.

Meara, P. (1992b) Network structures and vocabulary acquisition in a foreign language. In Arnaud, P. and H. Béjoint, H. (eds.) *Vocabulary and Applied Linguistics*. London: Macmillan, 62–72.

Meara, P. (1993) The bilingual lexicon and the teaching of vocabulary. In Schreuder, R. and Weltens, B. (eds.) *The Bilingual Lexicon*. Amsterdam and Philadelphia, PA: Benjamins, 279–97.

Meara, P. (1997) Towards a new approach to modeling vocabulary acquisition. In Schmitt, N. and McCarthy. M. (eds.) *Vocabulary: Description, Acquisition and Pedagogy*. Cambridge: Cambridge University Press.

Meara, P. (2003) *V_Tools* (computer software) Swansea: Lognostics.

Meara, P. and Babí, A. (2001) Just a few words: how assessors evaluate minimal texts. *IRAL* 39, 75–83.

Meara, P. and Bell, H. (2001) P-Lex: a simple and effective way of describing the lexical characteristics of short L2 texts. *Prospect* 16 (3), 323–37.

Meara, P. and Buxton, B. (1987) An alternative to multiple choice vocabulary tests. *Language Testing* 4, 142–51.

Meara, P. and Fitzpatrick, T. (2000) Lex-30: an improved method of assessing productive vocabulary in an L2. *System* 28, 19–30.

Meara, P. and Jones, G. (1990) *Eurocentre's Vocabulary Size Test, Version E1.1/K10*. Zurich: Eurocentres Learning Service.

Meara, P.M. and Milton, J.L. (2003a) *X-Lex: Swansea Vocabulary Levels Test* (Version 2.02) (Computer software). Swansea: Lognostics.

Meara, P. and Milton, J.L. (2003b) *The Swansea Levels Test*. Newbury: Express.

Meara, P. and Schur, E. (2002) Random association networks: a baseline measure of lexical complexity. In Miller, K.S. and Thompson, P. (eds.) *Unity and Diversity in Language Use*. London: Continuum, 169–82.

Meara, P. and Wolter, B. (2004) V_Links: beyond vocabulary depth. *Angles on the English Speaking World* 4, 85–97.

Meara, P., Lightbown, P.M. and Halter, R.H. (1994) The effect of cognates on the applicability of Yes/No vocabulary tests. *The Canadian Modern Language Review/La Revue canadienne des langues vivantes* 50 (2), 296–311.

Meara, P., Milton, J. and Lorenzo-Dus, N. (2001) *Language Aptitude Tests*. Newbury: Express.

Melka, F. (1997) Receptive vs. productive aspects of vocabulary. In Schmitt, N. and McCarthy, M. (eds.) *Vocabulary: Description, Acquisition and Pedagogy*. Cambridge: Cambridge University Press, 82–102.

Ménard, N. (1983) *Mesure de la richesse lexicale*. Geneva: Slatkine.

Miller, J.F. and Chapman, R. (1993) *SALT: Systematic Analysis of Language Transcripts, Version 3.0*. Baltimore, MD: University Park Press.

Milton, J. (2004) Lexical profiles, learning and style. Paper presented at BAAL/CUP *Workshop in Vocabulary Knowledge and Use*. Bristol: niversity of the West of England, 8–9 January.

Milton, J. (2004) Comparing the lexical difficulty of French reading comprehension exam texts. *Language Learning Journal* 30, 5–11.

Milton, J. (2005) Aural word recognition and vocabulary size. Paper presented to EuroSLA, September 14–17. Dubrovnik, Croatia.

Milton, J. (2006) Language lite: learning French vocabulary in school. *Journal of French Language Studies* 16(2), 187–190.

Milton, J. and Meara, P. (1995) How periods abroad affect vocabulary growth in a foreign language. *ITL Review of Applied Linguistics*, vols. 107–8, 17–34.

Milton, J. and Vassiliu, P. (2000) Frequency and the lexis of low-level EFL texts. In Nicolaidis, K. and Mattheoudakis, M. (eds.) *Proceedings of the 13th Symposium in Theoretical and Applied Linguistics*, Aristotle University of Thessaloniki, 444–55.

Mitchell, R. and Martin, C. (1997) Rote learning, creativity, and 'understanding' in classroom foreign language teaching. *Language Teaching Research* 1, 1–27.

Motter, A.E., de Moura, A.P.S., Lai, Y.C. and Dasgupta, P. (2002) Topology as the conceptual network of language. *Physical Review* 65, 1–4.

Mushait, S.A. (2003) The relationship of L1 reading and L2 language proficiency with the L2 reading comprehension and strategies of Saudi EFL university students. Unpublished PhD thesis, University of Essex.

Nagy, W.E., Anderson, R., Schommer, M., Scott, J.A. and Stallman, A. (1989) Morphological families in the internal lexicon. *Reading Research Quarterly* 24 (3), 263–82.

Nation, I.S.P. (1983) Testing and teaching vocabulary. *Guidelines* 5, 12–25.

Nation, I.S.P. (ed.) (1984) *Vocabulary Lists: Words, Affixes and Stems*. English University of Wellington, New Zealand: English Language Institute.

Nation, I.S.P. (1986) *Vocabulary Lists: Words, Affixes and Stems, Revised Edition*. Wellington, New Zealand: University of Wellington, English Language Institute.

Nation, I.S.P. (1990) *Teaching and Learning Vocabulary*. Boston, MA: Heinle and Heinle.

Nation, I.S.P. (1993) Vocabulary size, growth and use. In Schreuder, R. and Weltens B. (eds.) *The Bilingual Lexicon*. Amsterdam and Philadelphia, PA: John Benjamins, 115–34.

Nation, I.S.P. (2001) *Learning Vocabulary in Another Language*. Cambridge: Cambridge University Press.

Nation, I.S.P. (2004) A study of the most frequent word families in the British National Corpus. In Bogaards, P. and Laufer, B. *Vocabulary in a Second Language*. Amsterdam and Philapdelphia, PA: John Benjamins, 3–13.

Nation, I.S.P. and Heatley, A. (2002) RANGE: a program for vocabulary analysis. Available at http://www.vuw.ac.nz/lals/staff/paul-nation/nation.aspx.

Nation, I.S.P. and Waring, R. (1997) Vocabulary size, text coverage and word lists. In Schmitt, N. and McCarthy, M. (eds.) *Vocabulary: Description, Acquisition, Pedagogy*. Cambridge: Cambridge University Press, 6–19.

Nation, I.S.P. (2003) http://www.vuw.ac.nz/lals/staff/paul-nation/nation. aspx.

Neather, T., Woods, C., Rodriguez, I., Davis, M. and Dunne, E. (1995) *Target Language Testing in Modern Foreign Languages: Report of a Project Commissioned by the School Curriculum and Assessment Authority.* London: SCAA.

Nemser, W. (1971) Approximative systems of FL learners. *International review of Applied linguistics* 9, 115–23.

Nesi, H. and Meara, P. (1994) Patterns of misinterpretation in the productive use of EFL dictionary definitions. *System* 22 (1), 1–15, (*nieuwsbrief* 4, 29–45).

Norris, L. and Ortega, L. (2003) Defining and measuring SLA. In Doughty, C.J. and Long, M.H. (eds.) *The Handbook of Second Language Acquisition.* Oxford: Blackwell, 717–61.

O'Loughlin, K. (2000) The impact of gender in the IELTS oral interview. In Tulloh, R. (ed.) *IELTS Research Reports 3*, Canberra: IELTS Australia, 1–28.

Orlov, J. (1982) Ein Model der Häufigkeitstruktur des Vokabulars. In: Guiter, H. and Arapov, M. (ed.) *Studies on Zipf's Law.* Bochum: Brockmeier, 154–233.

Page, E.B. (1993) The target language and examinations. *Language Learning Journal* 8, 6–7.

Page, E.B., Poggio, J.P. and Keith, T.Z. (1997) Computer analysis of student essays: finding trait differences in the student profile. Paper presented at the annual meeting of the American Educational Research Association, March. Chicago, IL.

Palmer, H.E. (1917) *The Scientific Study and Teaching of Languages,* London: Harrap.

Picoche, J. (1993) *Didactique du vocabulaire français.* Paris: Nathan.

Picoche, J. (2001) L'outillage lexical. *Cahiers de Lexicologie* 78 (1), 127–38.

Pine, J.M., Lieven, E.V.M. and Rowland, C. (1996) Observational and checklist measures of vocabulary composition: what do they mean? *Journal of Child Language* 23, 573–90.

Pinker, S. (1999) *Words and Rules: the Ingredients of Language.* London: Weidenfeld and Nicolson.

Plauen, E.O. (1996 [1952]) *Vater und Sohn* (vol. 2). Ravensburg: Ravensburger Taschenbuchverlag.

Plunkett, K. and Marchman, V.A. (1991) U-shaped learning and frequency effects in a multi-layered perception: implications for child language acquisition. *Cognition* 38 (1), 43–102.

Poehner, M.E. and Lantolf, J.P. (2003) Dynamic assessment of L2 development: bringing the past into the future. *CALPER Working Papers Series, No.1.* The Pennsylvania State University: Center for Advanced Language Proficiency, Education and Research.

Politzer, R. (1978) Paradigmatic and syntagmatic associations of first year French students. In Honsa, V. and Hardman-de-Bautista, M.J. (eds.)

Papers on Linguistics and Child Language: Ruth Hirsch Weir Memorial Volume. The Hague: Mouton, 203–10.

Pollio, H.R. (1963) A simple matrix analysis of associative structure. *Journal of Verbal Learning and Verbal Behavior* 2, 166–9.

Porter, D. (1997) Dimensions in the diversity of language: a language testing perspective. *The Language Teacher* 21, 51–4.

Postman, L. and Keppel, G. (1970) *Norms of Word Association*. New York City: Academic Press.

Powell, B., Barnes, A. and Graham, S. (1996) *Using the Target Language to Test Modern Foreign Language skills*. Warwick: University of Warwick, The Language Centre.

Qian, D.D. and Schedl, M. (2004) Evaluation of an in-depth vocabulary knowledge measure for assessing reading performance. *Language Testing* 21, 28–52.

Rapoport, An., Rapoport, Am., Livant, W.P. and Boyd, J. (1966) A study of lexical graphs. *Foundations of Language* 2, 338–76.

Reed, D.J. (1992) The relationship between criterion-based levels of oral proficiency and norm-referenced scores of general proficiency in English as a second language. *System* 20, 329–45.

Read, J. (2000) *Assessing Vocabulary*. Cambridge: Cambridge University Press.

Read, J. (2004) Plumbing the depths: how should the construct of vocabulary knowledge be defined? In Bogaards, P. and Laufer, B. *Vocabulary in a Second Language*. Amsterdam and Philadelphia, PA: John Benjamins, 209–27.

Read, J. and Nation, I.S.P. *An Investigation at the Lexical Dimension of the IELTS Speaking Test*. Report to IELTS Australia, November 2004.

Richards, B.J. (1987) Type/token ratios: what do they really tell us? *Journal of Child Language* 14, 201–9.

Richards, B.J. (1990) *Language Development and Individual Differences: A Study of Auxiliary Verb Learning*. Cambridge: Cambridge University Press.

Richards, B.J. and Malvern, D.D. (1997) *Quantifying Lexical Diversity in the Study of Language Development*. *The New Bulmershe Papers*. Reading: University of Reading.

Richards, B.J. and Malvern, D.D. (2000) Accommodation in oral interviews between foreign language learners and teachers who are *not* native speakers. *Studia Linguistica* 54, 260–71.

Richards, B.J. and Malvern, D.D. (2004) Investigating the validity of a new measure of lexical diversity for root and inflected forms. In Trott, K., Dobbinson, S. and Griffiths, P. (eds.) *The Child Language Reader*. London: Routledge, 81–9.

Riegel, K.F., Ramsey, R.M. and Riegel, R. (1967) A comparison of the first and second languages of American and Spanish Students. *Journal of Verbal Learning and Verbal Behavior* 6, 536–54.

Riegel, K.F. and Zivian, I.W.M. (1972) A study of inter- and intralingual associations in English and German. *Language Learning* 22, 51–63.

Rietveld, R. and van Hout, R. (1993) *Statistical Techniques for the Study of Language and Language Behaviour.* Berlin and New York: Mouton de Gruyter.

Rosenzweig, M. (1961) Comparisons among word association responses in English, French, German and Italian. *American Journal of Psychology* 74, 347–60.

Rosenzweig, M. (1964) Word associations of French workmen: comparisons of associations of French students and American workmen and students. *Journal of Verbal Learning and Verbal Behavior* 3, 57–69.

Ross, S. (1992) Accommodative questions in oral proficiency interviews. *Language Testing* 9 (2), 173–86.

Ross, S. (1998) Self-assessment in second language testing: a meta-analysis of experimental factors. *Language Testing* 15, 1–20.

School Curriculum and Assessment Authority (1994) *Papers from the School Curriculum and Assessment Authority. GCSE Criteria for Modern Foreign Languages: Draft Proposals.* London: SCAA.

Schrooten, W. and Vermeer, A. (1994) *Woorden in het Basisonderwijs. 15.000 woorden aangeboden aan leerlingen. Studies in Meertaligheid.* Tilburg: Tilburg University Press.

Schur, E. (2003) An exploration of the structural properties of L2 vocabulary networks: a graph theoretical approach. Unpublished PhD thesis, University of Wales, Swansea.

Scott, J. (1991) *Social Network Analysis: A Handbook.* London, Sage.

Shillaw, J. (1999) The application of the Rasch model to Yes/No vocabulary tests. Unpublished PhD thesis. University of Wales, Swansea.

Shiotsu, T. (2001) Individual differences in L2 word recognition speed: a measurement perspective. *Bulletin of the Institute of Foreign Language Education Kurume University* 8, 63–77.

Shohamy, E. (1994) The validity of direct versus semi-direct oral tests. *Language Testing* 11, 99–123.

Shohamy, E. (2001) *The Power of Tests: A Critical Perspective on the Uses of Language Tests.* Essex: Longman, Pearson Education Limited.

Sigman, M. and Cecchi, G.A. (2002) Global organization of the Wordnet lexicon. *Proceedings of the National Academy of Science* 99, 3, 1742–7.

Singleton, D. (1999) *Exploring the Second Language Mental Lexicon.* Cambridge: Cambridge University Press.

Skehan, P. (1989) *Individual Differences in Language Learning.* Oxford: Oxford Oxford University Press.

Söderman, T. (1993) Word associations of foreign language learners and native speakers: the phenomenon of a shift in response type and its relevance for lexical development. In Ringbom, H. (ed.) *Near Native Proficiency in English.* Abo, Abo Akademi, 81–182.

Stanovich, K.E. (1980) Towards an interactive compensatory model of individual differences in the development of reading fluency. *Reading Research Quarterly* 16 (1), 32–71f.

Stansfield, C.W. and Kenyon, D.M. (1992) Research on the comparability of the oral proficiency interview and the simulated oral proficiency interview. *System* 20 (3), 347–64.

Stoddard, G.D. (1929) An experiment in verbal learning. *Journal of Educational Psychology* 20, 452–7.

Stokes, S.F. and Fletcher, P. (2000) Lexical diversity and productivity in Cantonese-speaking children with specific language impairment. *International Journal of Language and Communication Disorders*, 35, 527–41.

Strogatz, S.H. (2001) Exploring complex networks. *Nature* 410, 268–76.

Szalay, L.B. and Deese, J. (1978) *Subjective Meaning and Culture: An Assessment Through Word Associations.* Hillsdale, NJ: Lawrence Erlbaum Associates.

Tardif, T., Gelman, S. and Xu, F. (1999) Putting the 'noun bias' in context: a comparison of English and Mandarin. *Child Development* 70, 620–35.

Thompson, B. (1998) Five methodology errors in educational research: the pantheon of statistical significance and other faux pas. Invited address presented at the annual meeting of the American Educational Research Association, San Diego, CA, April.

Thomson, G. and Thompson, R. (1915) Outlines of a method for the quantitative analysis of writing vocabularies. *British Journal of Psychology* 8, 52–69.

Treffers-Daller, J. and van Hout, R. (1999) De meting van woordenschatrijkdom in het Turks van Turks-Duits tweetaligen. In Huls, E. and Weltens, B. (eds.) *Artikelen van de derde Sociolinguïstische Conferentie.* Delft: Eburon, 429–40.

Tweedie, F.J. and Baayen, R.H. (1998) How variable may a constant be? Measures of lexical richness in perspective. *Computers and the Humanities* 32, 323–52.

Van de Velde, H. and Eyckmans, J. (2005) Het cognate-effect in de Ja/Nee woordenschattoets. In Ph. Hiligsmann, L. Beheydt, L. Degard., P. Godin and S. Vanderlinden (eds.) *Neerlandistiek in Frankrijk en in Franstalige België/Les études néerlandais en France et en Belgique francophone, Langues et Cultures* 1, Louvain-la-Neuve: Academia-Bruylant, 239–50.

Van Dijk, T. and Kintsch, W. (1983) *Strategies of Discourse Comprehension.* New York City: Academic Press.

Van Hout, R. and Vermeer, A. (1988) Spontane taaldata en het meten van lexicale rijkdom in tweede-taalverwerving. *Toegepaste taalwetenschap in artikelen* 32, 108–22.

Van Hout, R. and Vermeer, A. (1992) Frequenties van woorden en het geometrisch gemiddelde. (Frequencies of words and the geometric mean). *Gramma/TTT* 1 (2), 125–32.

Verhallen, M. and Schoonen, R. (1998) Lexical knowledge in L1 and L2 of Third and Fifth Graders. *Applied Linguistics* 19 (4), 452–70.

Vermeer, A. (1986) Tempo en struktuur van tweede-taalverwerving bij Turkse en Marokkaanse kinderen. (Success and structure in SLA of Turkish and Moroccan children). Unpublished PhD thesis, Tilburg University.

Vermeer, A. (1997) Breedte en diepte van woordenschat in relatie tot toenemende taalverwerving en frequentie van aanbod. *Gramma/TTT, tijdschrift voor taalwetenschap* 6 (3), 169–87.

Vermeer, A. (2000) Coming to grips with lexical richness in spontaneous speech data. *Language Testing* 17(1), 65–83.

Vermeer, A. (2001) Breadth and depth of vocabulary in relation to L1/L2 acquisition and frequency of input. *Applied Psycholinguistics* 22, 217–34.

Vermeer, A. (2004a) The relation between lexical richness and vocabulary size in Dutch L1 and L2 children. In Bogaards, P. and Laufer, B. (eds.) *Vocabulary in a Second Language.* Amsterdam and Philadelphia, PA: John Benjamins, 173–89.

Vermeer, A. (2004b) MLR: Maat voor Lexicale Rijkdom. (Measure of Lexical Richness). Available at: http://www.woordwerken.annevermeer. com.

Waring, R. (1997) A comparison of the receptive and productive vocabulary sizes of some second language learners. In *Immaculata: The Occasional Papers at Notre Dame Seishin University,* 94–114.

Waring, R. and Takaki, M. (2003) At what rate do learners learn and retain new vocabulary from reading a graded reader? *Reading in a Foreign Language* 15 (2), 130–63.

Watts, D.J. (1999) *Small Worlds: The Dynamics of Networks between Order and Randomness.* Princeton, NJ: Princeton University Press.

Watts, D.J. (2003) *Six Degrees: The Science of a Connected Age.* New York: W.W. Norton.

Watts, D.J. and Strogatz, S.H. (1998) Collective dynamics of 'small-world networks'. *Nature* 393, 440–2.

Webb, S. (2002) Investigating the effects of learning tasks on vocabulary knowledge. Unpublished PhD thesis, Victoria University of Wellington, New Zealand.

Weinert, R. (1995) The role of formulaic language in second language acquisition: a review. *Applied Linguistics* 15, 180–205.

Wells, C.G. (1985) *Language Development in the Pre-School Years.* Cambridge: Cambridge University Press.

Wesche, M. and Paribakht, T.A. (1996) Assessing second language vocabulary knowledge: depth versus breadth. *Canadian Modern Language Review* 53, 13–40.

West, M. (1953) *A General Service List of English Words.* London: Longman.

Wilks, C. (1999) Untangling word webs: graph theory approaches to L2 lexicons. Unpublished PhD thesis, University of Wales, Swansea.

Wilks, C. and Meara, P. (2002) Untangling word webs: graph theory and the notion of density in second language word association networks. *Second Language Research* 18 (4), 303–24.

Williamson, M.M. and Huot, B. (eds.) (1993) *Validating Holistic Scoring for Writing Assessment: Theoretical and Empirical Foundations.* Creskill, NJ: Hampton Press.

Woods, C. and Neather, T. (1994) Target language testing in KS4 examinations. *Language Learning Journal* 10, 19–21.

Woods, A., Fletcher, P. and Hughes, A. (1986) *Statistics in Language Studies.* Cambridge: Cambridge University Press.

WordNet Lexicon, available at: http://www.cogsci.princeton.edu/~wn/.

Young, R. (1995) Conversational styles in language proficiency interviews. *Language Learning* 45 (1), 3–42.

Young, R. and He, A.W. (eds.) (1998) *Talking and Testing: Discourse Approaches to the Assessment of Oral Proficiency.* Amsterdam and Philadelphia, PA: John Benjamins.

Zipf, G.K. (1949) *Human Behavior and the Principle of Least Effort.* Reading, MA: Addison Wesley.

Appendix 1

C-test

1. Les vaches folles

Selon une récente enquête, 45 % des Français auraient diminué ou cessé de manger de la viande de boeuf depuis le début de la crise de la vache folle. Ils se tournent vers les viandes blanches et la nourriture végétale. On court sans doute davantage de risques en prenant le volant de sa voiture qu'en consommant une entrecôte. Mais, comme le remarquait dernièrement un sociologue, «les Français veulent bien mourir en conduisant mais pas en mangeant».

2. Un nouveau défi : la mondialisation

On croise sur les autoroutes françaises de plus en plus de camions immatriculés à l'étranger. Les enseignes Gap, C & A, Ikea font partie du décor quotidien. Chacun d'entre nous, au supermarché, remplit son chariot de produits provenant des quatre coins du monde. La mondialisation est là, de plus en plus présente dans notre vie quotidienne. Le phénomène de la mondialisation n'est pas nouveau. Les marchands de Venise de la Renaissance vivaient, à leur façon, la mondialisation.

3. Que reste-t-il de la fête de l'internet?

C'était une jolie idée, il y a trois ans, que celle de la fête de l'internet. On voulait être au réseau ce que la fête de la musique est à la musique, un moment privilégié pendant lequel ceux qui savent font profiter de leurs talents ceux qui ne savent pas. C'est ainsi que, partout en France et dans plusieurs pays francophones, des associations, des collectivités locales, les administrations ont organisé des manifestations diverses et variées qui, pour la plupart d'entre elles, avaient l'ambition d'initier les foules ébahies à la magie du clic sur la toile et aux douceurs du courriel enchanté.

4. La vie en 35 heures . . .

On travaille de moins en moins. La semaine de travail – de 84 heures en 1900 – s'est fortement réduite dans tous les pays au cours du siècle dernier. La France a notamment adopté, il y a deux ans, la semaine d'une durée légale de 35 heures pour tous les salariés. « Je pense avec terreur au réajustement de ses habitudes que l'homme devra effectuer. Il lui faudra se débarrasser en quelques décennies de ce qui lui a été inculqué au cours des générations.

5. L'Europe niveau bac

Pour cesser d'être élève et devenir étudiant, chaque jeune Européen doit obtenir son passeport pour l'Université. Ce diplôme qui marque la fin des études secondaires prend des formes très variées selon les pays de l'Union. Dans chacun des 15 États membres de l'Union européenne, la fin de la scolarité, qui précède l'entrée à l'université, est validée par l'obtention d'un diplôme. On peut établir un portrait-type de ce diplôme: il est obtenu à la suite d'un examen général, national, constitué d'épreuves écrites et orales, et qui est associé aux notes de contrôle continu des années précédentes.

6. Le chanteur Tété

De temps en temps, dans la chanson, un jeune homme se met en route vers la gloire. Un écrivain de chansons, un compositeur, un jeune homme qui a de la voix et qui trace son chemin, aussi loin que possible du déjà dit. Cela faisait longtemps que ce n'était plus arrivé en France. Et puis sort un superbe album, poussé par un grand morceau, « Le meilleur des mondes ». De cette chanson, on retient surtout la voix chaude, aigüe, jouant sur de nombreuses harmonies, le jeu de guitare et la performance mélodique . . .

Appendix 2

@Begin
@Languages: French
@Participants: 605 Student
@Sex: Female
@Level: Erasmus
@File name: 605.CHA
@Stim: lake story and bank story
@Date: 09-MAR-2004
@Transcriber: JYC
@Coder: JYC

*605:   une [: un] petite [: petit] fille &um qui [/] qui se+promène
        [: se+promener] avec [/] &um avec son grand+père et son
        chien .
*605:   donc la [: le] petite [: petit] fille s'amuse [: s+amuser] à # à
        lancer un [/] # un bâton .
*605:   et [?] elle [: il] joue [: jouer] avec son chien .
*605:   et son chien bien+sûr &um <lui lui> [/] lui rapporte
        [: rapporter] le bâton .
*605:   <&um un> [/] un vieux monsieur <passe [: passer] passe
        [: passer]> [/] passe [: passer] à+côté du chien de la [: le] petite
        [: petit] fille .
*605:   et # et il est [: être] assez # <cela cela> cela l' [: le] amuse
        [: amuser] <de voir> [/] de voir la [: le] petite [: petit] fille
        jouer avec [/] avec son chien .
*605:   et donc &um il décide [: décider] &um de ce [/] ce vieux
        monsieur <a [: avoir] une [: un]> [/] a [: avoir] une [: un] canne
        pour marcher .
*605:   et <il dé(cide)> [/] il décide [: décider] <de lancer> [/] &um de
        lancer <la [: le]> [/] &um la [: le] canne au loin <dans dans
        dans> [/] dans la [: le] mer .
*605:   xxx et &um pour [/] pour que le chien # rapporte [: rapporter]
        la [: le] canne .

265

*605: comme il le fait [: faire] avec avec le bâton .

*605: et en fait [: en+fait] le chien ne réagit [: réagir] pas .

*605: et le vieux monsieur <ne comprend [: comprendre] pas> [/] ne comprend [: comprendre] pas pourquoi .

*605: et donc ainsi le [/] le vieux monsieur est [: être] obligé [: obliger] # d' [: de] enlever ses [: son] vêtements [: vêtement] pour aller chercher un chercher <sa [: son]> [/] sa [: son] canne # <dans la [: le]> [/] dans la [: le] mer .

*605: donc &um ensuite <la [: le] # la [: le]> [/] la [: le] deuxième histoire &um se+passe [: se+passer] se+passe [: se+passer] dans une [: un] banque .

*605: &um &um <un cambrioleur> [/] un cambrioleur entre [/] entre <dans la [: le]> [/] dans la [: le] banque .

*605: et <renverse [: renverser]> [/] &um renverse [: renverser] <une [: un]> [/] une [: un] petite [: petit] fille <qui tombe [: tomber] qui tombe [: tomber]> [/] # qui tombe [: tomber] par+terre .

*605: et &um son son grand+père arrive [: arriver] et <demande [: demander] demande [: demander]> [/] demande [: demander] à # <lui demande [: demander]> [/] lui demande [: demander] pourquoi [/] pourquoi elle [: il] pleure [: pleurer] .

*605: et donc elle [: il] lui explique [: expliquer] qu' [: que] il y a [: avoir] un méchant [/] méchant monsieur .

*605: qui l' [: le] a [: avoir] fait [: faire] tomber par+terre # donc &um <ils [: il] rentrent [: rentrer]> [/] ils [: il] rentrent [: rentrer] tous [: tout] les [: le] deux <dans dans> [/] dans la [: le] banque .

*605: et le grand+père est [: être] <très très> [/] # très énervé .

*605: le cambrioleur a [: avoir] avec lui deux pistolets [: pistolet] .

*605: et <menace [: menacer]> [/] menace [: menacer] les [: le] employés [: employé] et # menace [: menacer] les [: le] employés [: employé] et les [: le] clients [: client] de la [: le] banque .

*605: mais [/] mais le grand+père <n' [: ne] a [: avoir]> [/] n' [: ne] a [: avoir] pas peur <du du> [/] du de l' [: le] agresseur .

*605: et <va [: aller]> [/] va [: aller] lui donner un coup+de+poing .

*605: et &um # <va [: aller]> [/] va [: aller] réussir à <le # le> [/] le maîtriser .

*605: et donc la [: le] # le grand+père <va [: aller]> [/] # va [: aller] devenir un [/] # un héros &um dans cette [: ce] banque auprès <des [: de]> des [: de] [//] de la [: le] clientèle et <des [: de]> [/] des [: de] employés [: employé] de la [: le] banque

@   End

Appendix 3

Basic types added to FF1

aide 'help'
banque 'bank'
célèbre 'famous'
chic 'stylish, smart'
cinquième 'fifth'
malheureusement 'unfortunately'
normal 'normal'
objet 'object'
parapluie 'umbrella'
parc 'park'
plage 'beach'
population 'population'
prison 'prison'
probablement 'probably'
problème 'problem'
promenade 'walk'
quatrième 'fourth'
rapidement 'fast'
situation 'situation'
sixième 'sixth'

Appendix 4

Key to transcription conventions

(laughs)	Non-verbal, paralinguistic, prosodic and contextual information
[	Simultaneous starting talk
WORD	Increased loudness
<slow>	Marked slower speech delivery
°quiet°	Quiet delivery
=	Overlapping talk with no discernible break between utterances
(.)	Short pause (half a second or under)
(2.0)	Longer pause, in seconds
?	Speech act having the illocutionary force of eliciting information; also rising intonation
wor-	Word cut off abruptly
[. . .]	Lines/words omitted from transcript
E	Examiner
C	Candidate

Index